THE STAR WARS DEBATE

edited by STEVEN ANZOVIN

THE REFERENCE SHELF

Volume 58 Number 1

D1253448

THE H. W. WILSON COMPANY

New York   1986

THE REFERENCE SHELF

The books in this series contain reprints of articles, excerpts from books, and addresses on current issues and social trends in the United States and other countries. There are six separately bound numbers in each volume, all of which are generally published in the same calendar year. One number is a collection of recent speeches; each of the others is devoted to a single subject and gives background information and discussion from various points of view, concluding with a comprehensive bibliography. Books in the series may be purchased individually or on subscription.

Library of Congress Cataloging in Publication Data

Main entry under title:

The Star Wars debate.

    (The Reference shelf ; v. 58, no. 1)
    Bibliography: p.
    1. Strategic Defense Initiative—Addresses, essays, lectures. I. Anzovin, Steven. II. Series.
UG743.S72   1986   358'.1754   85–29603
ISBN 0–8242–0723–8

Printed in the United States of America

CONTENTS

Preface 5

I. The Challenge

Editor's Introduction 7
Ronald Reagan. Peace and National Security: A New
    Defense .... Vital Speeches of the Day   8
The President's Strategic Defense Initiative ....
.... Department of State Bulletin   11

II. Can It Be Done?

Editor's Introduction 31
James C. Fletcher. The Technologies for Ballistic Mis-
    sile Defense ...... Issues in Science and Technology   32
Hans A. Bethe, Richard L. Garwin, Kurt Gottfried, and
    Henry W. Kendall. Space-based Ballistic Missile De-
    fense .... Scientific American   52
Robert Jastrow. The War against Star Wars ....
.... Commentary   74
Gary L. Guertner. What Is "Proof?" ... Foreign Policy   90

III. Should It Be Done?

Editor's Introduction 101
George A. Keyworth II. The Case for Strategic Defense:
    An Option for a World Disarmed ....
.... Issues in Science and Technology   102

Fred C. Ikle. Is the Administration's "Star Wars" Strate-
gic Defense Initiative Sound National Policy?—Pro ..
.... Congressional Digest   122
William Proxmire. Is the Administration's "Star Wars"
Strategic Defense Initiative Sound National Policy?—
Con .... Congressional Digest   127
David E. Sanger. Campuses' Role in Arms Debated As
'Star Wars' Funds Are Sought .... New York Times   133
Matthew Rothschild and Keenen Peck. Star Wars: The
Final Solution .... Progressive   143

IV. WORLD OPINION

Editor's Introduction   160
John Newhouse. Test .... New Yorker   161
Dave Griffiths, Ronald Taggiasco, Thane Peterson, and
Frederic A. Miller. The Selling of Star Wars to Busi-
nesses Abroad .... Business Week   185
K. Subrahmanyam. The 'Star Wars' Delusion ....
.... Times of India (World Press Review)   189
G. Arbatov. Playing with Fire ....
.... Pravda (Current Digest of the Soviet Press)   196
David B. Rivkin, Jr. What Does Moscow Think? ......
.... Foreign Policy   200

BIBLIOGRAPHY   219

PREFACE

In March 1983 President Ronald Reagan startled the world by announcing an ambitious plan to develop a space-based multi-billion-dollar defense against strategic ballistic-missile attack that would protect American cities as well as military targets from a Soviet first strike. An effective strategic defense, in the President's view, would allow the world to awaken from its nuclear nightmare by rendering nuclear weapons "impotent and obsolete." Reagan's Strategic Defense Initiative (SDI), as it is officially known, was immediately dubbed the "Star Wars" defense after the popular 1977 science-fiction film. Like the film, the Star Wars defense features orbiting battle stations, automated "death stars" ready to blast enemy missiles with laser beams, atomic rays, and killer robots.

To its many critics, Star Wars bears a further resemblance to its namesake: They say it is a childish fantasy whose appeal lies primarily in its high-priced special effects, not a rational plan on which to base the defense of the nation. Originally the pet project of a small group of scientists and military experts, Star Wars was dismissed by most people, including many scientists, at the time of its announcement. Not only did the plan appear to be vague and unworkable, but Reagan appeared to have caught the American military establishment, which would have to implement it, completely by surprise. Initially, some observers thought Star Wars was a bluff to put pressure on the U.S.S.R. in upcoming arms talks. But the President has been unflinching in his support, and the Soviets themselves have taken Star Wars very seriously. In only two years it has come to dominate arms negotiations between the superpowers, and with the continued vigorous advocacy of the most popular postwar president, Star Wars now promises to alter fundamentally the nuclear strategy that America has pursued for the past thirty years.

The President's vision of a nuclear-free future made safe by an unbreachable space shield leaves unanswered the many complex technological, moral, and political questions that need to be addressed before Star Wars can become a reality, if indeed it should. These questions, about which there is much uncertainty and disagreement at all levels, include what form a Star Wars defense should take; how effective it would be; what it would cost; when it could be ready; whether it would stabilize or destabilize the balance of power; and whether some other course, such as disarmament, might not be better. The major aspects of the ongoing Star Wars debate are discussed in this compilation of speeches, articles, and essays. The first section presents the Reagan Strategic Defense Initiative in the President's own words and in an official White House pamphlet. Section II covers the controversy raging among experts as to the scientific feasibility of Star Wars: Can exotic technologies as yet undeveloped be made the centerpiece of national defense? The articles in Section III discuss the moral and political issues raised by Star Wars: Even if an effective defense is possible, should it be built? Star Wars and world opinion is dealt with in the final section. Will the Allies support it, and how will Moscow react?

The editor wishes to thank the authors and publishers who have kindly granted permission to reprint the material in this collection. Special thanks are also due to Diane Podell of the B. Davis Schwartz Memorial Library, C. W. Post Center, Long Island University, and to the staffs of the public libraries of Englewood and Teaneck, New Jersey.

STEVEN ANZOVIN

February 1986

I. THE CHALLENGE

EDITOR'S INTRODUCTION

The signing of the Anti-Ballistic Missile (ABM) treaty between the United States and the Soviet Union in 1972 was hailed at the time as a milestone in nuclear arms control. A new arms race to develop a defense against intercontinental ballistic missiles had been forestalled; the superpowers had agreed to continue to rely on the threat of mutually assured destruction (the MAD doctrine) to deter a nuclear first strike by either power. MAD was profoundly frightening but had the virtue of being familiar; the development of a strategic defense against ballistic missiles was viewed as dangerously destabilizing, as well as very difficult or perhaps impossible.

Despite the apparent success of the ABM treaty, however, neither the United States nor the U.S.S.R. had completely abandoned the concept of strategic defense—it was like an itch unscratched. By the early 1980s it was widely believed in the West that the Soviets had deployed an ABM system of interceptor missiles around Moscow and that special "phased-array" radars were being built deep in Soviet territory to aid in ABM guidance. In the United States, by contrast, strategic defense was taken seriously only by a small but vocal conservative faction in the military led by Lt. Gen. Daniel O. Graham, former director of the Pentagon's Defense Intelligence Agency, and by a few weapons scientists, notably Edward Teller, "father" of the H-bomb. In late 1982 President Reagan saw the right-wing Heritage Foundation's study, "High Frontier: A New National Strategy," which advocated applying directed-energy and computer technology to the development of an advanced ballistic-missile defense. The High Frontier study strongly favored replacing "the dangerous doctrine of mutually assured destruction with a strategy of assured survival." So taken was President Reagan with this concept that, with virtually no internal consultation with Administration advisors or the military, he decided to push for a Star Wars defense in a televised speech on March 23, 1983. The relevant portion of that speech is reprinted as the first selection in this section.

Also included is the text of a pamphlet on the SDI released by the White House in January 1985. This pamphlet amplifies and explains many aspects of the Administration's program that were only hinted at by President Reagan in his 1983 address.

PEACE AND NATIONAL SECURITY: A NEW DEFENSE[1]

Thus far tonight I have shared with you my thoughts on the problems of national security we must face together. My predecessors in the Oval Office have appeared before you on other occasions to describe the threat posed by Soviet power and have proposed steps to address that threat. But since the advent of nuclear weapons, those steps have been directed toward deterrence of aggression through the promise of retaliation—the notion that no rational nation would launch an attack that would inevitably result in unacceptable losses to themselves. This approach to stability through offensive threat has worked. We and our allies have succeeded in preventing nuclear war for three decades. In recent months, however, my advisers, including in particular the Joint Chiefs of Staff, have underscored the bleakness of the future before us.

Over the course of these discussions, I have become more and more deeply convinced that the human spirit must be capable of rising above dealing with other nations and human beings by threatening their existence. Feeling this way, I believe we must thoroughly examine every opportunity for reducing tensions and for introducing greater stability into the strategic calculus on both sides. One of the most important contributions we can make is, of

[1]Speech by President Ronald Reagan from the White House, March 23, 1983. Reprinted from *Vital Speeches of the Day* 49:386–90, Ap. 15, '83, with permission.

course, to lower the level of all arms, and particularly nuclear arms. We are engaged right now in several negotiations with the Soviet Union to bring about a mutual reduction of weapons. I will report to you a week from tomorrow my thoughts on that score. But let me just say I am totally committed to this course.

If the Soviet Union will join us in our effort to achieve major arms reduction we will have succeeded in stabilizing the nuclear balance. Nevertheless it will still be necessary to rely on the specter of retaliation—on mutual threat, and that is a sad commentary on the human condition.

Would it not be better to save lives than to avenge them? Are we not capable of demonstrating our peaceful intentions by applying all our abilities and our ingenuity to achieving a truly lasting stability? I think we are—indeed, we must!

After careful consultation with my advisers, including the Joint Chiefs of Staff, I believe there is a way. Let me share with you a vision of the future which offers hope. It is that we embark on a program to counter the awesome Soviet missile threat with measures that are defensive. Let us turn to the very strengths in technology that spawned our great industrial base and that have given us the quality of life we enjoy today.

Up until now we have increasingly based our strategy of deterrence upon the threat of retaliation. But what if free people could live secure in the knowledge that their security did not rest upon the threat of instant U.S. retaliation to deter a Soviet attack; that we could intercept and destroy strategic ballistic missiles before they reached our own soil or that of our allies?

I know this is a formidable technical task, one that may not be accomplished before the end of this century. Yet, current technology has attained a level of sophistication where it is reasonable for us to begin this effort. It will take years, probably decades, of effort on many fronts. There will be failures and setbacks just as there will be successes and breakthroughs. And as we proceed we must remain constant in preserving the nuclear deterrent and maintaining a solid capability for flexible response. But is it not worth every investment necessary to free the world from the threat of nuclear war? We know it is!

In the meantime, we will continue to pursue real reductions in nuclear arms, negotiating from a position of strength that can be insured only by modernizing our strategic forces. At the same time, we must take steps to reduce the risk of a conventional military conflict escalating to nuclear war by improving our nonnuclear capabilities. America does possess—now—the technologies to attain very significant improvements in the effectiveness of our conventional, nonnuclear forces. Proceeding boldly with these new technologies, we can significantly reduce any incentive that the Soviet Union may have to threaten attack against the United States or its allies.

As we pursue our goal of defensive technologies, we recognize that our allies rely upon our strategic offensive power to deter attacks against them. Their vital interests and ours are inextricably linked—their safety and ours are one. And no change in technology can or will alter that reality. We must and shall continue to honor our commitments.

I clearly recognize that defensive systems have limitations and raise certain problems and ambiguities. If paired with offensive systems, they can be viewed as fostering an aggressive policy and no one wants that.

But with these considerations firmly in mind, I call upon the scientific community who gave us nuclear weapons to turn their great talents to the cause of mankind and world peace: to give us the means of rendering these nuclear weapons impotent and obsolete.

Tonight, consistent with our obligations under the ABM Treaty and recognizing the need for close consultation with our allies, I am taking an important first step. I am directing a comprehensive and intensive effort to define a long-term research and development program to begin to achieve our ultimate goal of eliminating the threat posed by strategic nuclear missiles. This could pave the way for arms control measures to eliminate the weapons themselves. We seek neither military superiority nor political advantage. Our only purpose—one all people share—is to search for ways to reduce the danger of nuclear war.

My fellow Americans, tonight we are launching an effort which holds the purpose of changing the course of human history.

There will be risks, and results take time. But with your support, I believe we can do it.

THE PRESIDENT'S STRATEGIC DEFENSE INITIATIVE[2]

Presidential Foreword

December 28, 1984

Since the advent of nuclear weapons, every President has sought to minimize the risk of nuclear destruction by maintaining effective forces to deter aggression and by pursuing complementary arms control agreements. This approach has worked. We and our allies have succeeded in preventing nuclear war while protecting Western security for nearly four decades.

Originally, we relied on balanced defensive and offensive forces to deter. But over the last twenty years, the United States has nearly abandoned efforts to develop and deploy defenses against nuclear weapons, relying instead almost exclusively on the threat of nuclear retaliation. We accepted the notion that if both we and the Soviet Union were able to retaliate with devastating power even after absorbing a first strike, that stable deterrence would endure. That rather novel concept seemed at the time to be sensible for two reasons. First, the Soviets stated that they believed that both sides should have roughly equal forces and neither side should seek to alter the balance to gain unilateral advantage. Second, there did not seem to be any alternative. The state of the art in defensive systems did not permit an effective defensive system.

Today both of these basic assumptions are being called into question. The pace of the Soviet offensive and defensive buildup has upset the balance in the areas of greatest importance during crises. Furthermore, new technologies are now at hand which may make possible a truly effective non-nuclear defense.

For these reasons and because of the awesome destructive potential of nuclear weapons, we must seek another means of deterring war. It is both militarily and morally necessary. Certainly, there should be a better way to strengthen peace and stability, a way to move away from a future that relies so heavily on the prospect of rapid and massive nuclear retaliation and toward greater reliance on defensive systems which threaten no one.

---

[2]From a pamphlet released by the White House in January 1985. Reprinted from *Department of State Bulletin*. 85:65–72. Mr. '85.

On March 23, 1983, I announced my decision to take an important first step toward this goal by directing the establishment of a comprehensive and intensive research program, the Strategic Defense Initiative, aimed at eventually eliminating the threat posed by nuclear armed ballistic missiles.

The Strategic Defense Initiative (SDI) is a program of vigorous research focused on advanced defensive technologies with the aim of finding ways to provide a better basis for deterring aggression, strengthening stability, and increasing the security of the United States and our allies. The SDI research program will provide to a future President and a future Congress the technical knowledge required to support a decision on whether to develop and later deploy advanced defensive systems.

At the same time, the United States is committed to the negotiation of equal and verifiable agreements which bring real reductions in the power of the nuclear arsenals of both sides. To this end, my Administration has proposed to the Soviet Union a comprehensive set of arms control proposals. We are working tirelessly for the success of these efforts, but we can and must go further in trying to strengthen the peace.

Our research under the Strategic Defense Initiative complements our arms reduction efforts and helps to pave the way for creating a more stable and secure world. The research that we are undertaking is consistent with all of our treaty obligations, including the 1972 Anti-Ballistic Missile Treaty.

In the near term, the SDI research program also responds to the ongoing and extensive Soviet anti-ballistic missile (ABM) effort, which includes actual deployments. It provides a powerful deterrent to any Soviet decision to expand its ballistic missile defense capability beyond that permitted by the ABM Treaty. And, in the long-term, we have confidence that SDI will be a crucial means by which both the United States and the Soviet Union can safely agree to very deep reductions and, eventually, even the elimination of ballistic missiles and the nuclear weapons they carry.

Our vital interest and those of our allies are inextricably linked. Their safety and ours are one. They, too, rely upon our nuclear forces to deter attack against them. Therefore, as we pursue the promise offered by the Strategic Defense Initiative, we will continue to work closely with our friends and allies. We will ensure that, in the event of a future decision to develop and deploy defensive systems—a decision in which consultation with our allies will play an important part—allied, as well as U.S. security against aggression would be enhanced.

Through the SDI research program, I have called upon the great scientific talents of our country to turn to the cause of strengthening world peace by rendering ballistic missiles impotent and obsolete. In short, I propose to channel our technological prowess toward building a more secure and stable world. And I want to emphasize that in carrying out this research program, the United States seeks neither military superiority nor political advantage. Our only purpose is to search for ways to reduce the danger of nuclear war.

As you review the following pages, I would ask you to remember that the quality of our future is at stake and to reflect on what we are trying to achieve—the strengthening of our ability to preserve the peace while shifting away from our current dependence upon the threat of nuclear retaliation. I would also ask you to consider the SDI research program in light of both the Soviet Union's extensive, ongoing efforts in this area and our own government's constitutional responsibility to provide for the common defense. I hope that you will conclude by lending your own strong and continuing support to this research effort—an effort which could prove to be critical to our nation's future.

RONALD REAGAN

The President's Vision

In his March 23rd address to the nation, the President described his vision of a world free of its overwhelming dependence on nuclear weapons, a world free once and for all of the threat of nuclear war. The Strategic Defense Initiative, by itself, cannot fully realize this vision nor solve all the security challenges we and our allies will face in the future; for this we will need to seek many solutions—political as well as technological. A long road with much hard work lies ahead of us. The President believes we must begin now. The Strategic Defense Initiative takes a crucial first step.

The basic security of the United States and our allies rests upon our collective ability to deter aggression. Our nuclear retaliatory forces help achieve this security and have deterred war for nearly forty years. Since World War II, nuclear weapons have not been used; there has been no direct military conflict between the two largest world powers, and Europe has not seen such an extended period of peace since the last century. The fact is, however, that we have no defense against nuclear ballistic missile attack. And, as the Soviet building program widens the imbalance in key offensive capabilities, introducing systems whose status and characteristics are more difficult to confirm, our vulnerability and that of our allies to blackmail becomes quite high. In the event deterrence failed, a President's only recourse would be to surrender or to retaliate. Nuclear retaliation, whether massive or limited, would result in the loss of millions of lives.

The President believes strongly that we must find a better way to assure credible deterrence. If we apply our great scientific and engineering talent to the problem of defending against ballistic missiles, there is a very real possibility that future Presidents will be able to deter war by means other than threatening devastation to any aggressor—and by a means which threatens no one.

The President's goal, and his challenge to our scientists and engineers, is to identify the technological problems and to find the technical solutions so that we have the option of using the potential of strategic defenses to provide a more effective, more stable means of keeping the United States and our allies secure from aggression and coercion. The Joint Chiefs of Staff, many respected scientists, and other experts believe that, with firm leadership and adequate funding, recent advances in defensive technologies could make such defenses achievable.

What Is the President's Strategic Defense Initiative?

The President announced his Strategic Defense Initiative (SDI) in his March 23, 1983, address to the nation. Its purpose is to identify ways to exploit recent advances in ballistic missile defense technologies that have potential for strengthening deterrence—and thereby increasing our security and that of our allies. The program is designed to answer a number of fundamental scientific and engineering questions that must be addressed before the promise of these new technologies can be fully assessed. The SDI research program will provide to a future President and a future Congress the technical knowledge necessary to support a decision in the early 1990s on whether to develop and deploy such advanced defensive systems.

As a broad research program, the SDI is not based on any single or preconceived notion of what an effective defense system would look like. A number of different concepts, involving a wide range of technologies, are being examined. No single concept or technology has been identified as the best or the most appropriate. A number of non-nuclear technologies hold promise for dealing effectively with ballistic missiles.

We do feel, however, that the technologies that are becoming available today may offer the possibility of providing a layered defense—a defense that uses various technologies to destroy attacking missiles during each phase of their flight.

• Some missiles could be destroyed shortly after they launch as they burn their engines and boost their warheads into space. By destroying a missile during this boost phase, we would also destroy all of the nuclear warheads it carries at the same time. In the case of ICBMs [intercontinental ballistic missiles], they would probably be destroyed before leaving the territory of the aggressor.

• Next, we could destroy those nuclear warheads that survive the boost phase by attacking them during the post-boost phase. During this phase we would target the device that sits on top of the missile and is used to dispense its warheads while it is in the process of releasing its cargo. By destroying this device, the post-boost vehicle, we can destroy all the warheads not yet released.

• Those warheads that have been released and survive travel for tens of minutes in the void of space on their ballistic trajectories towards their targets. While we would now have to locate, identify, and destroy the individual nuclear warheads themselves, this relatively long mid-course phase of flight again offers us time to exploit advanced technologies to do just that.

• Finally, those warheads that survive the outer layers of defense could be attacked during the terminal phase as they approach the end of their ballistic flight.

The concept of a layered defense could be extremely effective because the progressive layers would be able to work together to provide many opportunities to destroy attacking nuclear warheads well before they approach our territory or that of our allies. An opponent facing several separate layers of defenses would find it difficult to redesign his missiles and their nuclear warheads to penetrate all of the layers. Moreover, defenses during the boost, post-boost, and mid-course phases of ballistic missile flight make no distinction in the targets of the attacking missiles—they simply destroy attacking nuclear warheads, and in the process protect people and our country. The combined effectiveness of the defense provided by the multiple layers need not provide 100% protection in order to enhance deterrence significantly. It need only create sufficient uncertainty in the mind of a potential aggressor concerning his ability to succeed in the purposes of his attack. The concept of a layered defense certainly will help do this.

There have been considerable advances in technology since U.S. ballistic missile defenses were first developed in the 1960's. At the time the ABM Treaty was signed (1972), ballistic missile defense prospects were largely confined to the attacking nuclear warheads during the terminal phase of their flight using nuclear-tipped interceptor missiles. Since that time, emerging technologies offer the possibility of non-nuclear options for destroying missiles and the nuclear warheads they carry in all phases of their flight. New technologies may be able to permit a layered defense by providing: sensors for identifying and tracking missiles and nuclear warheads; advanced group and spaceborne interceptors and directed energy weapons to destroy both missiles and nuclear warheads; and the technology to permit the command, control, and communications necessary to operate a layered defense.

In the planning that went into the SDI research program, we consciously chose to look broadly at defense against ballistic missiles as it could be applied across all these phases of missile flight: boost, post-boost, mid-course, and terminal. Although it is too early to define fully those individual technologies or applications which will ultimately prove to be most effective, such a layered approach maximizes the application of emerging technology and holds out the possibility of destroying nuclear warheads well before they reach the territory of the United States or our allies.

As President Reagan made clear at the start of this effort, the SDI research program will be consistent with all U.S. treaty obligations, including the ABM Treaty. The Soviets, who have and are improving the world's only existing antiballistic missile system (deployed around Moscow), are continuing a program of research on both traditional and advanced anti-ballistic missile technologies that has been underway for many years. But while the President has directed that the United States effort be conducted in a manner that is consistent with the ABM Treaty, the Soviet Union almost certainly is violating that Treaty by constructing a large ballistic missile early warning radar in Siberia (at Krasnoyarsk) which is located and oriented in a manner prohibited by the Treaty. This radar could contribute significantly to the Soviet Union's considerable potential to rapidly expand its deployed ballistic missile defense capability.

The United States has offered to discuss with the Soviet Union the implications of defensive technologies being explored by both countries. Such a discussion would be useful in helping to clarify both sides' understanding of the relationship between offensive and defensive forces and in clarifying the purposes that underlie the United States and Soviet programs. Further, this dialogue could lead to agreement to work together toward a more stable strategic relationship than exists today.

Why SDI?

SDI and Deterrence. The primary responsibility of a government is to provide for the security of its people. Deterrence of aggression is the most certain path to ensure that we and our allies survive as free and independent nations. Providing a better, more stable basis for enhanced deterrence is the central purpose of the SDI program.

Under the SDI program, we are conducting intensive research focused on advanced defensive technologies with the aim of enhancing the basis of deterrence, strengthening stability, and thereby increasing the security of the United States and our allies. On many occasions, the President has stated his strong belief that "a nuclear war cannot be won and must never be fought." U.S. policy has always been one of deterring aggression and will remain so even if a decision is made in the future to deploy defensive systems. The purpose of SDI is to strengthen deterrence and lower the level of nuclear forces.

Defensive systems are consistent with a policy of deterrence both historically and theoretically. While today we rely almost exclusively on the threat of retaliation with offensive forces for our strategic deterrence, this has not always been the case. Throughout the 1950's and most of the 1960's, the United States maintained an extensive air defense network to protect North America from attack by Soviet bomber forces. At that time, this network formed an important part of our deterrent capability. It was allowed to decline only when the Soviet emphasis shifted to intercontinental ballistic missiles, a threat for which there was previously no effective defense. Recent advances in ballistic missile defense technologies, however, provide more than sufficient reason to believe that defensive systems could eventually provide a better and more stable basis for deterrence.

Effective defenses against ballistic missiles have potential for enhancing deterrence in the future in a number of ways. First, they could significantly increase an aggressor's uncertainties regarding whether his weapons would penetrate the defenses and destroy our missiles and other military targets. It would be very difficult for a potential aggressor to predict his own vulnerability in the face of such uncertainties. It would restore the condition that attacking could never leave him better off. An aggressor will be much less likely to contemplate initiating a nuclear conflict, even in crisis circumstances, while lacking confidence in his ability to succeed.

Such uncertainties also would serve to reduce or eliminate the incentive for first strike attack. Modern, accurate ICBMs carrying multiple nuclear warheads—if deployed in sufficiently large numbers relative to the size of an opponent's force structure, as the Soviets have done with their ICBM force—could be used in a rapid first strike to undercut an opponent's ability to retaliate effectively. By significantly reducing or eliminating the ability of ballistic missiles to attack military forces effectively, and thereby rendering them impotent and obsolete as a means of supporting aggression, advanced defenses could remove this potential major source of instability.

Finally, in conjunction with air defenses, very effective defenses against ballistic missiles could help reduce or eliminate the apparent military value of nuclear attack to an aggressor. By preventing an aggressor from destroying a significant portion of our country, an aggressor would have gained nothing by attacking in the first place. In this way, very effective defenses could reduce substantially the possibility of nuclear conflict.

If we take the prudent and necessary steps to maintain strong, credible military forces, there is every reason to believe that deterrence will continue to preserve the peace. However, even with the utmost vigilance, few things in this world are absolutely certain, and a responsible government must consider the remote possibility that deterrence could fail. Today, the United States and our allies have no defense against ballistic missile attack. We also have very limited capability to defend the United States against an attack by enemy bombers. If deterrence were to fail, without a shield of any kind, it could cause the death of most of our population and the destruction of our nation as we know it. The SDI program provides our only long-term hope to change this situation.

Defenses also could provide insurance against either accidental ballistic missile launches or launches by some future irrational leader in possession of a nuclear armed missile. While such events are improbable, they are not inconceivable. The United States and other nuclear-capable powers have instituted appropriate safeguards against inadvertent launches by their own forces and together have formulated policies to preclude the proliferation of nuclear weapons. Nonetheless, it is difficult to predict the future course of events. While we hope and expect that our best efforts will continue to be successful, our national security interests will be well served by a vigorous SDI research program that could provide an additional safeguard against such potentially catastrophic events.

Today our retaliatory forces provide a strong sword to deter aggression. However, the President seeks a better way of maintaining deterrence. For the future, the SDI program strives to provide a defensive shield which will do more than simply make that deterrence stronger. It will allow us to build a better, more stable basis for deterrence. And, at the same time, that same shield will provide necessary protection should an aggressor not be deterred.

Insurance against Soviet Defensive Technology Program. While we refer to our program as the President's Strategic Defense Initiative some have the misconception that the United States alone is pursuing an increased emphasis on defensive systems—a unilateral U.S. action which will alter the strategic balance. This is not the case. The Soviet Union has always considered defense to be a central and natural part of its national security policy. The extensive, advanced Soviet air defense network and large civil defense program are obvious examples of this priority.

But in addition to this, the Soviets have for many years been working on a number of technologies, both traditional and advanced, with potential for defending against ballistic missiles. For example, while within the constraints of the ABM Treaty, the Soviet Union currently is upgrading the capability of the only operational ABM system in the world today—the Moscow ABM defense system.

The Soviets are also engaged in research and development on a rapidly deployable ABM system that raises concerns about their potential ability to break out of the ABM Treaty and deploy a nationwide ABM defense system within the next ten years should they choose to do so. Were they to do so, as they could, deterrence would collapse, and we would have no choices between surrender and suicide.

In addition to these ABM efforts, some of the Soviet Union's air defense missiles and radars are also of particular concern. The Soviet Union already possesses an extensive air defense network. With continued improvements to this network, it could also provide some degree of ABM protection for the Soviet Union and its Warsaw Pact allies—and do so all nominally within the bounds prescribed by the ABM Treaty.

Since the late 1960's, the Soviet Union also has been pursuing a substantial, advanced defensive technologies program—a program which has been exploring many of the same technologies of interest to the United States in the SDI program. In addition to covering a wide range of advanced technologies, including various laser and neutral particle beams, the Soviet program apparently has been much larger than the U.S. effort in terms of resources invested—plant, capital, and manpower. In fact, over the last two decades, the Soviet Union has spent roughly as much on defense as it has on its massive offensive program.

The SDI program is a prudent response to the very active Soviet research and development activities in this field and provides insurance against Soviet efforts to develop and deploy unilaterally an advanced defensive system. A unilateral Soviet deployment of such advanced defenses, in concert with the Soviet Union's massive offensive forces and its already impressive air and passive defense capabilities, would destroy the foundation on which deterrence has rested for twenty years.

In pursuing the Strategic Defense Initiative, the United States is striving to fashion a future environment that serves the security interests of the United States and our allies, as well as the Soviet Union. Consequently, should it prove possible to develop a highly capable defense against ballistic missiles, we would envision parallel United States and Soviet deployments, with the outcome being enhanced mutual security and international stability.

Requirements for an Effective Defense

To achieve the benefits which advanced defensive technologies could offer, they must, at a minimum, be able to destroy a sufficient portion of an aggressor's attacking forces to deny him confidence in the outcome of an attack or deny an aggressor the ability to destroy a militarily significant portion of the target base he wishes to attack. The level of defense system capability required to achieve these ends cannot be determined at his time, depending as it does on the size, composition, effectiveness, and passive survivability of U.S. forces relative to those of the Soviet Union. Any effective defense system must, of course, be survivable and cost-effective.

To achieve the required level of survivability, the defensive system need not be invulnerable, but must be able to maintain a sufficient degree of effectiveness to fulfill its mission, even in the face of determined attacks against it. This characteristic is essential not only to maintain the effectiveness of a defense system, but to maintain stability.

Finally, in the interest of discouraging the proliferation of ballistic missile forces, the defensive system must be able to maintain its effectiveness against the offense at less cost than it would take to develop offensive countermeasures and proliferate the ballistic missiles necessary to overcome it. ABM systems of the past have lacked this essential capability, but the newly emerging technologies being pursued under the SDI program have great potential in this regard.

Current Programs

Today, deterrence against Soviet aggression is grounded almost exclusively in the capabilities of our offensive retaliatory forces, and this is likely to remain true for some time. Consequently, the SDI program in no way signals a near-term shift away from the modernization of our strategic and intermediate-range nuclear systems and our conventional military forces. Such modernization is essential to the maintenance of deterrence while we are pursuing the generation of technologically feasible defensive options. In addition, in the event a decision to deploy a defensive system were made by a future President, having a modern and capable retaliatory deterrent force would be essential to the preservation of a stable environment while the shift is made to a different and enhanced basis of deterrence.

Arms Control

As directed by the President, the SDI research program will be conducted in a manner fully consistent with all U.S. treaty obligations, including the 1972 ABM Treaty. The ABM Treaty prohibits the development, testing, and deployment of ABM systems and components that are space-based, air-based, and sea-based, or mobile land-based. However, as Gerard Smith, chief U.S. negotiator of the ABM Treaty, reported to the Senate Armed Services Committee in 1972, that agreement does permit research short of field testing of a prototype ABM system or component. This is the type of research that will be conducted under the SDI program.

Any future national decision to deploy defensive systems would, of course, lead to an important change in the structure of United States and Soviet forces. We are examining ways in which the offense/defense relationship can be managed to achieve a more stable balance through strategic arms control. Above all, we seek to ensure that the interaction of offensive and defensive forces removes first-strike options from either side's capability.

The United States does not view defensive measures as a means of establishing military superiority. Because we have no ambitions in this regard, deployments of defensive systems would most usefully be done in the context of a cooperative, equitable, and verifiable arms control environment that regulates the offensive and defensive developments and deployments of the United States and Soviet Union. Such an environment could be particularly useful in the period of transition from a deterrent based on the threat of nuclear retaliation, through deterrence based on a balance of offensive and defensive forces, to the period when adjustments to the basis of deterrence are complete and advanced defensive systems are fully deployed. During the transition, arms control agreements could help to manage and establish guidelines for the deployment of defensive systems.

The SDI research program will complement and support U.S. efforts to seek equitable, verifiable reductions in offensive nuclear forces through arms control negotiations. Such reductions would make a useful contribution to stability, whether in today's deterrence environment or in a potential future deterrence environment in which defenses played a leading role.

A future decision to develop and deploy effective defenses against ballistic missiles could support our policy of pursuing significant reductions in ballistic missile forces. To the extent that defensive systems could reduce the effectiveness and, thus, value of ballistic missiles, they also could increase the incentives for negotiated reductions. Significant reductions in turn would serve to increase the effectiveness and deterrent potential of defensive systems.

SDI and the Allies

Because our security is inextricably linked to that of our friends and allies, the SDI program will not confine itself solely to an exploitation of technologies with potential against ICBMs and SLBMs [submarine-launched ballistic missiles], but will also carefully examine technologies with potential against shorter range ballistic missiles.

An effective defense against shorter range ballistic missiles could have a significant impact on deterring aggression in Europe. Soviet SS-20's, SCALEBOARD's and other shorter range ballistic missiles provide overlapping capabilities to strike all of NATO Europe. Moreover, Soviet doctrine stresses the use of conventionally armed ballistic missiles to initiate rapid and wide-ranging attacks on crucial NATO military targets throughout Europe. The purpose of this tactic would be to reduce significantly NATO's ability to resist the initial thrust of a Soviet conventional force attack and to impede NATO's ability to resupply and reinforce its combatants from outside Europe. By reducing or eliminating the military effectiveness of such ballistic missiles, defensive systems have the potential for enhancing deterrence against not only strategic nuclear war, but against nuclear and conventional attacks on our allies as well.

Over the next several years, we will work closely with our allies to ensure that, in the event of any future decision to deploy defensive systems (a decision in which consultation with our allies will play an important part), allied, as well as U.S., security against aggression would be enhanced.

Assertions and Facts about SDI

A key fact ignored by many critics of the Strategic Defense Initiative is that SDI is a research program, not a program to deploy weapons. The question of whether to proceed to deployment of an actual ballistic missile defense system would arise in the years to come when the SDI research generates options for effective defenses that are achievable and affordable.

Many misleading claims and charges are often made by critics of SDI.

Assertion: SDI means a radical change in the fundamental concepts of U.S. military-political strategy.

Fact: Fundamental U.S. and NATO defense policy is to avoid war through deterrence. A mix of offensive and defensive systems is fully compatible with that objective.

The purpose of SDI is to determine whether there are cost-effective defensive technologies that could enhance deterrence and increase stability.

Technological advances inevitably have profound military and political effects. The course of statesmanship is not to ignore the advance of technology, but to look ahead, to study the promise and potential pitfalls of these advances, especially in their implications for international security. That is precisely what SDI is designed to do.

Assertion: SDI will leave our allies defenseless and mean a return to "Fortress America."

Fact: The President made clear that no change in technology can or will alter our commitments to our allies. In particular, NATO's strategy of flexible response, which is the basis for deterrence and peace in Europe, remains as valid today as when it was first adopted in 1967. The President made our continuing commitment to our allies explicit in his March 1983 speech announcing SDI. Consequently, SDI is looking at the entire ballistic missile threat, including the shorter-range threat to our allies.

Assertion: The experts "know" that there is no point in even trying to defend against attack.

Fact: The history of the development of technology argues strongly against those who make flat statements that something is technologically impossible. Advances in physics, data processing, and other fields offer ample justification to explore whether technologies in these and other fields can be applied to defend the United States and its allies. Arguments made by Western scientists over the feasibility of defending against ballistic missiles can only be resolved with further research.

This argument is also a favorite theme of the "concerned Soviet scientists" who argue in the West that the United States should refrain from even exploring whether it is possible to defend against offensive nuclear systems. In doing so, they carefully and intentionally refrain from noting the Soviet Union's own efforts at defense.

Assertion: Through SDI, the United States is unilaterally accelerating the arms race.

Fact: As noted, the Soviets are already hard at work on advanced technologies for BMD [ballistic missile defense], including lasers and other directed-energy weapons. They also have active programs on more conventional approaches to BMD, including upgrading the anti-ballistic missile (ABM) system in place around Moscow (the only ABM system in the world), and research and development on a new rapidly deployable ABM system.

These Soviet programs have been going on without regard to U.S. efforts. Most were underway many years before the President's speech on strategic defense. There is no reason to believe they would stop if we now decided to do no research of our own.

Moreover, during the past decade the Soviets have engaged in a massive build-up of all categories of offensive weaponry as well, despite the existence of the ABM Treaty and the Treaty's commitment to corresponding reductions in offensive (as well as defensive) capabilities.

Assertion: Effective BMD would be fantastically expensive, and easily negated by countermeasures.

Fact: Judgments of technological feasibility of possible costs (including offense/defense cost ratios) are highly premature. When not the product of prejudgment or bias, many critics' assertions betray a static approach to complex questions of evolving technology and strategic deterrence, both of which are, by their nature, highly dynamic.

Assertion: Ballistic missile defenses are intended to give the United States a first-strike capability.

Fact: The United States does not seek a "first-strike capability" and we will not attempt to acquire one. The President has reaffirmed that we do not aim for a unilateral advantage in BMD.

In fact, effective defenses against ballistic missiles, by increasing the uncertainty a potential attacker must confront, would be a powerful disincentive to anyone contemplating a nuclear first strike. This disincentive to first-strike can be further enhanced by reductions of offensive ballistic missiles—precisely the objective we have been trying to achieve in arms control.

The basic U.S. arms control objective is to achieve balanced outcomes at the lowest possible level, with the forces of both sides deployed in a way that increases crisis stability. The U.S. strategic modernization program is designed both to provide incentives for the Soviets to move toward such an outcome, and to enhance deterrence and stability whether they do so or not.

Soviet commentators, of course, can be counted on to call any new U.S. weapon a "first-strike" system—they have even applied the term to the Space Shuttle. Comparable Soviet systems—including many deployed for years before their U.S. counterparts—never earn this sobriquet. Their discussion of the SDI research program is fully consistent with this pattern.

Assertion: SDI violates the ABM Treaty.

Fact: The United States does not and will not violate its treaty obligations. The ABM Treaty explicitly permits the kind of research envisaged under SDI, and all such research will be conducted within its constraints. Critics who claim that SDI would violate this treaty or others are simply wrong—often because they are critiquing an SDI program of a nature and direction of their own invention, rather than the research program the United States will actually carry out. Moreover, the Soviets have been conducting analogous research for many years. They have not called their research program a violation of the ABM Treaty—nor have we for that matter.

In contrast, the Soviet Union is constructing a large phased-array radar that will contribute to its ABM potential. Because of the location and orientation of this radar, it almost certainly constitutes a violation of the 1972 ABM Treaty.

The ABM Treaty provides for possible amendments and periodic review sessions in which possible changes can be discussed. When the SDI research has produced specific options to develop and deploy a BMD system, we would then address the question of availing ourselves of these procedures in order to modify the Treaty.

Meanwhile, however, the ABM Treaty specifically calls on the United States and U.S.S.R. to take effective measures to reduce offensive nuclear weapons. The United States welcomes the Soviet Union's decision to return to such negotiations, which it has boycotted since late 1983.

Moreover, we have repeatedly told the Soviets we would like to discuss the implications of these new defensive technologies with them in a government-to-government forum. We have made suggestions about the venue and invited their ideas.

Assertion: SDI will mean "the militarization of outer space."

Fact: Recent Soviet propaganda has stressed the supposed need "to prevent the militarization of outer space." In fact, the Soviets have had a fully deployed anti-satellite (ASAT) weapon for over a decade; it is the only such operational system in the world (A U.S. ASAT is still under development.) In the late 1960's the Soviets developed a Fractional Orbiting Bombardment System, involving an orbiting nuclear warhead—a system with no U.S. counterpart, then or now. Moreover, the "militarization of space" began in the late 1950's when the first Soviet ballistic missiles were tested. Thus, professed Soviet concerns about preventing the United States from "militarizing space" are disingenuous at best.

If a decision were made at some future time to deploy a BMD system, some components might well be based in space. Any such deployments would be defensive systems, aimed at preventing the use of weapons, which themselves go through space to attack targets on earth. It is hard to understand why it is wrong even to consider possible ways to use space to prevent nuclear devastation on earth.

Today, there are considerable "military" uses of space which directly help maintain stability and preserve the peace. Both the United States and the U.S.S.R. for instance, use space for such purposes as early warning and the monitoring of arms control agreements.

Questions and Answers about SDI

Q. What is the Administration's Strategic Defense Initiative (SDI) which is sometimes referred to as "Star Wars"? Does it mean we have lost confidence in deterrence?

A. Our nuclear deterrent has kept the peace for almost forty years. It has prevented not only nuclear conflict but also direct military conflict between the United States and the Soviet Union and between East and West in Europe. At the same time, as President Reagan pointed out in March 1983, it is important to examine the potential contribution of defensive technologies to see if we can reduce the risk of war even further. He described the vision underlying his initiative in this way: "What if free people could live secure in the knowledge that their security did not rest upon the threat of instant U.S. retaliation to deter a Soviet attack, that we could intercept and destroy strategic ballistic missiles before they reach our own soil or that of our allies?"

The Strategic Defense Initiative (SDI) is a research program to vigorously pursue important new technologies that can be used to create a defense against ballistic missiles which could strengthen deterrence and increase our security and that of our allies. The research effort is designed to allow a future President and Congress to decide whether to go ahead with such a system. The Strategic Defense Initiative is fully consistent with all of our arms control treaty obligations.

Q. Why is the Administration pursuing the Strategic Defense Initiative now?

A. For three basic reasons. First, a defense against ballistic missiles could significantly enhance deterrence and stability. Second, recent technological breakthroughs suggest that it may be possible to overcome the difficulties in defending against ballistic missiles. Third, the Soviets have long been hard at work in this area. We cannot afford to risk letting them gain a significantly technological advantage that could in time be converted to a military advantage over us.

By pursuing SDI research now we learn more about the prospect for defense against ballistic missiles and have a prudent hedge against the possibility of a Soviet breakthrough in defensive technologies and breakout or abrogation of the ABM Treaty.

Q. Specifically, what are the Soviets doing in the area of strategic defense?

A. The U.S.S.R. has long devoted many more financial and human resources than we have to strategic defenses. The Soviets maintain and are upgrading the world's only operational antiballistic missile (ABM) system, which is in place around Moscow. They are building a new large phased-array radar in Siberia which almost certainly violates the ABM Treaty. The Soviets are also engaged in research and development on a potential ABM system which could be quickly installed and could form the basis of a nationwide defense if they chose to go ahead with such a system. In addition, for more than a decade and a half, the Soviets have been vigorously pursuing research in advanced technologies—including lasers and neutral particle beams—with application to ballistic missile defense.

Q. What is the difference between the Strategic Defense Initiative and ASATs?

A. Both the Strategic Defense Initiative and our anti-satellite program aim at enhancing deterrence and strengthening strategic stability, both in different ways. Many of the technologies involved in the Strategic Defense Initiative research and the ASAT program are related. However, the ASAT program is a near-term effort to develop an anti-satellite weapon intended to redress a specific military imbalance. The Strategic Defense Initiative is a long-term research program to explore the future potential for defense against the threat of ballistic missiles and to provide insurance against any potential Soviet decision to deploy additional anti-ballistic missile (ABM) systems.

Q. Is the Strategic Defense Initiative permitted under the ABM Treaty?

A. Yes. The Strategic Defense Initiative is a research program. The ABM Treaty permits research. The United States and, to a greater extent, the U.S.S.R. have had research programs since the signing of the Treaty.

II. CAN IT BE DONE?

EDITOR'S INTRODUCTION

Despite the President's claims, it is not at all clear that an effective Star Wars defense—one that fits Reagan's definition of rendering nuclear weapons obsolete—can be built. An array of spectacular new technologies—most as yet undeveloped and unproven—has been proposed as the basis for strategic defense. These include "smart bullets" that guide themselves toward their targets, high-powered lasers and particle beams that can burn the skin off a missile or destroy its electronics, and remote-sensing satellites using superconducting computers that can detect missile launches within seconds and faultlessly direct the operations of scores of orbiting battle stations. Even those scientists who, like the President, are optimistic about these technologies tend to disagree vehemently about their applicability, ultimate cost, and readiness to be used. But many experts feel that strategic defense is completely unattainable at any foreseeable level of technological expertise. In fact, Star Wars has polarized the scientific community to a greater extent than almost any other recent issue.

James C. Fletcher, the former head of NASA, is the author of this section's first article, reprinted from *Issues in Science and Technology*. He reviews the results of his study of Star Wars technologies and outlines the concept of "defense in depth" that is at the heart of an effective defense. In the next article, from *Scientific American*, physicists Hans Bethe, Richard Garwin, Kurt Gottfried, and Henry Kendall, all members of the Union of Concerned Scientists, give a pessimistic assessment of Star Wars. A Star Wars defense could not protect the entire nation, they claim, but instead would initiate a dangerous escalation of the arms race. Astrophysicist Robert Jastrow, a prominent supporter of Star Wars, rebutts the conclusions of the UCS in the next selection, reprinted from *Commentary*. Opponents of Star Wars, in his view, are giving way to "ideological preconceptions." Finally, Gary L. Guertner,

a political scientist writing in *Foreign Policy*, analyzes the raging
scientific debate. At issue, says Guertner, is whether any aspect
of Star Wars has been or can be proven to be a realistic possibility.

THE TECHNOLOGIES FOR BALLISTIC MISSILE DEFENSE[1]

I

In March of 1983, President Reagan appealed to the scientific
community to devise new methods for countering the threat of nuclear ballistic missiles. Shortly after his speech, Reagan directed
that two studies be conducted, one to assess the technologies necessary for ballistic missile defense, the other to examine the policy
implications of such a system.

I was asked to lead the Defensive Technologies Study. Over
a period of four-and-a-half months, our team of 50 scientists and
engineers reviewed the emerging technologies relevant to ballistic
missile defense. We looked at infrared, laser, and radar sensors
for tracking missiles high in space; at high-speed projectiles and
powerful laser and particle beams for intercepting missiles minutes after they are launched. Furthermore, we examined concepts
for fashioning these technologies into a robust, reliable system.

At the end of our study, we concluded that although enormous
hurdles remain, the technological advances of the past two decades
show great promise for ballistic missile defense. We recommended
that a vigorous research and development program be pursued.
The goal of that program is to demonstrate the key technologies
by the early 1990s, allowing a decision to be made at that time on
whether to proceed with a ballistic missile defense for the twenty-
first century. Since that time, the Strategic Defense Initiative Organization has been established within the Defense Department

[1]Reprint of an article by James C. Fletcher, former head of NASA. *Issues in Science and Technology.*
1:15+. Fall '84. ©1984, National Academy of Sciences. Reprinted by permission.

to pursue a technology development program very similar to the one we recommended.

This article describes the technologies for ballistic missile defense. It identifies the most promising approaches and system components, as well as the critical technologies—those emerging systems and capabilities that must be demonstrated before we will know whether an effective defense is feasible.

The various system concepts described in this article, as in the study on which it is based, are designed to counter a massive, full-scale Soviet attack, which, at current force levels, would involve thousands of intercontinental and submarine-launched ballistic missiles and the tens of thousands of warheads that they carry. Smaller portions of a comprehensive defense system could be deployed in different combinations to protect against limited nuclear ballistic missile attacks, as described later.

The emphasis in this defensive effort is on ballistic missiles, rather than on other offensive forces, because they are the most threatening of the strategic nuclear weapons. Given their extremely short flight time (ballistic missiles launched from the Soviet Union can reach the United States in approximately 30 minutes), these missiles provide the capability for a preemptive attack that could potentially overwhelm our strategic forces, eliminating the chance of an effective retaliatory response. By contrast, bombers and cruise missiles offer sufficient warning time for the United States to disperse, and thereby protect, its retaliatory assets. However, ballistic missiles launched from submarines a short distance off the U.S. coast could have even shorter flight times than intercontinental ballistic missiles; therefore they would have to be handled differently.

To understand the various defensive concepts under investigation, it is necessary to know something more about the typical trajectory of a ballistic missile, which consists of four phases. The estimates of flight time below are for an intercontinental ballistic missile and would vary for intermediate-range and submarine-launched ballistic missiles.

The *boost phase* spans the first several hundred seconds after launch, when the missile is lifted from its silo and thrust through and out of the atmosphere by its first, second, and third-stage booster rockets. Each rocket burns for about one minute, propelling the missile at increasing speeds to an altitude of about 200 kilometers, the altitude of the lowest earth-orbiting satellites. By the end of the boost phase, the missile is traveling at seven kilometers per second.

Once the third-stage booster burns out, the missile enters the *post-boost phase,* which lasts another several hundred seconds. The third-stage booster falls away, leaving the post-boost vehicle and its cargo, up to ten multiple independently targeted reentry vehicles, or MIRVs, each carrying a nuclear warhead directed at a separate target. Powered by a low-thrust rocket, the post-boost vehicle, or "bus," maneuvers through space, dropping off its reentry vehicles in programmed sequence and directing them on their distinct trajectories. The post-boost vehicle can also carry decoys and other penetration aids to confuse or overwhelm the defense; hundreds of these may be deployed by each booster along with each reentry vehicle.

Once released from the bus, the reentry vehicles and decoys begin their ballistic, or freefall, flight, arcing up to their apogee at 1,000 kilometers or so, then falling back to Earth. This 20-minute unguided ascent and descent of the reentry vehicles is known as the *midcourse phase.* In addition to its nuclear warhead, each reentry vehicle contains sufficient heat shielding to allow it to survive reentry through the atmosphere and a fusing system to detonate the warhead at the right time.

The *terminal phase* begins when the reentry vehicles, decoys, penetration aids, and debris begin to reenter Earth's upper atmosphere at an altitude of about 100 kilometers. Lightweight objects, including some decoys and debris, are slowed by atmospheric drag and then broken apart by the force of deceleration. The heavier reentry vehicles, which are "hardened" to survive the heat and deceleration, continue on their trajectories. The terminal phase ends some two minutes after it begins when the reentry vehicles, by this time a glowing red, detonate over their targets.

An effective defense against a massive Soviet ballistic missile attack will require a multilayered system capable of attacking missiles in all phases of their trajectory. Each of these multiple layers, corresponding to one of the four phases of a missile's flight, would use its own combination of sensors and weapons to track and intercept missiles as they streak through space. Each layer serves as a back-up to the previous layer: those missiles that penetrate or "leak" through the first line of defense, the boost-phase defense, will be intercepted by post-boost, midcourse, and then terminal-phase defenses. By contrast, the earlier antiballistic missile (ABM) concepts attacked oncoming missiles primarily in their reentry phase.

The fundamental premise of today's "defense-in-depth" concept is that a series of moderately effective layers can produce extremely high system effectiveness. For example, four layers that are each 70 percent effective produce an overall intercept effectiveness of greater than 99 percent. In addition, a single layer of 70 or 90 percent effectiveness is far less costly to construct than a single layer of 90 to 99.9 percent effectiveness.

Another assumption is that a multilayered defense, with its combination of different weapons and sensors, will vastly complicate the task of the attacker. Any tactic, usually called a countermeasure, that the offense might use to degrade or circumvent one defensive weapon or sensor would have little or no effect on the other elements of the defense. Indeed, certain countermeasures may actually limit the attacker's ability to penetrate other defenses. For instance, a coat of heat-shielding material applied to the skin of a missile can reduce the effects of a laser attack. This shield also increases the missile's weight, however, which means it can carry fewer warheads and decoys.

Each phase of missile flight presents advantages and disadvantages to the defensive planner. By intercepting missiles in the boost phase, the defense can eliminate the entire cargo of reentry vehicles and decoys, which can mean the difference between one or hundreds of targets. In this phase, tracking the missile is simple: once the booster rises above the cloud deck its red-hot exhaust flames are readily visible to space-based sensors. In addition, the unprotected booster is vulnerable to attack by either impact weapons or lasers and particle beams. The difficulty of boost-phase defense is that the system must be able to respond to a simultaneous launch of as many as several thousand missiles, which must be intercepted within the two or three minutes that they rise above the atmosphere.

There is an obvious advantage to attacking early in the next phase, the post-boost phase, before the bus has deployed all of its reentry vehicles and penetration aids. As in the boost-phase defense, the post-boost system must intercept a large—and increasing—number of targets within a few minutes. The task is complicated in this phase, however, because the colder flame of the bus's low-thrust rocket is difficult to detect. Another disadvantage is that the post-boost vehicle may be hardened to withstand attacks by lasers and other weapons.

Midcourse defense offers the advantage of a long, 20-minute engagement time and the predictability of the freefall trajectory. The disadvantage is that the defense must discriminate warheads from debris and hundreds of thousands of decoys, and detection is still more difficult. In addition, the shielding that enables the reentry vehicles to survive atmospheric reentry protects them from weapons as well.

In the terminal phase, the atmosphere filters out the decoys and debris, simplifying the task of target identification. The relatively modest range at which the interceptors have to operate poses fewer demands on weapon design. The disadvantage of terminal defense is that very few, if any, of the remaining reentry vehicles can be allowed through, and there is only a short time available for the defenses to act.

II

A ballistic missile defense system must perform certain essential functions in each phase. These are surveillance, acquisition, and discrimination; pointing and tracking; target intercept and destruction; and battle management.

Surveillance and acquisition involves search and detection of any potentially threatening objects. Sensors are used to detect an attack and define its intensity, destination, and probable targets. *Discrimination* involves processing signals and data to identify an object, and in the later stages, to determine whether it is a warhead that should be intercepted or a nonthreatening decoy or booster fragment. The same sensors can also be used to determine whether a missile or reentry vehicle has been successfully destroyed or damaged.

Pointing and tracking, which is usually performed by sensors built into the defense weapons, involves taking a series of measurements of the position and velocity of the target—the booster or reentry vehicle, for instance—to determine its future trajectory. These measurements are then used to guide the interceptor to its target.

Target intercept and destruction is the use of any one of a number of weapons to intercept and destroy the booster or reentry vehicle.

Battle management encompasses all the data management, communication, and decisionmaking functions necessary to coordinate the defensive efforts.

To illustrate how ballistic missile defense might work, a hypothetical system is described below. This description is intended to convey the scope of such a system—to show, for example, how the individual components might function and how the sensors and weapons in the various layers might interact. It should not be seen as a precise blueprint. A number of diverse technologies show promise for ballistic missile defense, and others will undoubtedly be brought to light by the current research effort. At this point, it is too early to know which components will prove the most effective or how a system might be configured from them.

This is especially true for the boost and post-boost phase weapons, which pose some of the most technically challenging design questions. The candidates for boost and post-boost intercept include space-based hypervelocity guns and chemical rockets, both of which are kinetic-energy weapons that accelerate a projectile toward the target at very high speeds, and the more publicized directed-energy weapons, lasers or particle beams, that direct energy toward their targets. The hypervelocity gun is described in the following conceptual design; the chemical rocket and directed-energy weapons will be discussed in a later section.

In this conceptual design, satellite-borne sensors in geosynchronous orbit approximately 36,000 kilometers up perform global, fulltime surveillance. These infrared sensors, which detect the thermal radiation of an object, scan specific corridors for an enemy attack. Within seconds of the missile launch, these sensors and their computers determine the general characteristics of the attack—the number and type of boosters and their general target areas. Throughout this time, rocket-powered interceptors on board the surveillance satellite protect it from attack by antisatellite weapons.

As soon as it is analyzed, information about the attack is beamed to the boost-phase weapon platforms, perhaps 100 satellites stationed in lower earth orbit. At the same time, the sensor satellites also pass on their data to a series of midcourse sensor satellites, in orbits 5,000 to 25,000 kilometers up, which will monitor the deployment of reentry vehicles and decoys by any missiles that slip through the first layer of defense.

Each boost-phase weapon platform contains a hypervelocity gun or guns. Sensors built into the hypervelocity guns begin tracking the boosters as they climb through the atmosphere and then fire into their path. These guns use electromagnetic energy to accelerate at high speed projectiles that can destroy a target on impact. The projectiles themselves are equipped with homing devices and maneuvering capabilities that guide them during the last few kilometers to the target; for that reason, they are often called "smart bullets." The kinetic energy of the head-on collision is sufficient to tear apart the missile before it completes its ascent.

Once the third-stage booster rockets burn out, the infrared sensors on high-altitude satellites lose sight of the remaining missiles. In their place, the various sensors on the midcourse satellites detect the colder plume of the post-boost vehicle, then begin tracking and the difficult process of discriminating real targets from decoys.

The hypervelocity guns on the boost-phase platform are used again to attack the targets in the post-boost phase, striking first against the buses in an effort to intercept as many as possible before they deploy their full allotment of warheads and decoys.

Throughout midcourse, the 20-minute freefall ascent and descent of the reentry vehicles, an increasing number of sensing and imaging devices on the midcourse satellites are called into play to discriminate the active targets from the large number of other objects. Scanners that operate at many different electromagnetic wavelengths—including radar, optical (light) sensors, and infrared sensors—provide a variety of distinctive "signatures" from the objects; these combined clues enable computers to discriminate the balloons, heavier decoys, debris, and weapons.

In addition, active laser probes beamed from space, or perhaps from the ground, are used to identify the most convincing decoys. These moderate-energy lasers scan the engagement area, illuminating hundreds of objects. Then specialized sensors on the midcourse platform observe how the objects reflect that light, providing information about their weight, size, temperature, and other characteristics.

Once the targets are identified, signals relayed from the space-based sensors guide thousands of very small, ground-based chemical rockets to the vicinity of the reentry vehicles. As they near their targets, the chemical rockets release their warheads, non-nuclear homing projectiles, or smart bullets, that home in on the target outside of the atmosphere and destroy it by impact. In addition, any gun platforms that have now orbited into range are brought to bear against the reentry vehicles.

In the final line of defense, the terminal-phase sensors detect and discriminate all objects that have leaked through the earlier layers. Information is handed over from space-based midcourse sensors to infrared sensors located aboard high-altitude aircraft, launched on warning of attack.

Ground-based radars work in conjunction with the airborne sensors to define the precise trajectory of the warheads before the interceptor rockets are committed. The terminal interceptors are ground-based, high-acceleration chemical rockets, capable of reaching their targets while they are still high in the atmosphere. (Reentry vehicles must be intercepted at high altitudes to ensure that even those warheads that are "salvage-fused"—that is, designed to detonate when intercepted—will not substantially damage targets on the ground.) The terminal defense rockets are equipped with onboard sensors and guidance systems that scan and home in on the reentry vehicle to which they have been assigned. As it nears the target, the interceptor warhead explodes, scattering thousands of pellets in the path of the reentry vehicle. Even if the rocket is blown off course at the last instant, some of the cloud of pellets will collide with the target. Alternately, these interceptors might also use smart bullets as their warheads.

Throughout the engagement, the actions of the various sensors and weapons are coordinated by the battle management and command, control, and communication system—a network of extremely fast, high-capacity interconnected computers located in space and on Earth. This system provides the communication link between the myriad components of the defense. It performs the data processing, or analysis, necessary to identify targets and support other operations.

Each defensive layer has its own semiautonomous battle management system, composed of its sensors, weapons, and data-processing equipment, that monitors the global situation, allocates the defensive weapons, directs their fire, and records the results of each attempted intercept. The battle management systems in each phase are interconnected, allowing for redundant, decentralized command and control of the entire defensive effort. The overall system maintains a master file that provides birth-to-death tracking of every potentially threatening object—the hundreds of thousands of warheads, decoys, penetration aids, and pieces of debris. This system provides global summaries of the progress of battle and in most cases replaces human decisionmaking.

Of the technologies described in this hypothetical ballistic missile defense system, those for midcourse and terminal defense are the best understood. The generic approaches identified here—that is, space-based sensors and ground-based rockets for midcourse defense, and airborne surveillance and ground-based rockets for terminal-phase defense—would likely be sufficiently advanced by the 1990s so that a decision could be made on whether to build a defensive system, should strategic policy warrant it.

Greater uncertainty surrounds the concepts for boost-phase defense. In addition to the hypervelocity guns and smart bullets, the candidates for boost-phase intercept include space-based chemical rockets; space-based lasers; ground-based lasers relayed off of mirrors in space; "pop-up" lasers; and space-based particle beams.

Like the hypervelocity gun, space-based chemical rockets are designed to accelerate smart projectiles that destroy their targets by impact. The rockets are clustered in groups in a "rocket pod" aboard a platform in lower earth orbit. Once the sensors have detected the missile launch, the rockets are fired into the path of the boosters. As the rocket nears the target, it releases its homing projectile, which uses its own sensors and maneuvering capabilities to accelerate and smash into a booster.

At this stage, the hypervelocity gun may offer a distinct advantage over the chemical rocket for boost-phase defense: it is estimated that these guns will be capable of accelerating the projectile at a speed of tens of kilometers per second, far faster than what appears possible for a chemical rocket. Higher velocities extend both the capabilities and the range of a weapon. Consequently, if chemical rockets were used for boost-phase intercept, the system might require five times the number of weapon platforms than would be necessary for hypervelocity guns. The hypervelocity gun has its own disadvantages, however. To achieve its high speeds the gun requires a considerable pulse of electric power, which might be costly to supply in space.

To varying extents, both of these kinetic-energy weapons concepts are based on existing technologies. Although much technology work remains to be done on these weapons, especially on the hypervelocity gun, in my opinion they might offer the potential for relatively near-term deployment.

Another candidate for boost-phase intercept is chemical laser weapons, operating at the infrared portion of the spectrum, based on 50 to 100 platforms in lower earth orbit. Traveling at literally the speed of light, the laser beams are able to destroy in sequence perhaps thousands of boosters launched in a mass attack. Each weapon requires a generator to produce the laser beam, an optics system, which consists of mirrors and lenses to focus and direct the beam, systems for acquisition, pointing, and tracking, and a considerable power supply. This adds up to a weight of tens of metric tons for each laser platform.

To intercept the booster, the laser must be aimed accurately— to within one meter over several thousand kilometers—and then held steady on a moving target. This might be accomplished using a low-energy laser to scan for the target. Light from this laser probe is reflected back by the target and used as a guide to lock the main laser onto the missile. The missile is destroyed when the laser burns a hole in its skin or raises its temperature to a level that damages the internal components—both of which might require several seconds of a continuous beam, depending on laser power and range.

Other directed-energy concepts for a space-based defense include x-ray lasers and particle-beam weapons. Particle-beam weapons, which are beams of charged or neutral atomic particles, deposit their energy within the target and cause damage through irradiation.

An alternative to the space-based system uses ground-based lasers and a series of orbiting mirrors in space that reflect laser light back to attack the rising boosters. Short wavelength lasers, such as free-electron or excimer lasers, can be used to penetrate the Earth's atmosphere with sufficient power. When a missile launch is detected, the laser energy is directed to relay mirrors in high orbit that carry the beam around the curve of the Earth. The beam is then sent to intercept mirrors at lower altitudes that guide it to the target.

Another option, sometimes called the "pop-up" scheme, bases x-ray lasers in the nose cones of ballistic missiles, which would be launched into space on early warning of an enemy attack.

III

An effective multilayered system for ballistic missile defense, such as the conceptual design described here, could not be built today. It depends upon certain technological systems and capabilities that have yet to be developed or demonstrated in these particular applications. These critical technologies, the weak links in the chain, are: weapons for boost-phase intercept; low-cost midcourse and terminal interceptors; sensors and software for tracking and discrimination; survivability techniques; and computer capability for battle management.

The Defensive Technologies Study Team proposed a long-term research and development plan to evaluate and demonstrate the technical feasibility of these key technologies. The outcome of this research will determine whether an effective ballistic missile defense is possible. The critical technologies are described below.

Boost-phase intercept. Without the ability to intercept missiles in their boost phase, a highly reliable, low-leakage defense would be exceedingly difficult to achieve. Consequently, a high priority of the new initiative is to demonstrate the directed-energy and kinetic-energy weapons for boost-phase intercept.

For directed-energy weapons, the current goal is to demonstrate the feasibility of these beam generators on a laboratory scale by the late 1980s or early 1990s, and their ability to be scaled to a weapon-level performance by the early 1990s. The generation of the beam itself is not the most critical task; indeed, technologies for beam control, optics, and pointing and tracking represent the greatest challenges. Research is under way in all of these areas.

It is also crucial to determine the lethality of these lasers and particle-beam weapons against "responsive" threats. The offense can use a number of countermeasures to withstand or evade defensive weapons. For instance, a booster can be "hardened" against laser attack: a reflective coat can deflect laser light and a heat-shielding material can provide some protection against damaging laser energy. Research is under way to determine the minimum energy needed to penetrate these shields or to overcome other offensive countermeasures.

"Fast-burn" booster rockets might also be used to evade boost-phase weapons. These are rockets that burn out in 100 seconds or less. Equipped with fast-burn rockets, a missile can complete most of the boost phase within the atmosphere. This complicates the task for both directed-energy and kinetic-energy weapons: given the short engagement time, additional interceptors might be necessary to destroy the same number of warheads. In addition, it would make the missiles largely invulnerable to certain types of boost-phase weapons, such as neutral particle beams, that cannot penetrate the atmosphere. Several beam weapons that have the potential for penetrating the atmosphere to intercept even fast-burn rockets are being investigated.

For the kinetic-energy weapons, research is focusing on the development of space-based hypervelocity guns, interceptor rockets, and homing projectiles. Key issues include systems for fire control, guidance, and space-based energy supply.

Midcourse and terminal intercept. The issue is not whether these interceptors—ground-based chemical rockets carrying homing projectiles—can be designed, but whether the cost can be kept relatively low. The goal is to design midcourse and terminal interceptors inexpensive enough to permit an attack on all threatening objects that cannot be discriminated—in other words, on decoys as well as warheads. Cost depends on the size of the rocket: the smaller it is, the less expensive to build and power.

Discrimination and tracking. Unless thousands of objects can be tracked simultaneously and active warheads can be discriminated from destroyed warheads, decoys, and debris, the attacker can saturate the defensive system by increasing the number of warheads and decoys. Discrimination and tracking in boost phase is relatively straightforward, as the booster flame is easy to detect and the number of targets is relatively small. Discrimination in the midcourse and terminal phases will depend on advances in both sensing technologies and computer software. The technology for sensing is quite complex. The research and development program calls for work on infrared sensors, laser sensors, space-based radar, and imaging techniques, as well as the requisite software capabilities.

Survivability. The space-based assets of a defense system—the boost-phase weapons and sensors, the midcourse sensors, and the battle management satellites—must be able to withstand direct enemy attack or the offense will simply remove them in the first phase of an attack. The possible threats to the system are ground- or space-based lasers or particle-beam weapons, direct-ascent antisatellite weapons, fragment clouds, and space mines. In addition, the electronics of these components are vulnerable to the effects of small nuclear explosions, which can be used to disable the system.

Ensuring the survivability of the space-based components of the defense is one of the toughest design challenges. The solution will require a combination of technologies and tactics specific to each weapon or sensor. In general, the approaches to enhancing survivability against a determined attacker are the classic ones that have been used for years to protect aircraft and surface ships: hardening, evasion, proliferation, deception, and active defense.

Using these approaches, there is reason to believe that space elements can be made highly survivable.

Battle management. The design of a battle management system will be a formidable task. It must keep track of tens of thousands of objects and allocate defense resources in a constantly changing situation. It must communicate with authorities external to the defense system and, for instance, coordinate these defensive actions with those of U.S. offensive forces.

The computers must be very fast, performing on the order of one billion operations a second. They should be designed to be maintenance-free for ten years and to avoid a sudden failure of the entire system in case any single element fails. In addition, the computers must be able to operate in a nuclear environment and must be hardened to survive radiation and shock. To keep crucial command, control, and communication capabilities out of the fray, some of the computers would be placed in high orbit halfway to the moon. These hardware requirements for a battle management system, although demanding, are almost within the state of the art. In fact, work has already begun on developing hardened computers.

The software requirements, however, strain present capabilities. Battle management for a multilayered defense is clearly one of the largest software problems ever tackled, requiring an enormous and error-free program, on the order of ten million lines of code. At present, tools are not available to write such software. The task will require the development of techniques for automated software development—in essence, a computer program that can write another computer program. Similarly, existing "debugging" procedures are inadequate for determining if the program is error-free. Fifty million tests might conceivably be run, again requiring automated testing.

These critical technologies may well require research programs of 10 to 20 years before they are ready for deployment in a ballistic missile defense system. In addition, the successful deployment and operation of a defense system will depend on a number of support capabilities whose development may take 5 to 10 years. For instance, a heavy-lift launch vehicle might be necessary for satellites of up to 100 metric tons. The current capability is

20 to 30 metric tons. Advanced orbital transfer vehicles will be needed to ferry materials from one orbit to another. And finally, a power source capable of supplying multimegawatts of electric power to run space-based weapons and sensors must be developed. Compact nuclear reactors and non-nuclear technologies are now being investigated.

It is the cost-effectiveness of a ballistic missile defense system, however, that may ultimately determine whether it is deployed. Obviously, it would be desirable for it to cost the defense less to destroy a warhead than it costs the offense to deploy one. If not, the offense could simply deploy additional warheads and decoys to saturate the defense, unless, of course, the size of their offensive force were limited by arms control agreements. Cost is closely tied to a number of technical capabilities, including the discrimination and the verification of target destruction. If warheads can be discriminated from all but the most sophisticated decoys, and if sensors can provide positive verification of target kill, then interceptors can be economically allocated to only the real targets.

IV

The technological challenges of strategic defense are great but not insurmountable. In the Defensive Technologies Study, we took an optimistic view of the emerging technologies and concluded that "a robust, multitiered ballistic missile [defense] system can eventually be made to work." We also realized that "the ultimate utility, effectiveness, cost, complexity, and degree of technical risk in this system will depend not only on the technology itself, but also on the extent to which the Soviet Union either agrees to mutual defense arrangements or offense limitations." For instance, if the Soviet Union agreed to reduce its force of intercontinental ballistic missiles, then an effective missile defense would be less expensive and would pose fewer technical challenges.

Although the complete, four-phase defense probably will not be feasible until after the year 2000, it may be possible to begin deploying portions of the system in the 1990s, should Congress and the president decide to do so. The technologies for terminal and midcourse defense are already relatively well understood. Indeed, it should be possible by the end of the decade to demonstrate some of the components for these defenses, including a space-based system for acquisition, pointing, and tracking; a megawatt-class, ground-based laser weapon operating at the visible light wavelength; an airborne sensing system; and a high-speed, non-nuclear interceptor to function within the atmosphere.

Such intermediate versions of a ballistic missile defense system, while unable to provide the protection available from a full, multitiered system, could nonetheless offer meaningful levels of defense, especially against limited nuclear attacks. Terminal or midcourse defenses could be deployed incrementally as part of the full, four-phase system. It would be essential to maintain effective, survivable offensive weapons in conjunction with these initial defense systems.

A terminal defense could provide protection for some high-value assets. The goal of most of the earlier terminal ABM concepts, such as Safeguard, the system partially installed in the early 1970s at the Grand Forks Air Force Base in North Dakota, was defense of our intercontinental ballistic missile silos, an approach known as *hardpoint* defense. The terminal defense systems now envisioned could be used to protect wider areas. These *area* defenses might be used to defend military forces, their command, control, and communication (C^3) facilities, and such support systems as munitions factories and power plants. In addition, a terminal defense system using near-term technology, such as non-nuclear interceptors and airborne surveillance, could perform well against shorter range missiles and could be appropriate for defense of our European allies.

A two-phase system, consisting of terminal and midcourse defenses, or possibly terminal and boost-phase defenses, could be effective enough, in my opinion, to protect most—perhaps 90 or even 99 percent—of the nation's population and infrastructure, including factories, transportation and communication systems, and power supplies—even against a full-scale nuclear attack. It could also provide significant additional protection for military forces and C^3 facilities. If properly constructed, a two-layer system could provide enhanced deterrence, as it would reduce the utility of a missile attack. A key factor relating to the effectiveness of a ballistic missile defense is its cost-exchange ratio: the cost of the defense in relation to the cost of additional offensive measures to overcome it. This remains to be worked out for the two-layer defense systems.

A complete four-phase system (or perhaps a three-phase boost, midcourse and reentry system) has the potential for protecting nearly all of the population—perhaps even greater than 99 percent, in my opinion—against massive nuclear attacks. It could also provide a near-perfect defense against limited attacks. In addition, both of these multitiered systems could save most lives in the event that nuclear weapons were launched by accident or miscalculation or for some irrational, nonmilitary purpose.

There has been much confusion and public debate over the goals of the current Strategic Defense Initiative—whether it is a more limited defense of our strategic forces or a near-perfect population defense. The Defensive Technologies Study Team concluded that, in fact, the two goals are not contradictory. The new program has as its near-term goal the development of technologies for defense of our strategic forces, which would include, among other things, silos, submarine bases, air defenses, intelligence facilities, military bases, factories, and communication and power systems. However, the same area defense technologies for protecting large military installations can also be used to protect cities, and the ultimate goal of the new program is to develop the technical option to deploy a thoroughly reliable population defense for both the United States and its allies.

V

Since this new ballistic missile defense effort was first announced, it has been the subject of much public debate. I would like to address some of the misconceptions about this program and the technologies under development.

The public discussion of defensive technologies has tended to focus on the more exotic weapons, such as lasers and particle beams. In fact, only about 25 percent of the current research budget is devoted to directed-energy weapons. Less than half of the program is concerned with weapons at all; the largest single area is surveillance and tracking research. Although the precise architecture of a future ballistic missile defense system cannot be predicted at this time, it is entirely possible that such a system will not include any directed-energy weapons, relying instead on kinetic-energy weapons. Moreover, if the two superpowers agree to limitations of their offensive forces, then an effective defense might be constructed without any weapons in space.

Another misconception is that offensive countermeasures are so easy, cheap, and effective that no defensive system can be effective. This argument seems to rest on three principal assumptions: first, that simple proliferation of weapons and decoys is a cost-effective method of overwhelming any defense; second, that the Soviets can build a new generation of offensive missiles capable of evading boost-phase defenses; and third, that the space-based assets of the system are inherently vulnerable.

All of these assumptions were addressed early in the Defensive Technologies Study. In evaluating the feasibility of ballistic missile defense—and in defining performance goals for various components of the system—we assumed that the Soviet Union would expand its offensive force at the maximum pace possible. That would mean that within our lifetimes, the Soviet offensive force could grow to two or three times its present size.

Some critics have performed "systems analyses" that seem to show that ballistic missile defenses cannot work against this increased threat. However, in constructing their hypothetical defense systems, these critics have made fundamental errors in choosing the parameters and orbital placement of the space-based components. This has led them to overestimate by a factor of two to ten the number of required satellites. Furthermore, arbitrary performance assumptions are frequently made on laser power, mirror size, and lethal range.

The current research program is designed to demonstrate affordable technologies capable of handling an expanded Soviet offensive force. Until this work is complete, any "systems analyses" will be conjectural at best.

Furthermore, we also devoted substantial effort to defining the countermeasures that might be incorporated in a new generation of Soviet missiles, which presumably would be constructed in re-

sponse to U.S. progress on a defense system. Of the potential countermeasures, the "fast-burn" booster, which could complete most
of its boost-phase within the atmosphere, has perhaps been the
most widely discussed.

Some critics assume that no defense system would be effective
against the fast-burn boosters. However, several issues should be
considered in evaluating the actual threat they pose. For one, the
technical feasibility and cost of building a new generation of missiles has yet to be determined. In addition, a fast-burn booster
might be less efficient and therefore limited to a smaller payload
and fewer decoys and penetration aids. These boosters might also
be less accurate than existing Soviet intercontinental ballistic missiles.

Many of the boost-phase weapons now under development
have substantial potential against fast-burn boosters. And it may
well be true, given the limitations of fast-burn boosters, that a Soviet offensive force composed entirely of these missiles could be effectively countered by midcourse and terminal defense systems
alone. Finally, if the Soviets are indeed faced with the possibility
of completely replacing their intercontinental and submarine-
launched ballistic missiles, an excellent opportunity would exist
for new and substantial arms limitation agreements.

Clearly, the potential threat of fast-burn boosters and all other
countermeasures must be fully assessed. That assessment is one
of the primary objectives of the current research and development
program.

Another issue of concern is whether command and control for
ballistic missile defense can be structured to allow national command authorities (the president and designated chain of command) to activate the system—especially the boost-phase system,
which must respond minutes after a launch is detected. Extensive
research will be required in this area. Nonetheless, it is by no
means clear that a multilayered defense cannot be structured to
allow human control.

An offensive strike would most likely be preceded by a crisis
of some kind. The system can be structured so that it can be activated in stages during a crisis, much as our military forces are now
activated. When the crisis reached a certain level, the president

might choose to activate the terminal defenses. This would provide full presidential control of any weapons deployment. As the crisis intensified, the president might choose to activate the midcourse and ultimately the boost-phase defenses. These steps would be taken with the full knowledge of the opponent. The boost-phase defenses could be set to hold fire until a massive attack was unambiguously confirmed. Any lower intensity attacks could be handled by the midcourse and terminal defenses alone. Furthermore, even an "automatic" response of a boost-phase defense could be structured to allow the president to halt its activation at any point.

VI

Clearly, there are many uncertainties as the United States embarks on its strategic defense effort. We could not now with confidence construct effective ballistic missile defenses. Conversely, we have not been presented with any compelling technical reasons that show that such defenses are not possible. The technical issues surrounding the development of effective defenses have many possible solutions and should not at this stage be the primary focus of the debate.

Rather, the debate should center on the implications of ballistic missile defense for our strategic policy. For the past two decades, the United States has relied exclusively on offensive weapons and the threat of nuclear retaliation as a deterrent to nuclear war. The underlying rationale of this doctrine is that neither superpower is likely to initiate a nuclear war if vulnerable to attack by the surviving strategic forces of the other.

Defensive technologies offer new opportunities for strengthening deterrence and new possibilities for arms limitations. Intermediate defense capabilities, such as a one- or two-phase defense, would reduce the Soviets' confidence in their ability to destroy key military targets, thereby increasing deterrence against a nuclear attack. Fully effective defenses would significantly reduce the utility of a major Soviet preemptive strike—and of ballistic missiles themselves. And by reducing the intrinsic value of ballistic missiles, defensive technologies could provide a strong inducement for reaching agreements to reduce these nuclear weapons.

Work during the past few years has shown that the technological promise is rich, and that effective defenses may indeed be possible. Moreover, the increased Soviet offensive and defensive threat offers a powerful motive for reassessing the role of ballistic missile defense in U.S. deterrent policy. The Soviets now are upgrading the world's only operational ballistic missile defense system, currently in place around Moscow. And they have been pursuing with undeniable vigor research on directed-energy weapons for a more advanced system. Unilateral deployment of such a system would have grave consequences for the security of the United States and its allies. At a minimum, we must pursue a comprehensive technology program to ensure that we are not caught unprepared by a Soviet deployment of advanced ballistic missile defenses.

Moreover, I believe that we have a strong moral imperative to base our strategic relationships on effective defenses, rather than on the threat of inflicting horrendous damage on the attacker. I believe that effective defenses, when deployed by both the United States and the Soviet Union, could lead to a safer world, a world with the possibility for nuclear disarmament. The current technology program can provide the option for this transition to strategic defense. The final decision, however, will be made by the American people.

SPACE-BASED BALLISTIC-MISSILE DEFENSE[2]

For two decades both the U.S. and the U.S.S.R. have been vulnerable to a devastating nuclear attack, inflicted by one side on the other in the form of either a first strike or a retaliatory second strike. This situation did not come about as the result of careful military planning. "Mutual assured destruction" is not a policy

[2]Reprint of an article by physicists Hans A. Bethe, Richard L. Garwin, Kurt Gottfried, and Henry W. Kendall. *Scientific American.* 251:39+. O. '84. © 1984 by *Scientific American.* Reprinted with permission.

or a doctrine but rather a fact of life. It simply descended like a medieval plague—a seemingly inevitable consequence of the enormous destructive power of nuclear weapons, of rockets that could hurl them across almost half of the globe in 30 minutes and of the impotence of political institutions in the face of such momentous technological innovations.

This grim development holds different lessons for different people. Virtually everyone agrees that the world must eventually escape from the shadow of mutual assured destruction, since few are confident that deterrence by threat of retaliation can avert a holocaust indefinitely. Beyond this point, however, the consensus dissolves. Powerful groups in the governments of both superpowers apparently believe that unremitting competition, albeit short of war, is the only realistic future one can plan for. In the face of much evidence to the contrary they act as if the aggressive exploitation for military purposes of anything technology has to offer is critical to the security of the nation they serve. Others seek partial measures that could at least curb the arms race, arguing that this approach has usually been sidetracked by short-term (and short-sighted) military and political goals. Still others have placed varying degrees of faith in radical solutions: novel political moves, revolutionary technological advances or some combination of the two.

President Reagan's Strategic Defense Initiative belongs in this last category. In his televised speech last year calling on the nation's scientific community "to give us the means of rendering these nuclear weapons impotent and obsolete" the president expressed the hope that a technological revolution would enable the U.S. to "intercept and destroy strategic ballistic missiles before they reached our own soil or that of our allies." If such a breakthrough could be achieved, he said, "free people could live secure in the knowledge that their security did not rest upon the threat of instant U.S. retaliation."

Can this vision of the future ever become reality? Can any system for ballistic-missile defense eliminate the threat of nuclear annihilation? Would the quest for such a defense put an end to the strategic-arms race, as the president and his supporters have suggested, or is it more likely to accelerate that race? Does the presi-

dent's program hold the promise of a secure and peaceful world
or is it perhaps the most grandiose manifestation of the illusion
that science can re-create the world that disappeared when the
first nuclear bomb was exploded in 1945?

These are complex questions, with intertwined technical and
political strands. They must be examined carefully before the U.S.
commits itself to the quest for such a defense, because if the president's dream is to be pursued, space will become a potential field
of confrontation and battle. It is partly for this reason the Strategic
Defense Initiative is commonly known as the "Star Wars" program.

This article, which is based on a forthcoming book by a group
of us associated with the Union for Concerned Scientists, focuses
on the technical aspects of the issue of space-based ballistic-missile
defense. Our discussion of the political implications of the president's Strategic Defense Initiative will draw on the work of two
of our colleagues, Peter A. Clausen of the Union for Concerned
Scientists and Richard Ned Lebow of Cornell University.

The search for a defense against nuclear-armed ballistic missiles began three decades ago. In the 1960's both superpowers developed anti-ballistic-missile (ABM) systems based on the use of
interceptor missiles armed with nuclear warheads. In 1968 the
U.S.S.R. began to operate an ABM system around Moscow based
on the Galosh interceptor, and in 1974 the U.S. completed a similar system to protect Minuteman missiles near Grand Forks Air
Force Base in North Dakota. (The U.S. system was dismantled
in 1975.)

Although these early efforts did not provide an effective defense against a major nuclear attack, they did stimulate two developments that have been dominant features of the strategic
landscape ever since: the ABM Treaty of 1972 and the subsequent
deployment of multiple independently targetable reentry vehicles
(MIRV's), first by the U.S. and later by the U.S.S.R.

In the late 1960's a number of scientists who had been involved
in investigating the possibility of ballistic-missile defense in their
capacity as high-level advisers to the U.S. Government took the
unusual step of airing their criticism of the proposed ABM sys-

tems both in congressional testimony and in the press. Many scientists participated in the ensuing debate, and eventually a consensus emerged in the scientific community regarding the flaws in the proposed systems.

The scientists' case rested on a technical assessment and a strategic prognosis. On the technical side they pointed out that the systems then under consideration were inherently vulnerable to deception by various countermeasures and to preemptive attack on their exposed components, particularly their radars. On the strategic side the scientists argued that the U.S.S.R. could add enough missiles to its attacking force to ensure penetration of any such defense. These arguments eventually carried the day, and they are still germane. They were the basis for the ABM Treaty, which was signed by President Nixon and General Secretary Brezhnev in Moscow in May, 1972. The ABM Treaty formally recognized that not only the deployment but also the development of such defensive systems would have to be strictly controlled if the race in offensive missiles was to be contained.

MIRV's were originally conceived as the ideal countermeasure to ballistic-missile defense, and in a logical world they would have been abandoned with the signing of the ABM Treaty. Nevertheless, the U.S. did not try to negotiate a ban on MIRV's. Instead it led the way to their deployment in spite of repeated warnings by scientific advisers and the Arms Control and Disarmament Agency to senior Government officials that MIRV's would undermine the strategic balance and ultimately be to the advantage of the U.S.S.R. because of its larger ICBM's. The massive increase in the number of nuclear warheads in both strategic arsenals during the 1970's is largely attributable to the introduction of MIRV's. The result, almost everyone now agrees, is a more precarious strategic balance.

The president's Strategic Defense Initiative is much more ambitious than the ABM proposals of the 1960's. To protect an entire society a nationwide defense of "soft" targets such as cities would be necessary; in contrast, the last previous U.S. ABM plan—the Safeguard system proposed by the Nixon Administration in 1969—was intended to provide only a "point" defense of "hard" targets such as missile silos and command bunkers. The latter mission could be accomplished by a quite permeable terminal-defense system that intercepted warheads very close to their targets, since a formidable retaliatory capability would remain even if most of the missile silos were destroyed. A large metropolitan area, on the other hand, could be devastated by a handful of weapons detonated at high altitude; if necessary, the warheads could be designed to explode on interception.

To be useful a nationwide defense would have to intercept and eliminate virtually all the 10,000 or so nuclear warheads that each side is currently capable of committing to a major strategic attack. For a city attack it could not wait until the atmosphere allowed the defense to discriminate between warheads and decoys. Such a high rate of attrition would be conceivable only if there were several layers of defense, each of which could reliably intercept a large percentage of the attacking force. In particular, the first defensive layer would have to destroy most of the attacking warheads soon after they left their silos or submerged submarines, while the booster rockets were still firing. Accordingly boost-phase interception would be an indispensable part of any defense of the nation as a whole.

Booster rockets rising through the atmosphere thousands of miles from U.S. territory could be attacked only from space. That is why the Strategic Defense Initiative is regarded primarily as a space-weapons program. If the president's plan is actually pursued, it will mark a turning point in the arms race perhaps as significant as the introduction of ICBM's.

Several quite different outcomes of the introduction of space weapons have been envisioned. One view (apparently widely held in the Reagan Administration) has been expressed most succinctly by Robert S. Cooper, director of the Defense Advanced Research Projects Agency. Testifying last year before the Armed Services Committee of the House of Representatives, Cooper declared: "The policy for the first time recognizes the need to control space as a military environment." Indeed, given the intrinsic vulnerability of space-based systems, the domination of space by the U.S. would be a prerequisite to a reliable ballistic-missile defense of the entire nation. For that reason, among others, the current policy also calls for the acquisition by the U.S. of antisatellite weapons.

The notion that the U.S. could establish and maintain supremacy in space ignores a key lesson of the post-Hiroshima era: a technological breakthrough of even the most dramatic and unexpected nature can provide only a temporary advantage. Indeed, the only outcome one can reasonably expect is that both superpowers would eventually develop space-based ballistic-defense systems. The effectiveness of these systems would be uncertain and would make the strategic balance more precarious than it is today. Both sides will have expanded their offensive forces to guarantee full confidence in their ability to penetrate defenses of unknown reliability, and the incentive to cut one's own losses by striking first in a crisis will be even greater than it is now. Whether or not weapons deployed in space could ever provide a reliable defense against ballistic missiles, they would be potent antisatellite weapons. As such they could be used to promptly destroy an opponent's early-warning and communications satellites, thereby creating a need for critical decisions at a tempo ill suited to the speed of human judgment.

Our analysis of the prospects for a space-based defensive system against ballistic-missile attack will focus on the problem of boost-phase interception. It is not only an indispensable part of the currently proposed systems but also what distinguishes the current concept from all previous ABM plans. On the basis of our technical analysis and our assessment of the most likely response of the U.S.S.R. we conclude that the pursuit of the president's program would inevitably stimulate a large increase in the Russian strategic offensive forces, further reduce the chances of controlling events in a crisis and possibly provoke the nuclear attack it was designed to prevent. In addition the reliability of the proposed defense would remain a mystery until the fateful moment at which it was attacked.

Before assessing the task of any defense one must first examine the likely nature of the attack. In this case we shall concentrate on the technical and military attributes of the land-based ICBM and on how a large number of such missiles could be used in combination to mount a major strategic attack.

The flight of an ICBM begins when the silo door opens and hot gases eject the missile. The first-stage booster then ignites. After exhausting its fuel the first stage falls away as the second stage takes over; this sequence is usually repeated at least one more time. The journey from the launch point to where the main rockets stop burning is the boost phase. For the present generation of ICBM's the boost phase lasts for three to five minutes and ends at an altitude of 300 to 400 kilometers, above the atmosphere.

A typical ICBM in the strategic arsenal of the U.S. or the U.S.S.R. is equipped with MIRV's, which are dispensed by a maneuverable carrier vehicle called a bus after the boost phase ends. The bus releases the MIRV's one at a time along slightly different trajectories toward their separate targets. If there were defenses, the bus could also release a variety of penetration aids, such as lightweight decoys, reentry vehicles camouflaged to resemble decoys, radar-reflecting wires called chaff and infrared-emitting aerosols. Once the bus had completed its task the missile would be in midcourse. At that point the ICBM would have proliferated into a swarm of objects, each of which, no matter how light, would move along a ballistic trajectory indistinguishable from those of its accompanying objects. Only after the swarm reentered the atmosphere would the heavy, specially shaped reentry vehicles be exposed as friction with the air tore away the screen of lightweight decoys and chaff.

This brief account reveals why boost-phase interception would be crucial: every missile that survived boost phase would become a complex "threat cloud" by the time it reached midcourse. Other factors also amplify the importance of boost-phase interception. For one thing, the booster rocket is a much larger and more fragile target than the individual reentry vehicles are. For another, its flame is an abundant source of infrared radiation, enabling the defense to get an accurate fix on the missile. It is only during boost phase that a missile reveals itself by emitting an intense signal that can be detected at a large distance. In midcourse it must first be found by illuminating it with microwaves (or possibly laser light) and then sensing the reflected radiation, or by observing its weak infrared signal, which is due mostly to reflection of the earth's infrared radiation.

Because a nationwide defense must be capable of withstanding any kind of strategic attack, the exact nature of the existing offensive forces is immaterial to the evaluation of the defense. At present a full-scale attack by the U.S.S.R. on the U.S. could involve as many as 1,400 land-based ICBM's. The attack might well begin with submarine-launched ballistic missiles (SLBM's), since their unpredictable launch points and short flight times (10 minutes or less) would lend the attack an element of surprise that would be critical if the national leadership and the ground-based bomber force were high-priority targets.

SLBM's would be harder to intercept than ICBM's, which spend 30 minutes or so on trajectories whose launch points are precisely known. Moreover, a space-based defense system would be unable to intercept ground-hugging cruise missiles, which can deliver nuclear warheads to distant targets with an accuracy that is independent of range. Both superpowers are developing sea-launched cruise missiles, and these weapons are certain to become a major part of their strategic forces once space-based ballistic-missile-defense systems appear on the horizon.

The boost-phase layer of the defense would require many components that are not weapons in themselves. They would provide early warning of an attack by sensing the boosters' exhaust plumes; ascertain the precise number of the attacking missiles and, if possible, their identities; determine the trajectories of the missiles and get a fix on them; assign, aim and fire the defensive weapons; assess whether or not interception was successful; and, if time allowed, fire additional rounds. This intricate sequence of operations would have to be automated, because the total duration of the boost phase, now a few minutes, is likely to be less than 100 seconds by the time the proposed defensive systems are ready for deployment.

If a sizable fraction of the missiles were to survive boost-phase interception, the midcourse defensive layer would have to deal with a threat cloud consisting of hundreds of thousands of objects. For example, each bus could dispense as many as 100 empty aluminized Mylar balloons weighing only 100 grams each. The bus would dispense reentry vehicles (and possibly some decoy reentry vehicles of moderate weight) enclosed in identical balloons. The balloons and the decoys would have the same optical and microwave "signature" as the camouflaged warheads, and therefore the defensive system's sensors would not be able to distinguish between them. The defense would have to disturb the threat cloud in some way in order to find the heavy reentry vehicles, perhaps by detonating a nuclear explosive in the path of the cloud. To counteract such a measure, however, the reentry vehicles could be designed to release more balloons. Alternatively, the midcourse defense could be designed to target everything in the threat cloud, a prodigious task that might be beyond the supercomputers expected a decade from now. In short, the midcourse defense would be overwhelmed unless the attacking force was drastically thinned out in the boost phase.

Because the boosters would have to be attacked while they could not yet be seen from any point on the earth's surface accessible to the defense, the defensive system would have to initiate boostphase interception from a point in space, at a range measured in thousands of kilometers. Two types of "directed energy" weapon are currently under investigation for this purpose: one type based on the use of laser beams, which travel at the speed of light (300,000 kilometers per second), and the other based on the use of particle beams, which are almost as fast. Nonexplosive projectiles that home on the booster's infrared signal have also been proposed.

There are two alternatives for basing such weapons in space. They could be in orbit all the time or they could be "popped up" at the time of the attack. There are complementary advantages and disadvantages to each approach. With enough weapons in orbit some would be "on station" whenever they were needed, and they could provide global coverage; on the other hand, they would be inefficient because of the number of weapons that would have to be actively deployed, and they would be extremely vulnerable. Pop-up weapons would be more efficient and less vulnerable, but they would suffer from formidable time constraints and would offer poor protection against a widely dispersed fleet of strategic submarines.

Pop-up interceptors of ICBM's would have to be launched from submarines, since the only accessible points close enough to the Russian ICBM silos are in the Arabian Sea and the Norwegian Sea, at a distance of more than 4,000 kilometers. An interceptor of this type would have to travel at least 940 kilometers before it could "see" an ICBM just burning out at an altitude of 200 kilometers. If the interceptor were lofted by an ideal instant-burn booster with a total weight-to-payload ratio of 14 to one, it could reach the target-sighting point in about 120 seconds. For comparison, the boost phase of the new U.S. MX missile (which has a weight-to-payload ratio of 25 to one) is between 150 and 180 seconds. In principle, therefore, it should just barely be possible by this method to intercept a Russian missile comparable to the MX, provided the interception technique employed a beam that moves at the speed of light. On the other hand, it would be impossible to intercept a large number of missiles, since many silos would be more than 4,000 kilometers away, submarines cannot launch all their missiles simultaneously and 30 seconds would leave virtually no time for the complex sequence of operations the battle-management system would have to perform.

A report prepared for the Fletcher panel, the study team set up last year by the Department of Defense under the chairmanship of James C. Fletcher of the University of Pittsburgh to evaluate the Strategic Defense Initiative for the president, bears on this question. According to the report, it is possible to build ICBM's that could complete the boost phase and disperse their MIRV's in only 60 seconds, at a sacrifice of no more than 20 percent of payload. Even with zero decision time a hypothetical instant-burn rocket that could pop up an interceptor system in time for a speed-of-light attack on such an ICBM would need an impossible weight-to-payload ratio in excess of 800 to one! Accordingly all pop-up interception schemes, no matter what kind of antimissile weapon they employ, depend on the assumption that the U.S.S.R. will not build ICBM's with a boost phase so short that no pop-up system could view the burning booster.

The time constraint faced by pop-up schemes could be avoided by putting at least some parts of the system into orbit. An antimissile satellite in a low orbit would have the advantage of having the weapon close to its targets, but it would suffer from the "absentee" handicap: because of its own orbital motion, combined with the earth's rotation, the ground track of such a satellite would pass close to a fixed point on the earth's surface only twice a day. Hence for every low-orbit weapon that was within range of the ICBM silos many others would be "absentees": they would be below the horizon and unable to take part in the defense. This unavoidable replication would depend on the range of the defensive weapon, the altitude and inclination of its orbit and the distribution of the enemy silos.

The absentee problem could be solved by mounting at least some components of the defensive system on a geosynchronous satellite, which remains at an altitude of some 36,000 kilometers above a fixed point on the Equator, or approximately 39,000 kilometers from the Russian ICBM fields. Whichever weapon were used, however, this enormous range would make it virtually impossible to exploit the radiation from the booster's flame to accurately fix an aim point on the target. The resolution of any optical instrument, whether it is an observing telescope or a beam-focusing mirror, is limited by the phenomenon of diffraction. The smallest spot on which a mirror can focus a beam has a diameter that depends on the wavelength of the radiation, the aperture of the instrument and the distance to the spot. For infrared radiation from the booster's flame the wavelength would typically be one micrometer, so that targeting on a spot 50 centimeters across at a range of 39,000 kilometers would require a precisely shaped mirror 100 meters across—roughly the length of a football field. (For comparison, the largest telescope mirrors in the world today are on the order of five meters in diameter.)

The feasibility of orbiting a high-quality optical instrument of this stupendous size seems remote. The wavelengths used must be shortened, or the viewing must be reduced, or both. Accordingly it has been suggested that a geosynchronous defensive system might be augmented by other optical elements deployed in low orbits.

One such scheme that has been proposed calls for an array of ground-based excimer lasers designed to work in conjunction with orbiting optical elements. The excimer laser incorporates a pulsed electron beam to excite a mixture of gases such as xenon and chlorine into a metastable molecular state, which spontaneously reverts to the molecular ground state; the latter in turn immediately dissociates into two atoms, emitting the excess energy in the form of ultraviolet radiation at a wavelength of .3 micrometer.

Each ground-based excimer laser would send its beam to a geosynchronous mirror with a diameter of five meters, and the geosynchronous mirror would in turn reflect the beam toward an appropriate "fighting mirror" in low orbit. The fighting mirror would then redirect and concentrate the beam onto the rising booster rockets, depending on an accompanying infrared telescope to get an accurate fix on the boosters.

The main advantage of this scheme is that the intricate and heavy lasers, together with their substantial power supplies, would be on the ground rather than in orbit. The beam of any ground-based laser, however, would be greatly disturbed in an unpredictable way by ever present fluctuations in the density of the atmosphere, causing the beam to diverge and lose its effectiveness as a weapon. One of us (Garwin) has described a technique to compensate for these disturbances, making it possible, at least in principle, to intercept boosters by this scheme.

Assuming that such a system could be made to work perfectly, its power requirement can be estimated. Such an exercise is illuminating because it gives an impression of the staggering total cost of the system. Again information from the Fletcher panel provides the basis for our estimate. Apparently the "skin" of a booster can be "hardened" to withstand an energy deposition of 200 megajoules per square meter, which is roughly what is required to evaporate a layer of carbon three millimeters thick. With the aid of a geosynchronous mirror five meters in diameter and a fighting and viewing mirror of the same size, the beam of the excimer laser described above would easily be able to make a spot one meter across on the skin of a booster at a range of 3,000 kilometers from the fighting mirror; the resulting lethal dose would be about 160 megajoules.

A successful defense against an attack by the 1,400 ICBM's in the current Russian force would require a total energy deposition of 225,000 megajoules. (A factor of about 10 is necessary to compensate for atmospheric absorption, reflection losses at the mirrors and overcast skies.) If the time available for interception were 100 seconds and the lasers had an electrical efficiency of 6 percent, the power requirement would be more than the output of 300 1,000-megawatt power plants, or more than 60 percent of the current electrical generating capacity of the entire U.S. Moreover, this energy could not be extracted instantaneously from the national power grid, and it could not be stored by any known technology for instantaneous discharge. Special power plants would have to be built; even though they would need to operate only for minutes, an investment of $300 per kilowatt is a reasonable estimate, and so the outlay for the power supply alone would exceed $100 billion.

This partial cost estimate is highly optimistic. It assumes that all the boosters could be destroyed on the first shot, that the Russians would not have shortened the boost phase of their ICBM's, enlarged their total strategic-missile force or installed enough countermeasures to degrade the defense significantly by the time this particular defensive system was ready for deployment at the end of the century. Of course the cost of the entire system of lasers, mirrors, sensors and computers would far exceed the cost of the power plant, but at this stage virtually all the required technologies are too immature to allow a fair estimate of their cost.

The exact number of mirrors in the excimer scheme depends on the intensity of the laser beams. For example, if the lasers could deliver a lethal dose of heat in just five seconds, one low-orbit fighting mirror could destroy 20 boosters in the assumed time of 100 seconds. It follows that 70 mirrors would have to be within range of the Russian silos to handle the entire attack, and each mirror would need to have a corresponding mirror in a geosynchronous orbit. If the distance at which a fighting mirror could focus a small enough spot of light was on the order of 3,000 kilometers, there would have to be about six mirrors in orbit elsewhere for every one "on station" at the time of the attack, for a total of about 400 fighting mirrors. This allowance for absenteeism is also optimistic, in that it assumes the time needed for targeting would be negligible, there would be no misses, the Russian countermeasures would be ineffective and excimer lasers far beyond the present state of the art could be built.

The second boost-phase interception scheme we shall consider is a pop-up system based on the X-ray laser, the only known device light enough to be a candidate for this role. As explained above, shortening the boost phase of the attacking missiles would negate any pop-up scheme. In this case a shortened boost phase would be doubly crippling, since the booster would stop burning within the atmosphere, where X rays cannot penetrate. Nevertheless, the X-ray laser has generated a good deal of interest, and we shall consider it here even though it would be feasible only if the Russians were to refrain from adapting their ICBM's to thwart this threat.

The X-ray laser consists of a cylindrical array of thin fibers surrounding a nuclear explosive. The thermal X rays generated by the nuclear explosion stimulate the emission of X-radiation from the atoms in the fibers. The light produced by an ordinary optical laser can be highly collimated, or directed, because it is reflected back and forth many times between the mirrors at the ends of the laser. An intense X-ray beam, however, cannot be reflected in this way, and so the proposed X-ray laser would emit a rather divergent beam; for example, at a distance of 4,000 kilometers it would make a spot about 200 meters across.

The U.S. research program on X-ray lasers is highly classified. According to a Russian technical publication, however, such a device can be expected to operate at an energy of about 1,000 electron volts. Such a "soft" X-ray pulse would be absorbed in the outermost fraction of a micrometer of a booster's skin, "blowing off" a thin surface layer. This would have two effects. First, the booster as a whole would recoil. The inertial-guidance system would presumably sense the blow, however, and it could still direct the warheads to their targets. Second, the skin would be subjected to an abrupt pressure wave that, in a careless design, could cause the skin to shear at its supports and damage the booster's interior. A crushable layer installed under the skin could prolong and weaken the pressure wave, however, thereby protecting both the skin and its contents.

Other interception schemes proposed for ballistic-missile defense include chemical-laser weapons, neutral-particle-beam weapons and nonexplosive homing vehicles, all of which would have to be stationed in low orbits.

The brightest laser beam attained so far is an infrared beam produced by a chemical laser that utilizes hydrogen fluoride. The U.S. Department of Defense plans to demonstrate a two-megawatt version of this laser by 1987. Assuming that 25-megawatt hydrogen-fluoride lasers and optically perfect 10-meter mirrors eventually become available, a weapon with a "kill radius" of 3,000 kilometers would be at hand. A total of 300 such lasers in low orbits could destroy 1,400 ICBM boosters in the absence of countermeasures if every component worked to its theoretical limit.

A particle-beam weapon could fire a stream of energetic charged particles, such as protons, that could penetrate deep into a missile and disrupt the semiconductors in its guidance system. A charged-particle beam, however, would be bent by the earth's magnetic field and therefore could not be aimed accurately at distant targets. Hence any plausible particle-beam weapon would have to produce a neutral beam, perhaps one consisting of hydrogen atoms (protons paired with oppositely charged electrons). This could be done, although aiming the beam would still present formidable problems. Interception would be possible only above the atmosphere at an altitude of 150 kilometers or more, since collisions with air molecules would disintegrate the atoms and the geomagnetic field would then fan out the beam. Furthermore, by using gallium arsenide semiconductors, which are about 1,000 times more resistant to radiation damage than silicon semiconductors, it would be possible to protect the missile's guidance computer from such a weapon.

Projectiles that home on the booster's flame are also under discussion. They have the advantage that impact would virtually guarantee destruction, whereas a beam weapon would have to dwell on the fast-moving booster for some time. Homing weapons, however, have two drawbacks that preclude their use as boost-phase interceptors. First, they move at less than .01 percent of the speed of light, and therefore they would have to be deployed in uneconomically large numbers. Second, a booster that burned out within the atmosphere would be immune to them, since friction with the air would blind their homing sensors.

That such a homing vehicle can indeed destroy an object in space was demonstrated by the U.S. Army in its current Homing Overlay test series. On June 10 a projectile launched from Kwajalein Atoll in the Pacific intercepted a dummy Minuteman warhead at an altitude of more than 100 miles. The interceptor relied on a homing technique similar to that of the Air Force's aircraft-launched antisatellite weapon. The debris from the collision was scattered over many tens of kilometers and was photographed by tracking telescopes. The photographs show, among other things, the difficulty of evading a treaty that banned tests of weapons in space.

In an actual ballistic-missile-defense system such an interceptor might have a role in midcourse defense. It would have to be guided to a disguised reentry vehicle hidden in a swarm of decoys and other objects designed to confuse its infrared sensors. The potential of this technique for midcourse interception remains to be demonstrated, whereas its potential for boost-phase interception is questionable in view of the considerations mentioned above. On the other hand, a satellite is a larger and more fragile target than a reentry vehicle, and so the recent test shows the U.S. has a low-altitude antisatellite capability at least equivalent to the U.S.S.R.'s.

The importance of countermeasures in any consideration of ballistic-missile defense was emphasized recently by Richard D. DeLauer, Under Secretary of Defense for Research and Engineering. Testifying on this subject before the House Armed Services Committee, DeLauer stated that "any defensive system can be overcome with proliferation and decoys, decoys, decoys, decoys."

One extremely potent countermeasure has already been mentioned, namely that shortening the boost phase of the offensive missiles would nullify any boost-phase interception scheme based on X-ray lasers, neutral-particle beams or homing vehicles. Many other potent countermeasures that exploit existing technologies can also be envisioned. All of them rely on generic weaknesses of the defense. Among these weaknesses four stand out: (1) Unless the defensive weapons were cheaper than the offensive ones, any defense could simply be overwhelmed by a missile buildup; (2) the defense would have to attack every object that behaves like a booster; (3) any space-based defensive component would be far more vulnerable than the ICBM's it was designed to destroy; (4) since the booster, not the flame, would be the target, schemes based on infrared detection could be easily deceived.

Countermeasures can be divided into three categories: those that are threatening, in the sense of manifestly increasing the risk to the nation deploying the defensive system; those that are active, in the sense of attacking the defensive system itself; and those that are passive, in the sense of frustrating the system's weapons. These distinctions are politically and psychologically significant.

The most threatening response to a ballistic-missile-defense system is also the cheapest and surest: a massive buildup of real and fake ICBM's. The deployment of such a defensive system would violate the ABM Treaty, almost certainly resulting in the removal of all negotiated constraints on offensive missiles. Therefore many new missile silos could be constructed. Most of them could be comparatively inexpensive fakes arrayed in clusters about 1,000 kilometers across to exacerbate the satellites' absentee problem. The fake silos could house decoy ICBM's—boosters without expensive warheads or guidance packages—that would be indistinguishable from real ICBM's during boost phase. An attack could begin with a large proportion of decoys and shift to real ICBM's as the defense exhausted its weapons.

All space systems would be highly vulnerable to active countermeasures. Few targets could be more fragile than a large, exquisitely made mirror whose performance would be ruined by the slightest disturbance. If an adversary were to put a satellite into the same orbit as that of the antimissile weapon but moving in the opposite direction, the relative velocity of the two objects would be about 16 kilometers per second, which is eight times faster than that of a modern armor-piercing antitank projectile. If the satellite were to release a swarm of one-ounce pellets, each pellet could penetrate 15 centimeters of steel (and much farther if it were suitably shaped). Neither side could afford to launch antimissile satellites strong enough to withstand such projectiles. Furthermore, a large number of defensive satellites in low or geosynchronous orbits could be attacked simultaneously by "space mines": satellites parked in orbit near their potential victims and set to explode by remote control or when tampered with.

Passive countermeasures could be used to hinder targeting or to protect the booster. The actual target would be several meters above the flame, and the defensive weapon would have to determine the correct aim point by means of an algorithm stored in its computer. The aim point could not be allowed to drift by more than a fraction of a meter, because the beam weapon would have to dwell on one spot for at least several seconds as the booster moved several tens of kilometers. Aiming could therefore be impeded if the booster flame were made to fluctuate in an unpredictable way. This effect could be achieved by causing additives in the propellant to be emitted at random from different nozzles or by surrounding the booster with a hollow cylindrical "skirt" that could hide various fractions of the flame or even move up and down during boost phase.

Booster protection could take different forms. A highly reflective coating kept clean during boost by a strippable foil wrapping would greatly reduce the damaging effect of an incident laser beam. A hydraulic cooling system or a movable heat-absorbing ring could protect the attacked region at the command of heat sensors. Aside from shortening the boost phase the attacking nation could also equip each booster with a thin metallic sheet that could be unfurled at a high altitude to absorb and deflect an X-ray pulse.

Finally, as DeLauer has emphasized, all the proposed space weapons face formidable systemic problems. Realistic testing of the system as a whole is obviously impossible and would have to depend largely on computer simulation. According to DeLauer, the battle-management system would face a task of prodigious complexity that is "expected to stress software-development technology"; in addition it would have to "operate reliably even in the presence of disturbances caused by nuclear-weapons effects or direct-energy attack." The Fletcher panel's report states that the *"survivability of the system components is a critical issue whose resolution requires a combination of technologies and tactics that remain to be worked out."* Moreover, nuclear attacks need not be confined to the battle-management system. For example, airbursts from a precursor salvo of SLBM's could produce atmospheric disturbances that would cripple an entire defensive system that relied on the ground-based laser scheme.

Spokesmen for the Reagan Administration have stated that the Strategic Defense Initiative will produce a shift to a "defense-dominated" world. Unless the move toward ballistic-missile defense is coupled with deep cuts in both sides' offensive forces, however, there will be no such shift. Such a coupling would require one or both of the following conditions: a defensive technology that was so robust and cheap that countermeasures or an offensive buildup would be futile, or a political climate that would engender arms-control agreements of unprecedented scope. Unfortunately neither of these conditions is in sight.

What shape, then, is the future likely to take if attempts are made by the U.S. and the U.S.S.R. to implement a space-based system aimed at thwarting a nuclear attack? Several factors will have a significant impact. First, the new technologies will at best take many years to develop, and, as we have argued, they will remain vulnerable to known countermeasures. Second, both sides are currently engaged in "strategic modernization" programs that will further enhance their already awesome offensive forces. Third, in pursuing ballistic-missile defense both sides will greatly increase their currently modest antisatellite capabilities. Fourth, the ABM Treaty, which is already under attack, will fall by the wayside.

These factors, acting in concert, will accelerate the strategic-arms race and simultaneously diminish the stability of the deterrent balance in a crisis. Both superpowers have always been inordinately sensitive to real and perceived shifts in the strategic balance. A defense that could not fend off a full-scale strategic attack but might be quite effective against a weak retaliatory blow following an all-out preemptive strike would be particularly provocative. Indeed, the leaders of the U.S.S.R. have often stated that any U.S. move toward a comprehensive ballistic-missile-defense system would be viewed as an attempt to gain strategic superiority, and that no effort would be spared to prevent such an outcome. It would be foolhardy to ignore these statements.

The most likely Russian response to a U.S. decision to pursue the president's Strategic Defense Initiative should be expected to rely on traditional military "worst case" analysis; in this mode of reasoning one assigns a higher value to the other side's capabilities than an unbiased examination of the evidence would indicate, while correspondingly undervaluing one's own capabilities. In this instance the Russians will surely overestimate the effectiveness of the U.S. ballistic-missile defense and arm accordingly. Many near-term options would then be open to them. They could equip their large SS-18 ICBM's with decoys and many more warheads; they could retrofit their deployed ICBM's with protective countermeasures; they could introduce fast-burn boosters; they could deploy more of their current-model ICBM's and sea-launched cruise missiles. The latter developments would be perceived as unwarranted threats by U.S. military planners, who would be quite aware of the fragility of the nascent U.S. defensive system. A compensating U.S. buildup in offensive missiles would then be inevitable. Indeed, even if both sides bought identical defensive systems from a third party, conservative military analysis would guarantee an accelerated offensive-arms race.

Once one side began to deploy space-based antimissile beam weapons the level of risk would rise sharply. Even if the other side did not overrate the system's antimissile capability, it could properly view such a system as an immediate threat to its strategic satellites. A strategy of "launch on warning" might then seem unavoidable, and attempts might also be made to position space mines alongside the antimissile weapons. The last measure might in itself trigger a conflict since the antimissile system should be able to destroy a space mine at a considerable distance if it has any capability for its primary mission. In short, in a hostile political climate even a well-intentioned attempt to create a strategic defense could provoke war, just as the mobilizations of 1914 precipitated World War I.

Even if the space-based ballistic-missile defense did not have a cataclysmic birth, the successful deployment of such a defense would create a highly unstable strategic balance. It is difficult to imagine a system more likely to induce catastrophe than one that requires critical decisions by the second, is itself untested and fragile and yet is threatening to the other side's retaliatory capability.

In the face of mounting criticism Administration spokesmen have in recent months offered less ambitious rationales for the Strategic Defense Initiative than the president's original formulation. One theme is that the program is just a research effort and that no decision to deploy will be made for many years. Military research programs are not normally announced from the Oval Office, however, and there is no precedent for a $26-billion, five-year military-research program without any commitment to deployment. A program of this magnitude, launched under such auspices, is likely to be treated as an essential military policy by the U.S.S.R. no matter how it is described in public.

Another more modest rationale of the Strategic Defense Initiative is that it is intended to enhance nuclear deterrence. That role, however, would require only a terminal defense of hard targets, not weapons in space. Finally, it is contended that even an imperfect antimissile system would limit damage to the U.S.; the more likely consequence is exactly the opposite, since it would tend to focus the attack on cities, which could be destroyed even in the face of a highly proficient defense.

In a background report titled *Directed Energy Missile Defense in Space,* released earlier this year by the Congressional Office of Technology Assessment, the author, Ashton B. Carter of the Massachusetts Institute of Technology, a former Defense Department analyst with full access to classified data on such matters, concluded that "the prospect that emerging 'Star Wars' technologies, when further developed, will provide a perfect or near-perfect defense system . . . is so remote that it should not serve as the basis of public expectation or national policy." Based on our assessment of the technical issues, we are in complete agreement with this conclusion.

In our view the questionable performance of the proposed defense, the ease with which it could be overwhelmed or circumvented and its potential as an antisatellite system would cause grievous damage to the security of the U.S. if the Strategic Defense Initiative were to be pursued. The path toward greater security lies in quite another direction. Although research on ballistic-missile defense should continue at the traditional level of expenditure and within the constraints of the ABM Treaty, every effort should be made to negotiate a bilateral ban on the testing and use of space weapons.

It is essential that such an agreement cover all altitudes, because a ban on high-altitude antisatellite weapons alone would not be viable if directed-energy weapons were developed for ballistic-missile defense. Once such weapons were tested against dummy boosters or reentry vehicles at low altitude, they would already have the capability of attacking geosynchronous satellites without testing at high altitude. The maximum energy density of any such beam in a vacuum is inversely proportional to the square of the distance. Once it is demonstrated that such a weapon can deliver a certain energy dose in one second at a range of 4,000 kilometers, it is established that the beam can deliver the same dose at a range of 36,000 kilometers in approximately 100 seconds. Since the beam could dwell on a satellite indefinitely, such a device could be a potent weapon against satellites in geosynchronous orbits even if it failed in its ballistic-missile-defense mode.

As mentioned above, the U.S. interception of a Minuteman warhead over the Pacific shows that both sides now have a ground-based antisatellite weapon of roughly equal capability. Hence there is no longer an asymmetry in such antisatellite weapons. Only a lack of political foresight and determination blocks the path to agreement. Such a pact would not permanently close the door on a defense-dominated future. If unforeseen technological developments were to take place in a receptive international political climate in which they could be exploited to provide greater security than the current condition of deterrence by threat of retaliation provides, the renegotiation of existing treaties could be readily achieved.

THE WAR AGAINST "STAR WARS"[3]

President Reagan offered a new strategic vision to the American people in his "Star Wars" speech of March 23, 1983. The policy he had inherited from his predecessors relied on the threat of incinerating millions of Soviet civilians as the main deterrent to a Soviet nuclear attack on our country. The President was troubled by the moral dimensions of this policy. He said: "The human spirit must be capable of rising above dealing with other nations and human beings by threatening their existence." And he called on our scientists to find a way of defending the United States against a Soviet nuclear attack by intercepting the Soviet missiles before they reached our soil.

When I first heard the President's speech, I thought he had a great idea. I wrote an article commenting favorably on the proposal and then, a little later, I traveled to Washington to hear a talk by Dr. George Keyworth, the President's Science Adviser, on the strategic and technical implications of the President's plan.

Since Dr. Keyworth was rumored to have made a major contribution to the thinking behind the "Star Wars" speech, I felt that I would be getting an insider's view of the technical prospects for success in this difficult undertaking. That was particularly interesting to me, because several of my fellow physicists had expressed the gravest reservations about the technical feasibility of the proposal. In fact, Dr. Hans Bethe, a distinguished Nobel laureate in physics, had said bluntly, "I don't think it can be done."

Dr. Keyworth started by describing the circumstances that had led to the President's speech. Then he got into the technical areas I had come to hear about. "For more than five months," he told us, "some fifty of our nation's better technical minds [have] devoted their efforts almost exclusively to one problem—the defense against ballistic missiles." This group of specialists, which included some of the most qualified defense scientists in the coun-

[3]Reprint of an article by Robert Jastrow, professor of earth sciences at Dartmouth University and founder of the Goddard Institute for Space Studies. *Commentary*. 79:19–25. D. '84. ©1984 by Robert Jastrow.

try, had concluded that the President's goal was realistic—that it "probably could be done."

"The basis for their optimism," Dr. Keyworth went on, "is our tremendously broad technical progress over the past decade." He pointed specifically to the advances in computers and "new laser techniques." He also mentioned the promising new developments that might enable us to protect the vitally important satellites carrying all this laser weaponry and computing equipment, and prevent the Soviets from knocking these critical satellites out as a preliminary to a nuclear attack on the United States. "These and other recent technical advances," Dr. Keyworth concluded, "offer the possibility of a workable strategic [missile] defense system."

That was pretty clear language. Defense experts had given the President's proposal a green light on its technical merits. I went back to New York with a feeling that the President's vision of the future—a future in which nuclear weapons would be "impotent and obsolete"—was going to become a reality.

The following month a panel of university scientists came out with a report that flatly contradicted Dr. Keyworth's assessment. According to the panel, an effective defense of the United States against Soviet missiles was "unattainable." The report, prepared under the sponsorship of the Union of Concerned Scientists (UCS), leveled numerous criticisms at the "Star Wars" proposal. It pointed out, *inter alia,* that thousands of satellites would be needed to provide a defensive screen; that one of the "Star Wars" devices under consideration would require placing in orbit a satellite weighing 40,000 tons; that the power needed for the lasers and other devices proposed would equal as much as 60 percent of the total power output of the United States; and that, in any case, the Soviets would be able to foil our defenses with a large bag of relatively inexpensive tricks, such as spinning the missile to prevent the laser from burning a hole in it, or putting a shine on it to reflect the laser light.

DEVASTATING IMPACT

The signers of the report included physicists of world renown and great distinction. The impact of their criticisms seemed absolutely devastating.

Around the same time, another study of the feasibility of the "Star Wars" defense came out with more or less the same conclusion. According to that report, which had been prepared for the Office of Technology Assessment (OTA) of the Congress, the chance of protecting the American people from a Soviet missile attack is "so remote that it should not serve as the basis for public expectations or national policy."

These scientific studies, documented with charts and tables, apparently sounded the death knell of missile defense. Scientists had judged the President's proposal, and found it wanting. According to *Nature,* the most prestigious science journal in the world:

The scientific community knows that [the President's proposal] will not work. The President's advisers, including his science adviser, Dr. George Keyworth, know it too, but are afraid to say so.
Dr. Keyworth is employed to keep the President informed on these technical matters, but sadly, there is no evidence that he is willing to give Mr. Reagan the bad news.

A few weeks later, I received unclassified summaries of the blue-ribbon panels appointed by the Defense Department to look into the feasibility of a United States defense against Soviet missiles. These were the documents on which Dr. Keyworth had relied in part for his optimistic appraisal. The reports by the government-appointed consultants were as different from the reports by the university scientists as day is from night. One group of distinguished experts said no fundamental obstacles stood in the way of success; the other group, equally distinguished, said it would not work. Who was right? According to the UCS report, "any inquisitive citizen" could understand the technical issues. I decided to look into the matter. This is what I found.

A Multi-Layered Defense

Missiles usually consist of two or three separate rockets or "stages," also called boosters. On top of the uppermost stage sits the "bus" carrying the warheads. One by one, the stages ignite, burn out, and fall away. After the last stage has burned out and departed, the bus continues upward and onward through space.

At this point it begins to release its separate warheads. Each warhead is pushed off the bus in a different direction with a different velocity, so as to reach a different target. The missiles with this capability are said to be MIRVed (MIRV stands for multiple independently targetable reentry vehicle).

Most of the discussion of the "Star Wars" defense assumes a many-layered defense with three or four distinct layers. The idea behind having several layers is that the total defense can be made nearly perfect in this way, even if the individual layers are less than perfect. For example, if each layer has, say, an 80-percent effectiveness—which means that one in five missiles or warheads will get through—a combination of three such layers will have an overall effectiveness better than 99 percent, which means that no more than one warhead in 100 will reach its target.

The first layer, called the boost-phase defense, goes into effect as the Soviet missile rises above the atmosphere at the beginning of its trajectory. In the second layer, or mid-course defense, the booster has burned out and fallen away, and we concentrate on trying to destroy or disable the "bus" carrying the nuclear warheads, or the individual warheads themselves, as they arc up and over through space on their way to the United States. In the third layer, or terminal defense, we try to intercept each warhead in the final stages of its flight.

The boost-phase defense offers the greatest payoff to the defender because at this stage the missile has not yet sent any of its warheads on their separate paths. Since the largest Soviet missiles carry ten warheads each, if our defense can destroy one of these missiles at the beginning of its flight, it will eliminate ten warheads at a time. The defense catches the Soviet missiles when they have all their eggs in one basket, so to speak.

But the boost-phase defense is also the most difficult technically, and has drawn the most fire from critics. How can we destroy a Soviet missile thousands of miles away, within seconds or minutes after it has left its silo?

At the present time, one of the most promising technologies for doing that is the laser, which shoots a bolt of light at the missile as it rises. Missiles move fast, but light moves faster. A laser beam travels a thousand miles in less than a hundredth of a second. Focused in a bright spot on the missile's skin, the laser beam either burns a hole through the thin metal of the skin, which is only about a tenth of an inch thick, or it softens the metal sufficiently so that it ruptures and the missile disintegrates.

PROMISING TECHNOLOGY

Another very promising technology for the boost-phase defense is the Neutral Particle Beam, which shoots a stream of fast-moving hydrogen atoms at the missile. The atoms travel at a speed of about 60,000 miles a second, which is less than the speed of light but still fast enough to catch up to the missile in a fraction of a second. The beam of fast-moving atoms is very penetrating, and goes through the metal skin of the missile and into the electronic brain that guides it on its course. There the atoms create spurious pulses of electricity that can cause the brain to hallucinate, driving the missile off its course so that it begins to tumble and destroys itself. If the beam is intense enough, it can flip the bits inside the brain's memory so that it remembers the wrong things; or it can cause the brain to lose its memory altogether. Any one of these effects will be deadly to the Soviet missile's execution of its task.

The Neutral Particle Beam can also play havoc with the circuits in the electronic brain that guide the bus sitting on top of the missile. The mischief created here may prevent the bus from releasing its warheads; or it may cause the bus to send the warheads in the wrong directions, so that they miss their targets; or it may damage the electronic circuits in the warheads themselves, after they have been pushed off the bus, so that when they reach their targets they fail to explode. The Neutral Particle Beam can be lethal to the attacker in the boost phase, the mid-course phase, and the terminal phase. All in all, it is a most useful device.

Now for an important point: to be effective, the laser or the Neutral Particle Beam must have unobstructed views of all the Soviet missile fields. One of the best ways of achieving that is to put the device that produces these beams on a satellite and send it into orbit.

So this, then, is the essence of the plan for a boost-phase defense against Soviet missiles: a fleet of satellites, containing equipment that generates laser beams or Neutral Particle Beams, circles the earth, with enough satellites in the fleet so that several satellites are over the Soviet missile fields at all times—a sufficient number to shoot down, in the worst case, all 1,400 Soviet missiles if they are launched against us simultaneously.

Critics' Errors

The plan looks good on paper. Yet according to the UCS report, it has absolutely no practical value. This study shows that because of the realities of satellite orbits, the satellites needed to protect the United States against Soviet attack would "number in the thousands." The report's detailed calculations put the precise number at 2,400 satellites.

Now, everyone acknowledges that these satellites are going to be extremely expensive. Each one will cost a billion dollars or more—as much as an aircraft carrier. Satellites are the big-ticket items in the plan for a space-based defense. If thousands are needed, the cost of implementing the plan will be many trillions of dollars. A defense with a price tag like that is indeed a "turkey," as a spokesman for the UCS called it.

If the numbers put out by the UCS were right, there would be no point in looking into the plan further. But after the UCS report hit the papers, I began to hear rumors from professionals in the field that the numbers were not right. Since the whole "Star Wars" plan rested on this one point, I thought I would just check out the calculations myself. So I got hold of a polar-projection map of the northern hemisphere and a piece of celluloid. I marked the positions of the North Pole and the Soviet missile fields on the celluloid, stuck a pin through the North Pole, and rotated the celluloid around the Pole to imitate the rotation of the earth carrying the missile fields with it. Then I played with the map, the moving celluloid, and different kinds of satellite orbits for a day or two, to get a feel for the problem.

ADEQUATE COVERAGE

It was soon clear that about 50 evenly spaced satellite orbits, with four satellites in each orbit, would guarantee adequate coverage of the missile fields. In other words, 200 satellites would do the job, and "thousands" were certainly not needed. I could also see that it might be possible to get down to fewer than 100 satellites, but I could not prove that with my celluloid "computer."

I talked again with my friends in the defense community and they told me that my answers were in the right ballpark. The experts had been looking at this problem for more than ten years, and the accurate results were well known. As I had suspected, a hundred or so satellites were adequate. According to careful computer studies done at the Livermore laboratory, 90 satellites could suffice, and if the satellites were put into low-altitude orbits, we might get by with as few as 45 satellites.

So the bottom line is that 90 satellites—and perhaps somewhat fewer—are needed to counter a Soviet attack. That cuts the cost down from many trillions of dollars to a level that could be absorbed into the amount already earmarked by the government for spending on our strategic forces during the next ten or fifteen years. It removes the aura of costliness and impracticality which had been cast over the President's proposal by the Union of Concerned Scientists' report.

The scientists who did these calculations for the UCS had exaggerated the number of satellites by a factor of about twenty-five. How did they make a mistake like that? A modicum of thought should have indicated that "thousands" of satellites could not be the right answer. Apparently the members of the panel did begin to think more carefully about the matter later on—but only after they had issued their report—because in testimony before a congressional committee a UCS spokesman lowered his organization's estimate from 2,400 satellites to 800 satellites. In their most recent publication on the matter, the members of the panel lowered their estimate again, to 300 satellites. That was getting closer. Another factor of three down and they would be home.

But the Union of Concerned Scientists never said to the press or the Congress: "We have found important mistakes in our calculations, and when these mistakes are corrected the impact is to cut the cost of the missile defense drastically. In fact, correcting these errors of ours has the effect of making the President's idea much more practical than we thought it was when we issued our report." Months after the publication of the report, *Science 84*, published by the American Association for the Advancement of Science, was still referring to the need for "2,400 orbiting laser stations."

The work by the Union of Concerned Scientists on the question of the satellite fleet is the poorest that has appeared in print, to my knowledge. The report prepared for the Office of Technology Assessment, which does a better job on this particular question, says that 160 satellites are needed for our defense. That is only about double the accurate result that came out of the computer studies at Livermore.

But the report to the OTA has a different failing. Because of an error in reasoning—an extremely inefficient placement of the satellites in their orbits—it concludes that if the Soviets were to build more missiles in an effort to overwhelm our defense, the United States would have to increase the number of its satellites in orbit in direct proportion to the increase in the number of Soviet missiles.

This seems like a technical detail, but it has a cosmic impact. It means that if the Soviets build twice as many missiles, we have to build twice as many satellites. If they build four times as many missiles, we have to build four times as many satellites. Since our satellites are going to be expensive, that can be a costly trade-off. In fact, it could enable the Soviets to overwhelm our defense simply by building more missiles. As the *New Republic* said: "They could just roll out more SS-18's" (the SS-18 is the biggest and most powerful missile in the Soviet arsenal).

But some fine work by the theoretical physicists at Los Alamos has shown that the report to the OTA is seriously in error. The Los Alamos calculations, which have been confirmed by computations at Livermore, show that the number of satellites needed to counter a Soviet attack does *not* go up in direct proportion to the number of Soviet missiles. It turns out instead that the number of satellites goes up approximately in proportion to the *square root* of the number of missiles.

SQUARE-ROOT
RULE

That also seems like a fine point—almost a quibble—but consider its significance. The square root means that if the Soviets build *four* times as many missiles, we only have to build *twice* as many satellites to match them. Suppose the United States built a defensive screen of 100 satellites that could shoot down—as a very conservative estimate—80 percent, or four-fifths, of the Soviet missiles. And suppose the Soviets decided they wanted to build enough missiles so that the number of missiles getting through our defensive screen would be the same as the number that would have reached the United States if we had no defense. That is what "overwhelming the defense" means. To do that, the Soviets would have to build more than 5,000 additional missiles and silos. The Los Alamos "square-root" rule tells us that if the Soviets went to that trouble and expense, the United States could counter those thousands of new missiles with only 100 additional satellites.

With numbers like that, the cost trade-offs are bound to favor the defense over the offense. If the Soviets tried to overwhelm our defense, they would be bankrupted before we were.

The report to the OTA has other defects. One is a peculiar passage in which the author exaggerates by a factor of roughly 50 the requirements for a terminal defense, i.e., a defense that tries to destroy the Soviet warheads toward the end of their passage, when they are already over the United States. Current planning assumes that as the warheads descend, they will be intercepted by smart mini-missiles with computer brains and radar or infrared "eyes," which maneuver into the path of the warhead and destroy it on impact. A smart missile of this kind destroyed an oncoming enemy warhead at an altitude of 100 miles on June 10, 1984, in a successful test of the technology by the Army.

The question is: how many smart missiles are required? Professionals sizing up the problem have concluded that at most 5,000 intercepting missiles will be needed. The answer according to the report to the OTA: 280,000 smart missiles. Though these smart missiles will not cost as much as aircraft carriers, they are not exactly throwaways. Thus the effect of this calculation, as with the studies by the Union of Concerned Scientists on the size of our fleet of laser-equipped satellites, is to create the impression that a defense against Soviet missiles will be so costly as to be impractical.

How did the report to the Office of Technology Assessment arrive at 280,000 missiles? First, the report assumed that about 1,000 sites in the United States—missile silos, command posts, and so on—need to be defended. That is reasonable.

Second, the report assumed the Soviets might choose to concentrate their whole attack on any one of these 1,000 sites. This means that every single site would have to have enough intercepting missiles to counter the Soviet attack, if the entire attack were aimed at this one location.

GIGO CALCULATION

That is not reasonable. Why would the Soviets launch thousands of warheads—their entire nuclear arsenal—against one American missile silo? This is known in the trade as a GIGO calculation (garbage in, garbage out). The theorist makes an absurd assumption, does some impeccable mathematics, and arrives at an absurd answer.

The Neutral Particle Beam

When theoretical physicists joust over ideas, a factor of two hardly counts; a factor of three matters a bit; factors of ten begin to be important; factors of 100 can win or lose an argument; and factors of 1,000 begin to be embarrassing. In a study of the practicality of the Neutral Particle Beam—that most promising destroyer of Soviet missiles and warheads—the panel of the Union of Concerned Scientists made a mistake by a cool factor of 1,600. As in the case of the panel's estimate of the size of our satellite fleet, the direction of its error was such as to make this promising "Star Wars" technology seem hopelessly impractical.

According to the scientists who wrote the UCS report, the device—called a linear accelerator—needed to generate the Neutral Particle Beam would weigh 40,000 tons. To be effective this enormous weight would have to be placed in a satellite. Of course, the idea of loading 40,000 tons onto an orbiting satellite is absurd. By comparison, the NASA space station will weigh about 40 tons. This finding by the Union of Concerned Scientists makes it clear that the plan to use the Neutral Particle Beam is ridiculous.

But the UCS's study panel made a mistake. The correct result for the weight of the linear accelerator is 25 tons, and not 40,000 tons. Now, 25 tons is quite a practical weight to put into an orbiting satellite. It is, in fact, about the same as the payload carried in a single flight of the NASA shuttle.

A UCS spokesman admitted his organization's rather large error in congressional testimony some months ago. But when he made the admission he did not say: "We have made a mistake by a factor of more than a thousand, and the correct weight of the accelerator for this Neutral Particle Beam is not 40,000 tons, but closer to 25 tons." He said, "We proposed to increase the area of the beam and accelerator, noting that would make the accelerator unacceptably massive for orbital deployment. Our colleagues have pointed out that the area could be increased after the beam leaves the small accelerator."

That was all he said about the mistake in his testimony.

False Conclusion

Now, this cryptic remark does not convey to a Senator attending the hearing that the scientist has just confessed to a mistake which changes a 40,000-ton satellite into a 25-ton satellite. There is nothing in his remark to indicate that the UCS's distinguished panel of scientists had reached a false conclusion on one of the best "Star Wars" defenses because the panel had made a whopping error in its calculations.

The report prepared for the OTA also makes a mistake on the Neutral Particle Beam, but this mistake is only by a factor of fifteen. According to the report, the Soviet Union can protect its missiles and warheads from the Neutral Particle Beam with a lead shield about one-tenth of an inch thick. The shield, the report states, would not weigh too much and therefore could be "an attractive countermeasure" for the Soviets.

But scientists at Los Alamos have pointed out that a layer of lead one-tenth of an inch thick will not stop the fast-moving atoms of the Neutral Particle Beam; they will go right through it. In fact, a table printed in the OTA report itself shows that the lead shield must be 15 times thicker—at least $1\frac{1}{2}$ inches thick—to stop these fast-moving particles.

A layer of lead as thick as that, wrapped around the electronics in the missile and its warheads, would weigh many tons—considerably more than the total weight of all the warheads on the missile. If the Soviets were unwise enough to follow the advice offered them in the report to the Office of Technology Assessment, their missile would be so loaded down with lead that it would be unable to get off the ground.

That would be a great plus for American security, and a nice response from our defense scientists to the President's call for ways of making the Soviet missiles "impotent and obsolete."

Possible Soviet Countermeasures

Other suggestions for the Soviets can be found in the report by the Union of Concerned Scientists. They include shining up the Soviet missiles, spinning them, attaching "band-aids" and "window shades," as the UCS report calls them, and launching "balloons" as fake warheads. I am not an expert in this dark area of "countermeasures," but I have talked with the experts enough to understand why the professionals in the defense community regard many of these proposals as bordering on inanity.

Putting a shine on the missile sounds like a good idea, because it reflects a part of the laser beam and weakens the beam's effect. However, it would be a poor idea for the Soviets in practice. One reason is that the Soviets could not count on keeping their missiles shiny; during the launch the missile gets dirty, partly because of its own exhaust gases, and its luster is quickly dulled. But the main reason is that no shine is perfect; some laser energy is bound to get through, and will heat the surface. The heating tends to dull the shine, so more heat gets through, and dulls the shine some more, and still more heat gets through . . . and very soon the shine is gone.

Spinning the missile spreads the energy of the laser beam over its whole circumference, and is a better idea than putting a shine on it. However, it only gains the Soviets a factor of pi, or roughly three, at most. And it does not gain them anything at all if the laser energy is transmitted in sharp pulses that catch the missile in one point of its spin, so to speak. The experts say there is no problem in building a laser that sends out its energy in sharp pulses.

More Proposals

Now to the other proposals by the scientists on the UCS panel. The "band-aid" is a metal skirt which slides up and down the outside of the missile, automatically picking out the spot that is receiving the full heat of the laser beam, and protecting the metal skin underneath. The "window shade" is a flexible, metallized sheet which is rolled up and fastened to the outside of the missile when it is launched, and then unrolled at altitudes above fifty miles. It is supposed to protect the missile against the X-ray laser, which is another exotic but promising defense technology.

The trouble with these suggestions is that they do not fit the realities of missile construction very well. A missile is a very fragile object, the ratio of its weight empty to its weight loaded being 10 or 15 to 1—nearly the same as an eggshell. Any attempt to fasten band-aids and window shades on the outside of the missile, even if their contours are smoothed to minimize drag, would put stresses on the flimsy structure that would require a major renovation of the rocket and a new series of test flights. If the Soviets tried to carry out all the suggestions made by the UCS's scientists—putting on band-aids and window shades, spinning their missiles and shining them up—their missile program would be tied up in knots. That would be another fine response from our scientists to the President's call for a way of rendering the Soviet weapons useless.

The "balloon" is still another trick to foil our defenses. The thought here is that after the boost phase is over, and the booster rocket has fallen away, the bus that normally pushes out the Soviet warheads will instead kick out a large number of "balloons"—light, metallized hollow spheres. Some balloons will have warheads inside them, and some will not. Since the empty balloons weigh very little, the Soviets can put out a great many of these. Not knowing which among this great multitude of balloons contain warheads, we will waste our mid-course defenses on killing every balloon in sight, empty or not.

A friend who works on these matters all the time explained to me what was wrong with this idea. He said that a modest amount of thought reveals that it is possible to tell very easily which balloons have warheads, and which do not. All the defense has to do is tap one, in effect, by directing a sharp pulse of laser light at it, and then observing how it recoils. An empty balloon will recoil more rapidly than a loaded one. Once the loaded balloons—the ones with the warheads—are picked out, we can go after them with our Neutral Particle Beams, or other warhead-killers.

This list of proposed countermeasures is not complete, but it is representative. The ideas put forward by the UCS—the band-aid, the window shade, the shining and spinning rockets, and the balloon—remind one of nothing so much as a group of bright students from the Bronx High School of Science getting together to play a game in which they pretend to be Soviet scientists figuring out how to defeat American missile defenses. The ideas they come up with are pretty good for a group of high-school students, but not good enough to stand up to more than a thirty-minute scrutiny by the defense professionals who earn their living in thinking about these matters.

Of course, there is no harm in these proposals. The harm comes in offering shoddy work—superficial analyses, marred by errors of fact, reasoning, and simple carelessness—as a sound scientific study bearing on a decision of vital importance to the American people. The work seems sound enough on casual examination, with its numbers, graphs, and theoretical arguments. Certainly the *New York Times* was impressed when it described the UCS report as "exhaustive and highly technical." It is only when you penetrate more deeply, and begin to talk with knowledgeable people who have thought long and hard about these problems, that you realize something is wrong here.

Why the Errors?

How did published work by competent scientists come to have
so many major errors? A theorist reviewing these reports on the
feasibility of the President's proposal cannot help noticing that all
the errors and rough spots in the calculations seem to push the results in one direction—toward a bigger and more costly defense,
and a negative verdict on the soundness of a "Star Wars" defense
against Soviet missiles. If the calculations had been done without
bias, conscious or otherwise, you would expect some errors to push
the result one way, and other errors to push it the other way.

But all the errors and omissions go in one direction only—
toward making the President's plan seem impractical, costly, and
ineffective.

This is not to say that the errors were made in a deliberate,
conscious effort to deceive. I do not think that for a moment. What
happens is quite different, and every theorist will recognize the
phenomenon. When you finish a calculation, you check your result against your intuitive feeling as to what the situation should
be. You ask yourself: "Does this result make sense, or not?" If the
result does not make sense, you know either that you have made
a great discovery which will propel you to Stockholm, or you have
made a mistake. Usually you assume the latter, and you proceed
to check your calculations very carefully. But if the result seems
to be in good agreement with everything you expected about the
behavior of the system you are investigating, you say to yourself,
"Well, that looks all right," and you go on to the next step.

Of course, a careful theorist always checks his calculations
anyway, whether the answer seems sensible or not. But he is apt
to check them just a mite less carefully if the results agree with
what he expected than if they do not.

I think this is what must have happened to the theorists who
wrote the report for the Union of Concerned Scientists. Clearly
they had a strong bias against the President's proposal from the
beginning, because they believed that a defense against Soviet missiles would, in their own words, "have a profoundly destabilizing
effect on the nuclear balance, increasing the risk of nuclear war,"
and that such a defense against missiles "could well produce
higher numbers of fatalities" than no defense at all.

So, when the calculations by the panel yielded the result that thousands of laser-equipped satellites would be needed to counter a Soviet attack—which meant that for this reason alone the whole plan was hopelessly impractical—the members of the panel were not surprised. Their technical studies had simply confirmed what they already knew to be true for other reasons, namely, that the President's idea was terrible.

Now, I would like to wager that if the theorists studying the matter for the UCS had found that only 10 satellites could protect the United States from a massive Soviet attack—if they had gotten a result that indicated the President's proposal was simple, effective, and inexpensive to carry out—then they would have scrutinized their calculations very, very carefully.

What is one to make of all this?

MISLEADING IMPRESSION

When I was a graduate student in theoretical physics, we revered some of the men who have lent their names to the report by the Union of Concerned Scientists. They are among the giants of 20th-century physics—the golden era in our profession. Yet these scientists have given their endorsement to badly flawed calculations that create a misleading impression in the minds of Congress and the public on the technical feasibility of a proposal aimed at protecting the United States from destruction.

Lowell Wood, a theorist at Livermore and one of the most brilliant of the younger generation of defense scientists, made a comment recently to the *New York Times* about what he also saw as a contradiction between the research talents of Dr. Hans Bethe—the most prominent physicist associated with the Union of Concerned Scientists—and the negative views of that great theorist on the technical merits of the proposal to defend the United States against Soviet missiles. Dr. Wood said:

Is Hans Bethe a good physicist? Yes, he's one of the best alive. Is he a rocket engineer? No. Is he a military-systems engineer? No. Is he a general? No. Everybody around here respects Hans Bethe enormously as a physicist. But weapons are my profession. He dabbles as a military systems analyst.

It seems to me that Dr. Wood has part of the answer. I think
the remainder of the answer is that scientists belong to the human
race. As with the rest of us, in matters on which they have strong
feelings, their rational judgments can be clouded by their ideological preconceptions.

WHAT IS "PROOF"?[4]

If you have such a thing, now, with this here available, why can't we both
reduce, or eliminate, the weapons since we've *proven* that it's possible to
be invulnerable to such an attack (emphasis added).

> —President Ronald Reagan
> Election Day interview
> November 6, 1984

Ever since its unveiling, the question of feasibility has shaped
judgments on and even the presentation of the Strategic Defense
Initiative (SDI). Reagan's own announcement of the program in
March 1983 recognized that "eliminating the threat posed by strategic nuclear missiles" would be "a formidable technical task . . .
that may not be accomplished before the end of this century."

Since the president's speech, administration officials have continually been confronted with the questions "Can it work?" and,
just as important, "How can we know?" The president's aides
have usually responded by stressing that the SDI is a research program and not a decision to deploy weapons. The question of deploying an actual strategic defense system, they have emphasized,
would arise only if and when SDI research generated options for
effective defenses that were achievable and affordable.

Yet great uncertainty rightly exists despite this apparently
prudent position. Partly to blame, no doubt, are the administration's constantly shifting rationales for the program, which make
it impossible to know how the SDI will affect future U.S. strategic
planning. After all, U.S. officials variously have predicted that the

[4]Reprint of an article by Gary L. Guertner, professor of political science at California State University,
Fullerton. *Foreign Policy*. p. 73+. Sum. '85. © 1985 by the Carnegie Endowment for International Peace.
Reprinted with permission.

SDI will replace deterrence, enhance deterrence, or defend retaliatory forces or possibly America's population. Congress has been told that strategic defense is not optional, but is central to American military planning, as well as that the SDI is simply a research program to see what develops.

The administration did not refine its position until preparations for the new Geneva arms control negotiations prompted a general coupling of the SDI and long-range strategic planning. The general call for a research program became the basis for a new "strategic concept" presented by Secretary of State George Shultz to Soviet Foreign Minister Andrei Gromyko during the January 1985 meeting that brought both sides back to the arms control negotiating table. The new concept, reportedly developed by Paul Nitze, special adviser to the president and secretary of state on arms control matters, calls for a "radical reduction" in offensive weapons over the next 10 years and for a period of mutual transition to effective, non-nuclear defense forces as technology makes such options available.

The uncertainty surrounding SDI's technical feasibility and cost-effectiveness, however, will persist for a more fundamental reason. Many of the answers that SDI critics and skeptics want can be provided only by the kind of field testing barred by the Anti-Ballistic Missile (ABM) Treaty of 1972 or by actual use during a nuclear war. If Congress authorizes all or most of the $26 billion that the administration plans to request for defensive research through fiscal year 1989, a great deal will undoubtedly be learned about promising new technologies that new American strategic concepts will require. But not even the most ambitiously funded research program will be able to provide the information needed to make a scientifically informed decision about strategic defense. Without understanding the ambiguities and controversies that will still remain, Congress and the public may succumb to a dangerous confidence that SDI research alone can illuminate a risk-free path to a safer, defense-dominated world. And an idea all too capable of fatally destabilizing today's nuclear balance may pass the point of no return, riding only bureaucratic momentum and the technically groundless optimism of vested political and professional interests.

Risks from SDI research, even in its current embryonic and seemingly innocent forms, can already be identified. In a speech last January 12 at the National Academy of Sciences, Gerald Yonas, senior scientist at the Strategic Defense Initiative Organization (SDIO), described his office's mission as a search for the limits of technology, for the vulnerability of systems to countermeasures, and for cost-effectiveness. Measured by these criteria, the least promising technologies will be subject to a "winnowing out" process. Yet winnowing out is the most that should be expected from SDIO scientists and engineers. The history of the attachment of project officers to systems to which they have devoted time, money, prestige, and perhaps future careers is a source of legitimate concern for SDI critics. Strong political commitment and sufficient technological ambiguity have worked in the past to sustain programs, even through periods of strong opposition and flawed performance. No matter how many approaches are winnowed out, these nonscientific factors will always fuel faith that an answer lies just around the corner.

Further, overt political pressures can easily distort technological objectivity when the time comes to make that so-called informed decision to deploy. Even if objectivity survives the political process, the political community may be too innocent of technical details and the uncertainties in scientific methods to evaluate innovations properly. Similarly, the technologically competent may be equally innocent of military strategy and unable to evaluate the impact of technology on war and strategy. These problems will usually be exacerbated by the dynamics of bureaucratic decision making. The scientists and engineers in the SDIO, in the Pentagon's Defense Advanced Research Projects Agency, and in the defense industry will almost certainly produce a system that generates major controversies, even from within. If there were a consensus within the scientific community, wise political leadership could reasonably defer. But when reputable scientists are divided, as they are likely to be, what will politicians do? They are likely to base their decisions on political preference rather than on scientific proof.

The primacy of politics over science is already apparent in optimistic administration statements about the status of emerging technologies required for a layered defense. In a January 1985 White House booklet entitled *The President's Strategic Defense Initiative*, for example, the president states that "new technologies are now at hand which may make possible a truly effective non-nuclear defense." The SDIO, in fact, is still evaluating what its director, General James Abrahamson, describes as "horse race" contracts. These contracts were awarded in a competition for the best—and most quickly produced—"concept" of mission and its required technical capabilities. References in public speeches to horse race contracts and "architectural design concepts" mean that the SDI is still in its formative stage. No one can predict what may result from this contractual laying of track on which the appropriations train may roll for the next two decades or more.

Most scientists agree that many individual components of a strategic defense system can be developed. Individual weapons could be tested and deployed in space or on the Earth's surface. Battle management satellites, radars, and millions of lines of computer instructions could be integrated into a real-time intelligence network to track a nuclear warhead from launch to the moment of its destruction. The problem, however, is that during the testing phases of the SDI, the success of individual components will not prove the reliability of the entire system.

The possibility of gaining a meaningful understanding of how defensive systems would operate in a wartime environment, for example, is almost nil, because of the fundamental difference between testing offensive and defensive weapons. Relatively reliable predictions of offensive-force performance can be gleaned from limited tests of individual weapons and components. Successfully firing individual intercontinental ballistic missiles (ICBMs) and submarine-launched ballistic missiles (SLBMs) down a long test range can give offensive planners confidence that a high percentage of deployed systems will reach their targets during wartime. Nevertheless, the operational uncertainties of launching large numbers of offensive weapons over previously untested trajectories to distant targets should not be minimized.

Yet the performance of defensive systems consists of much more than launching essentially identical individual weapons according to a particular targeting plan. Instead, defensive systems are integrated units that must be able to intercept large numbers of simultaneously launched weapons before they reach their targets. Full-scale tests against some 5,000 to 10,000 weapons are obviously impossible. Thus, because defense planners see only isolated pieces, they cannot discern the entire puzzle. Claims of systemic effectiveness will be matters of faith and inference, since only a full-scale attack could demonstrate the reliability of sensors, communications, and weapons operating together in the most complex battle management system ever devised.

Moreover, even if all these questions could be answered, the answers would be outdated almost instantly. The problems associated with strategic defense are not static obstacles that can be leaped or sidestepped. Instead, these problems are created by an adversary who is actively trying to overwhelm, circumvent, or in some way negate U.S. efforts. It is foolish to talk about low costs or favorable cost-exchange ratios between defense and offense as if there will be a time and a clearly delineated posture that, once reached, will permit the defense to declare final victory. The fog and friction of war—a sophisticated version of Murphy's Law— that Carl von Clausewitz described more than a century ago in his classic *On War*, still pertains to modern conflict. Complex technology and nuclear weapons create uncertainties even larger than those faced by military planners and soldiers who struggled bravely on 19th-century battlefields.

The primary effect of competition based on so much uncertainty is to push both sides toward worst-case judgments about the effectiveness of their own and their adversary's defensive systems. The same logic that drives one to doubt one's own capabilities results in inflation of the enemy's. Ironically, this tendency could have the salutary effect of diminishing the USSR's confidence in its ability to wage war successfully, but also might dangerously reduce U.S. and allied confidence in their ability to deter Soviet aggression. In order to remedy these perceived shortcomings and reduce uncertainties, both sides are likely to undertake defensive- and offensive-force improvements that could only prompt similar, redoubled efforts by the other side. These uncertainties combine to create a strategic environment in which crude estimates replace tangible evidence as building blocks of perceived reality.

Such uncertainty could complicate offensive and defensive arms control efforts by clouding judgments of what systems could be limited or foreclosed without jeopardizing national security. Offensive forces, for example, could be expanded by the side perceiving inferiority in defensive capability. Either side could seek countervailing advantages in offense or defense. Thus the competition could gain momentum not only through technological opportunism, but also from the fear of falling behind.

A Policy Quandary

SDI supporters should not forget the importance of maintaining the existing arms control regime and of preserving the negotiating process aimed at reducing offensive arms levels. The Defensive Technologies Study Team (also called the Fletcher panel), which examined the SDI's feasibility for the Pentagon, not only emphasized that the cost and technological complexity of strategic defenses would be open-ended without arms control agreements, but also stressed that interim deployments of ballistic missile defenses (BMDs), specifically "point defenses" designed to protect missile silos, would be cost-effective only against "constrained threats." The policy quandary sure to arise in the future will result from the panel's recommendations to pursue a vigorous research and development program and to demonstrate "intermediate technologies." Demonstrations are essential to proving the system's potential, but little can be done within the limits of the ABM Treaty—in other words, without destroying treaty constraints that the panel has identified as essential for establishing cost and technological boundaries to the SDI's development.

Article V of the ABM Treaty forbids the parties to "develop," "test," or "deploy" sea-based, air-based, space-based, or mobile land-based ABM systems or components. By failing specifically to proscribe it, the treaty tacitly permits some activity that could be called research. But the line between prohibited "development" and permitted "research" is often vague and subject to conflicting interpretations. Growing SDI research budgets will inevitably build pressures and create constituencies to assault that line either directly or under cover of treaty ambiguities.

During treaty ratification hearings, Gerard Smith, former director of the Arms Control and Disarmament Agency (ACDA) and negotiator of the ABM Treaty, told the Senate Committee on Armed Services that both sides understood "development" to mean "activities involved after a component moves from the laboratory development and testing stage to the field testing stage, wherever performed." Smith explained that the United States chose field testing as the dividing line largely because earlier stages of development and testing in the laboratory would be difficult to verify through national technical means. But his definition, which was not seriously challenged at the time, effectively classified laboratory development and testing, even of prototypes, as permitted research.

The Soviet definition of prohibited development is equally flexible. In the words of a September 30, 1972, *Pravda* article, former Defense Minister Andrei Grechko told a session of the Presidium of the Supreme Soviet that ratified the ABM Treaty that the accord "imposes no limitations on the performance of research and experimental work aimed at resolving the problem of defending the country against nuclear missile attack."

Both sides agree on the importance of maintaining research programs to provide both insurance against sudden advantages by the opponent and incentives for complying with current and future treaties. But new defensive technologies, such as lasers, particle beams, sensors, and kinetic energy weapons, spark new controversies over Article V prohibitions and the extent to which they should apply to activities inside the laboratory. Both sides have approached this point in their current research programs; like runners anticipating the starting gun, they seem poised to begin the race if and when treaty obstacles are removed.

Lawyers from the Pentagon, State Department, ACDA, and other national security agencies determine whether SDI activities comply with the ABM Treaty. Like other lawyers, however, they do not base their advice on some objective standard. They are not judges; they represent their organizations' (that is, their clients') positions within the bureaucracy. Legal analysis, therefore, is the captive of the same interagency conflicts that paralyzed nearly all other arms control issues during the first Reagan administration.

Although avoiding further erosion of the ABM Treaty has been a mutually declared goal in both capitals, current research programs increase the likelihood that Washington will attempt to negotiate treaty modifications that would permit more extensive testing of SDI technologies. Abrahamson has already anticipated the political pressures against current treaty constraints. In a speech before the American Institute of Aeronautics and Astronautics he argued: "As we take aboard [larger] budgets, we must demonstrate that we are responsible stewards. . . . There is no way, even if Congress believes in the idea . . . that it will continue to put out multiple billion dollar budgets" if the technologies cannot be demonstrated.

Yet pressure from administration officials and from a supportive faction in Congress to demonstrate the existence of real rather than theoretical bargaining chips will collide with the desire to maintain existing arms control agreements and will polarize opinion in Congress, the media, and the public at large. The prodevelopment forces will have a strong case because the feasibility of the transition to a defense-dominant world cannot be known until technical developments make possible clear choices of systems.

How Many Satellites?

The warring factions in Congress will be influenced most by SDI costs and by estimates of the cost-exchange ratios between defensive weapons and offensive countermeasures. The complexity of this debate is clear from the widely divergent estimates of the number of satellites required for a credible layered defense. No single issue in the strategic defense debate has been more divisive, as the following list of recent estimates indicates:

Union of Concerned Scientists	300
Office of Technology Assessment	160
Lawrence Livermore National Laboratory	90
Drell, Farley, and Holloway	320
High Frontier[a]	432
Brzezinski, Jastrow, and Kampelman	114

[a]The figure in this case refers to kinetic energy weapons; the other estimates refer to lasers.

The great variance in satellite-force size estimates stems from often unstated assumptions concerning such factors as a satellite's orbital time (low-flying satellites can orbit Earth in 90 minutes); the time it spends over the target area during a single orbit; its destructive payloads; the range of weapons on board; the time required for target acquisition; dwell time (the time required for destruction of an ICBM booster); slew, or retargeting, time; the dispersal of Soviet ballistic missiles; the sequence of launches (mass or phased); warning time; decision time; battle management capabilities; and the reliability of ground-based terminal defenses. Resolving these differences is essential to the future of the SDI, since each satellite could cost as much as an aircraft carrier but would have a considerably shorter operational life.

The methodological battle over calculating these numbers remains intense, and debate will not be easily closed, since satellite numbers must be responsive to unknown Soviet countermeasures. Prudent planners must apply the same technological optimism to countermeasures that they apply to emerging SDI technologies. Judgments of a system's costs and complexity, therefore, cannot be reached by estimating its effectiveness against a static level of Soviet forces.

A realistic estimate of the costs of strategic defense should include the costs of defending the system or making it survivable; of maintaining and replacing over time satellite battle stations and supporting command, communication, and control systems; of devising defenses against bombers and cruise missiles as well as ballistic missiles; and of larger conventional forces. In addition, clear limits on the growth of Soviet offensive forces must be established and codified by treaty.

Answering these questions may prove impossible. Many are being ignored entirely by supporters of strategic defense who, like physicists Robert Jastrow of Dartmouth College and Gregory Canavan of the Los Alamos Scientific Laboratory, have made optimistic estimates of satellite-force size and, therefore, of the costs of strategic defense. Once deployments have begun, however, today's optimists will probably revert to their more traditional tendency to issue worst-case assessments of Soviet capabilities to justify more resources for an ever-expanding program that includes offensive-force modernization.

Certainly the United States could not risk neglecting its own offensive forces in the face of a massive expansion and improvement of Soviet offensive forces to counter ballistic missile defenses. American technology may be quite capable of countering those countermeasures, but only at correspondingly increased systems complexity and cost. And even these defensive counters will represent just one more step in the never-ending contest between offense and defense. It may be instructive to recall the estimates that were made early in the Manhattan Project. The initial cost estimates for the first atomic bomb were only $100 million in 1942 dollars. Actual costs turned out to be $2 billion—and there were no Japanese countermeasures.

When confronting a powerful adversary rather than a nearly prostrate enemy, however, methodological and perceptual factors in cost calculations must be employed even more carefully. For example, offensive and defensive costs do not increase linearly. For the Soviets, the unit costs of offensive weapons may go down as they use their large, well-established infrastructure and hot ICBM production lines to turn out more missiles. By contrast, U.S. defensive systems are still in their research stage. Continuing research, development, testing, and production costs will exceed the unit costs of Soviet offensive increases for years to come until an equally solid base has been established in defensive design, performance, and production. Defense may eventually win the cost-exchange competition by achieving lower marginal costs, but only in the long run and after many uncertainties have been clarified. In short, Soviet per unit offensive costs could decrease while U.S. defensive expenditures increase rapidly.

Moreover, Moscow can be expected to spend whatever is necessary to maintain the forces required to execute its strategic doctrine, whatever the costs of overwhelming U.S. defenses. The Soviets will face technical hurdles, but their administrative superiority over the United States spares them the more formidable political obstacles confronted by American planners saddled with a highly pluralistic political and economic system that is far more difficult to squeeze and mobilize than its Soviet counterpart.

If Congress could clearly see the final price tag, strategic defense would have little chance of surviving the scrutiny of deficit-minded legislators. But incremental funding, technological optimism, ambiguous standards of proof—for example, validation of components rather than systems reliability—and predictably shrill Soviet reactions may combine to propel it through the appropriations process for many years. This process would resemble a recipe the late Illinois Senator Everett Dirksen once read during a Senate filibuster. His recipe (read "tactic") for cooking frogs cautioned against plopping them directly into boiling water because they would jump right out and mess up the kitchen. "It's better to put them in a pot of cool water, turn the heat on low, cover the pot, and bring the poor critters to a slow boil." Dirksen would have known how to get appropriations for the SDI.

Strategic defense may prove to be the wave of the future, but the scientists and engineers inside and outside government who can lead the way into this uncharted world have an obligation to hold their professions and their work to high standards. Scientific objectivity should rise above partisan political debate. Scientists should speak out when technological ambiguity is exploited to anchor political arguments that misrepresent science. Vast sums of money, a wall of secrecy that limits peer review, and strong political commitment to deployment are not the ideal ingredients for proving the reliability of a defensive system on which the future security of the United States may rest. There is a clear and present danger that scientists on both the inside and the outside may become more interested in advocacy than in proof. Those based in Washington would do well to visit the Albert Einstein memorial on the grounds of the National Academy of Sciences. Inscribed there is the standard they should all strive to reach: "The right to search for truth implies also a duty; one must not conceal any part of what one has recognized to be true."

III. SHOULD IT BE DONE?

EDITOR'S INTRODUCTION

Just as there is dissension over the technological feasibility of Star Wars, there is also heated disagreement over its desirability. Administration proponents point to strategic defense as the only way to make the United States safe from nuclear annihilation—especially since the Russians are already pursuing Star Wars research. Hawks believe that the Soviet Union will go bankrupt trying to develop countermeasures to an American strategic defense. Industrialists argue that spinoffs from Star Wars technology will aid American industry's bid to regain world technological and productivity dominance. The first two articles in this section, reprinted from *Issues in Science and Technology* and *Congressional Digest* respectively, by President Reagan's principal science advisor, George Keyworth, and U. S. Undersecretary of Defense for Policy, Fred C. Ikle, outline the pro–Star Wars position.

Critics of Star Wars, on the other hand, consider the program a "trillion-dollar boondoggle"—as Senator William Proxmire, whose views are recorded in *Congressional Digest,* calls it in the third selection—that will never yield a workable defense. Several government studies support his conclusion. The political views of Ikle and Proxmire reflect a larger national debate taking place on college campuses. As academic scientists scramble for some of the many billions of dollars in research grants Star Wars is likely to disburse, others are organizing efforts to bar Star Wars funding from their campuses altogether. University involvement in Star Wars is discussed in David Sanger's article for the *New York Times.* Closing this section is an essay from *The Progressive* that touches on the antinuclear movement's efforts to come to grips with Star Wars. Disarmament, claim the authors, is the only rational alternative to what promises to be "a new arms race; a greater danger of war; a scheme that will take Federal money from the needy and bloat the military-industrial establishment; increased secrecy and heightened repression."

THE CASE FOR STRATEGIC DEFENSE:
AN OPTION FOR A WORLD DISARMED[1]

Success/four flights Thursday morning/all against twenty-one mile wind/
started from level with engine power alone/average speed through air thirty-one miles/longest fifty-nine seconds/inform press/home Christmas
                                        Kittyhawk, December 17, 1903

I

The First World War started in 1914, lasted four years, and engaged approximately 14,000 combat aircraft on the western front. Not one was of American design or manufacture. My subject is not airplanes. Rather, it is the lessons that four generations of Americans since Kittyhawk should have learned. It is about opportunity, in some cases lost opportunity, and time. It is about fear. And it is about hope, which the opportunities we now possess could leave as a legacy for the next generation.

Early this year [1984], Freeman Dyson wrote a book entitled *Weapons and Hope*. In it he identified two philosophies of war: that of the warrior and that of the victim. He went on to explore his sense of the root human causes of modern war and some of the reasons the superpowers find themselves at odds. He found these are the same reasons that warriors and victims have difficulty communicating—they simply do not speak the same language. He also found that " . . . the world seems now to be approaching a fork in the road with two ways out marked by conspicuous signposts: 'Ban the Bomb!' and 'Don't Rock the Boat!'" Ban the Bomb, a slogan of the victims, says that our existing weapons and strategy are unacceptably dangerous. The warrior slogan, Don't Rock the Boat, says that it would be unacceptably dangerous to upset the

[1]Reprint of an article by George A. Keyworth II, science advisor to President Reagan. *Issues in Science and Technology.* 1:30+. Fall '84. © 1984, National Academy of Sciences. Reprinted by permission.

delicate political balance established by our existing weapons and strategy. As Dyson observed, both parties are right. It is this dilemma—and an opportunity to escape it—that I propose as my subject.

II

In 1984 the superpowers confront each other with a combined arsenal of approximately 17,000 ballistic missile warheads, based in both silos and submarines, and about 700 more bombers, which can carry an assortment of cruise missiles, short-range attack missiles, and bombs. All in all there are more than nine gigatons of combined arsenal—an explosive force equivalent to 9 billion tons of TNT—spread over a combined population of a little more than a half billion people. To date we have deliberately left ourselves exposed and hostage to these weapons.

In the warrior's world these are the tools of deterrence. The concept of deterrence is not new, though it has come to have an almost exclusive connotation associated with the nuclear age. Since time immemorial, rational men have used the two aspects of deterrence—deny the enemy his objectives and retaliate against him if he tries—to preserve peace. To date it has worked well; the warrior will correctly point to 35 years of nuclear peace.

The victim is not swayed by the complex arguments and analyses of deterrence strategists. Instead, he sees roughly 50,000 pounds of high explosive equivalent destined for every man, woman, and child in America, and about 20,000 pounds destined for every Soviet. The victim hears the warrior's argument of adverse exchange ratio but does not understand it. On the one hand, he knows very well the destructive power of thermonuclear weapons—and that they exist by the thousands, if not tens of thousands. He knows the delivery systems that carry them are currently unstoppable—deliberately so—to ensure that rational men will never consider their use. And he knows that the physical controls and safeguards on those systems make the probability of error extremely small.

On the other hand, the victim has an intuitive sense that there is no such thing as perfection, that man's history is more one of a series of irrational wars than it is one of reasoned peace. And that while one can always hope, leopards do not easily change their spots.

An even more deeply rooted barrier exists between the world of the victim and the world of the warrior: the difference in currency. The victims' currency is not weapons—it is the lives and suffering of their children.

It truly is the children that seem to be at the heart of the issue. Throughout man's history both individuals and nations have faced innumerable threats to their *present* existence. Rarely, however, have they faced a situation that foreshadows the end of their future. It is that vision of catastrophe that fuels the nuclear freeze movement, as well as calls for unilateral disarmament. In this respect, both the warriors and the victims share a common ground. As Meg Greenfield said in her April 30, 1984 *Newsweek* editorial "The Keepers of the Bomb": "I do not for a moment believe all those elaborate they-do-this-so-we-do-that scenarios the double-dome strategists expect these military men to put into effect could happen: a nuclear war wouldn't be so considerately tidy and tame. But that is not the fault of the men and women who preside over these [nuclear] installations. They are as much victims as we, and—my final observation—they truly embody the American nuclear dilemma."

This dilemma is exacerbated because we continue to judge Soviet perceptions and objectives by our own standards. We automatically assign to them our Western logic, cultural values, historical perspective, and demand for absolute guarantees reflected in a "number." As a result, we have been unable to steer Soviet actions and are thus frustrated by their reactions.

We have built a strategic system that tends to work at cross purposes to that of the Soviets. We compound the problem by further assuming a perpetually rational relationship between a perpetually limited club of superpowers—with no provision for mistakes, miscalculation, or madmen.

The American people seem to instinctively grasp these inconsistencies, probably because they are not mesmerized by the numbers or mathematical elegance of the proposed theories. And they are demanding change.

III

I do not argue with the past. Some have snidely remarked that we seem to have gone from "Assured Ascendancy" in the 1950s to "Assured Destruction" in the 1960s and 1970s, ending with "Assured Anxiety" in the 1980s. But this does not recognize the challenge met by the men at the dawn of the nuclear age. Without real technical or political alternatives, these men walked a razor's edge with delicate balance. Global peace attests to that balance, and that balance must be maintained; our nuclear deterrent posture must be kept healthy—for the immediate future.

I feel uncomfortable, however, with reasoning that says that mutual offensive deterrence—*wherein the promise of complete national destruction is presumed*—must remain as policy ad infinitum. I believe we must consider a transition.

I say this for several reasons. First, there is great concern among military analysts about the imbalance between the projected scale of loss in the United States versus that of the Soviet Union as a result of nuclear war. Make no mistake, the results on either side would be catastrophic. But differences in socioeconomic assets; the locations, density, structure, discipline, and civil defense of the populations; and weapons types, numbers, and targeting strategies all combine to produce reasonable estimates that the Soviets might expect 30 to 35 million casualties, while the United States could experience numbers four to five times that. These are staggering figures. After all, the United States has had only a little more than 1.2 million battle and battle-related deaths in all its wars *combined*—a period covering more than 200 years and ten generations. (Confederate deaths during the Civil War are estimated at two-thirds that of Union forces.)

By contrast, the Soviet Union lost a minimum of 2 million people in the First World War. During the 1917 Revolution, the 1920s purges, and the 1930s collectivization programs under Stalin, they lost 11 to 15 million. More than 20 million died as a result of the Second World War. This adds up to approximately 40 million dead, and probably twice that many total casualties, in two generations.

The Soviet people are tough. They have a history of tragedy and disaster—followed by recovery with renewed determination and increased strength. Their modern writings, organization, and preparation can leave little doubt that they view nuclear war as the ultimate ruin. But if it comes, they fully intend—and are prepared—to recover and prevail at all cost.

The Soviet people, however, stand no taller as individuals than the American people. When challenged, Americans have consistently shown that they also come from resilient stock. Although our commitment after Pearl Harbor is often cited, the Civil War best exemplifies how Americans have sustained horrendous losses and still retained their organization and purpose. At Chickamauga, the Union and Confederate Armies lost almost 40,000 men in 48 hours—about the same numbers lost at Waterloo 50 years earlier. The Confederates won, but it cost them 27 percent of their entire force. The Union Army, which lost 30 percent of its men, retreated. Yet Union General Thomas still held fast to prevent Southern pursuit, and the Union Army was ready to fight again the next day. By comparison, when Napoleon lost 31 percent of his men at Waterloo, his army was utterly destroyed.

It should be remembered that these battles were fought in an age when there were few means of communication and no hospitals or transportation facilities for the wounded. By necessity, the dead and dying were left on the battlefield, and both armies foraged daily in the field for provisions. It was utter horror by modern standards. A British officer—Cecil Battine, captain of the King's Hussars—observed:

This history of the American Civil War still remains the most important theme for the student and the statesman because it was waged between adversaries of the highest intelligence and courage, who fought by land and sea over an enormous area with every device within the reach of human ingenuity, and who had to create every organization needed for the purpose after the struggle had begun. . . . Justice has hardly been done to the armies which arose time and again from sanguinary repulses, and from *disasters more demoralizing than any repulse in the field, because they were caused by political and military incapacity in high places, to redeem which the soldiers freely shed their blood, as it seemed, in vain.* If the heroic endurance of the Southern people and the fiery valor of the Southern armies thrill us today with wonder and admiration, the stubborn tenacity and courage which succeeded in preserving intact the heritage of the American nation, which triumphed over foes so formidable, are not less worthy of praise and imitation. *The American people still hold the world record for hard fighting.* [original emphases]

The message here is that both the Americans and Soviets firmly believe the other will fight—and that is the essence of deterrence. Left to themselves, the peoples of the two nations would undoubtedly prosecute any conflict to its bloody conclusion.

But times change, as do weapons and leadership. Beginning in the late 1950s, ordinary citizens began to realize the futility of global thermonuclear war. More recently, the American Roman Catholic bishops consolidated a large body of thought in their discussion of the ethics of defending ourselves with weapons we cannot morally use, in a war we cannot possibly win.

Nevil Shute was probably the first to anticipate the demise of the policy of massive retaliatory deterrence in his book *On the Beach*. His message was simple: it does not matter who starts the conflict, for in his scenario neither the United States nor the Soviet Union is the initiator. Nor does it matter whose fault it is—his thesis is that the superpowers mistakenly retaliate against each other through unavoidable error. And no matter how much either side wants to stop the conflict after it starts, the war rapidly assumes its own momentum. Finally, it does not really matter who the combatants are: in Shute's vision, everybody dies.

It has been almost two decades—about one generation—since *On the Beach* was written. Shute's view can now be said to reflect the mood of the people. As Elie Wiesel put it, so simply and poignantly—they are scared.

They're scared because they watch a tremendous amount of money being spent on defense, yet they feel no more secure for it. They're scared by predictions that Armageddon, or something very like it, might result from nuclear explosions totaling only a few hundred megatons—and the gross stockpiles on both sides are at least two orders of magnitude larger than that already, and growing. They're scared because they can see no logical end to the arms race, because no balance of power has ever lasted forever, and because they want to leave more hope to their children.

IV

In A.D. 14 Tiberius became emperor of Rome. He succeeded Julius Caesar, who brutally reorganized and expanded Greco-Roman civilization, and Augustus, who had continued Caesar's expansion with unparalleled administrative genius. Although Tiberius inherited one of the greatest societal upheavals in history, he passed on 200 years of peace. In this context, Tiberius was often heard to comment: "As they say, I have got a wolf by the ears."

We, too, have our wolf by the ears. It is a world in which the superpowers have established a tense nuclear standoff. Each has an arsenal sufficient to destroy the other. Each has an abiding distrust of the other's intentions. Each views the other as preparing to strike first. For both nations, the future is growing less stable and predictable. And their leaders' technological options for maintaining stability are becoming increasingly marginal.

We chose this route two generations ago when we acquired a power we dared not turn away. Once we had nuclear weapons, deterrence as we know it evolved for several reasons. Some were political—to consolidate and maintain our world leadership after World War II. Some were military, such as the need to offset Soviet nuclear development. And some were monetary—conventional forces were too expensive. Our ride on the nuclear wolf, however, has become a balance of terror. To paraphrase Winston Churchill, we are riding to and fro on an animal that we dare not dismount, and the animal is getting hungry.

Because we have relied so heavily on offensive nuclear weapons, an aura of inevitability surrounds them, especially the ballistic missile. The Soviets have used this to great advantage to build a strategic force in which the intercontinental ballistic missile (ICBM) represents 75 percent of their capability. With its speed, increasing accuracy, and incredible payload, the Soviet ICBM fleet has six times the payload capacity of that of the United States.

Soviet reluctance to even discuss real limitations on this ICBM fleet points out the gulf between U.S. and Soviet views. We consider the use of nuclear weapons as unthinkable other than as a retaliatory *deterrent*—that is, to prevent war. The Soviet Union tends to regard nuclear weapons, and the ICBM in particular, more as a *preemptive* means by which to drastically curtail any retaliatory reprisal in the event of war.

The problem is compounded by the imbalance in allied and Soviet conventional forces. The Soviets have more than twice the combat divisions and related equipment and more than three times the tanks and artillery than does the United States. We must therefore contend not only with the possibility of strategic war with mismatched forces, but also with the difficulties of a conventional war occurring under the nuclear umbrella. Given a Soviet doctrine emphasizing both surprise and preemption, the distinction between conventional and nuclear war could blur very rapidly.

Perhaps more than any other person today, President Reagan appreciates this danger. But withdrawal from confrontation—and from our commitment to NATO—is out of the question, as is the unilateral discard of tactical or strategic deterrence. Nor can he or NATO consider massive conventional growth to match the Soviets. The fact remains, however, that today the Soviets are, for all intents and purposes, on a war footing. And while the West regards its nuclear force as retaliatory, the Warsaw Pact nations regard *both* U.S. and Soviet forces as preemptive. This situation can only be viewed as explosive.

Token arms control does absolutely nothing to reduce either the dangers or projected effects of nuclear war. Freezing the present posture only exacerbates the problem. And unilateral or unverifiable agreements are tantamount to suicide. We must take concerted action to maintain our balance on the nuclear wolf while we search for ways to get off it entirely. To do this we must drastically reduce both the utility of nuclear weapons and our reliance upon them. If we succeed, we will have our first real opportunity to bring about deep reductions in the two arsenals. President Reagan directed that we investigate just these options in his March 23 speech of a year ago.

Some immediately dubbed it the "Star Wars" speech, never listening to the president address not only the entire spectrum of nuclear weapons, but also " . . . technologies to attain very significant improvements in the effectiveness of our conventional non-nuclear forces."

Many remember him promising immediate results, ignoring his caution "that it will take years, probably decades . . . on many fronts [with] failures and setbacks, just as there will be successes and breakthroughs."

Many decry him as directing immediate deployment of an ultimate system, ignoring that he expressly " . . . direct[ed] a comprehensive and intensive effort to *define* a *long-term* research and development program to *begin* to achieve our ultimate goal."

Many have accused him of abandoning present policies, never heeding that " . . . we will continue to pursue real reductions in nuclear arms, negotiating from a position of strength that can be assured only by modernizing our strategic forces."

V

Seemingly, we have led ourselves back to Freeman Dyson's paradox. The victim says we cannot live with our present nuclear weapons and strategy; the warrior says we cannot live without them. The public sees itself trapped by weapons of mass destruction, a de facto policy of guaranteed delivery, and a de facto policy of massive retaliation. They perceive that both sides maintain a preemptive capability to curtail the damage of a retaliatory strike, that we proliferate our offensive weapons as a counter to preemption, and that proliferation and preemptive capabilities lead to increasing instability.

Can we get a handle on the first of these issues? Can we reject the weapons of destruction themselves? Regardless of the calls to disarm, I believe we are long past that stage. Nuclear weapons are too firmly established as the centerpiece of the world's balance of power. More important, many Third-World nations see nuclear weapons as an indisputable trump card in their scramble for ascending status and power. Although perhaps only six countries have built and tested nuclear weapons to date, it is estimated that there are at least ten more who *could* build them within six years, and eleven more who *might* within ten years. No matter how much one may want to return to the prenuclear era, we have eaten from that tree of knowledge.

Do we want to abandon deterrence? Even though many critics may state that those of us who advocate strategic defense are calling for such a policy, there is no question that we must retain a specific retaliatory capability. Nuclear weapons, because of their small size-to-destruction ratio, are a most precious commodity. The destruction resulting from just one weapon is so high that countries might consider any means to acquire one. Ultimately, the issue for countries considering initiating nuclear war is: Is it worth it?

Are the gains worth the risk of retaliation? I propose that if there were no risk of retaliation, then the chances that nuclear weapons might be used would be even greater than they are today. Even if one were to have perfect defenses, an overt no-retaliation posture would be precisely the fatal-fascination-of-the-fortress that has proved disastrous throughout history.

But do we have to maintain nuclear weapons as part of this posture? To retain its credibility, retaliation must balance itself against the potential damage that an enemy can inflict. Unless and until the world can completely rid itself of nuclear weapons, an admittedly unlikely prospect, the nuclear weapon will remain one aspect of any deterrent policy. But I submit that the *massive* retaliatory arsenals that threaten our future today can be made effectively obsolete if the defense technologies we can now foresee are allowed to emerge and evolve.

I propose here a central thesis: It is not deterrence, per se, that has caused the general public to lose faith in our policy and that has caused the buildup of our offensive weapons to turn cancerous. Rather, it is our deliberate and continued inability to protect the socioeconomic structure of our society—coupled with our growing inability to protect the retaliatory deterrent.

In particular, I do not believe the average citizen, Soviet or American, either understands or trusts a national security posture that promises to deliver everlasting stability through "parity," a calculated "adverse exchange ratio," and more than nine gigatons of potential catastrophe. For the same reason, I do not accept that the policymakers of 20 to 25 years ago believed we would face the situation we do today. Nor do I believe they considered the possibility that complete mutual destruction would have to remain the permanent basis of an otherwise reasonable evolution of stable deterrent relationships. In his often-quoted April 1965 Report to Congress, then Secretary of Defense McNamara said: "The Soviets have decided that they have lost the quantitative [nuclear] arms race, and they are not seeking to engage us in that contest. . . . There is no indication that the Soviets are seeking to develop a strategic nuclear force as large as our own."

At that time, policymakers did not believe the Soviets would call our bluff. As long as they did not, and the United States retained an unquestioned lead in strategic capability, mutual stand-off might suffice—at least until we could work out something else.

But the Soviets did call our bluff. Not only did they do that, but they immediately began to kick the props out from under the principles of deterrence as we knew it. Deterrence became less and less a matter of threatened retaliation and more and more a matter of possible preemption. We did not, however, respond flexibly to this change in the ground rules. We locked ourselves into an offensive spiral, we negotiated ourselves into a technical box, and we refused to recognize that defense is as much a part of an effective deterrent as is offense.

Advocates of the status quo are quick to point out the warrior's argument: to change is by definition to destabilize. "Don't look now," replies the victim, "but things are shifting out from under you regardless." Both sides pursue arms control, but neither side chooses to recognize why effective efforts have not taken root.

The Soviet Union has never conceded the certainty of a successful American retaliatory strike. While their existing ballistic missile defense system is small, it is the only game in town, one with a history of continuing improvements and more than ten years of operational experience. They have a massive air defense missile fleet, which many experts now suspect may have an effective antiballistic missile capability. They have built the world's largest fleet of aircraft for air defense, a truly prodigious (and disciplined) civil defense network, and an incredible set of facilities for protection of their national leadership. In short, they take national survival very seriously. John Collins, the senior specialist in national defense for the Library of Congress, has reported:

Nuclear war could occur, according to Soviet writings, if impulsive 'imperialists' launched a sudden attack, or a local conflict escalated out of control. Contrary to the U.S. notion that neither side could 'win' in any case, the Kremlin intends to try if preventive ploys fail. . . . Soviet decisionmakers further reject defeatist fatalism because it could foster moral decay among their countrymen. Illogical as it seems to some U.S. counterparts, they appear determined to fight for important political ends if nuclear war should result, rather than restrict Soviet strategy to punitive reprisals that serve the state poorly in their estimation. That stance does not bespeak belief that victory is preordained, but reflects a positive objective. . . . Brezhnev finds U.S. fears of Soviet first strike 'absurd and totally unfounded' because 'the Soviet Union has always been a convinced opponent of such concepts.' Soviet strategists, however, separate premeditated first strikes from preemption, which they depict as a form of active defense designed to attenuate the effects of imminent enemy attack. Costs of inaction, as they see it, could be cataclysmic in such cases. They seek to achieve military and psychological advantage through mass and shock at the onset, and seem to believe they stand a better chance of sustaining momentum by beating their opponents to the punch.

That brings us to the crux of the most immediate argument in favor of developing active defenses: they remove the preemptive option, both for the Soviet Union and the United States. Growing preemptive capability has been and continues to be the prime factor in the spiraling arms race. In Soviet eyes, U.S. technical know-how in the 1960s and 1970s provided a unique qualitative edge for preemption that could be overcome only by sheer mass and a strategic force that could get at the enemy fast—the ICBM.

In U.S. eyes, this Soviet ICBM force, coupled with its dramatically improving technological performance and survivability, gave the Soviets an overwhelming preemptive potential, unparalleled flexibility, and an unacceptable strategic reserve in times of conflict; hence, the concerted U.S. attempts to modernize its strategic forces starting in the late 1970s.

At that time, however, the United States was just beginning to emerge mentally from the Vietnam War. The defense budget as a portion of the gross national product was dropping precipitously from a peacetime expenditure of close to 10 percent a decade-and-a-half after World War II to 5 percent at the close of the 1970s, and SALT II was on everybody's lips.

Then came the realization that the Soviets had reached parity through an incredible acceleration in their nuclear weapons buildup following the Cuban missile crisis (never slowing down as they went by us in the mid-1970s). Nearly 600 ICBMs—the SS-17s, 18s, and 19s—carrying their full contingent of MIRVs or multiple independently targeted reentry vehicles, were suddenly discovered in place a half decade ahead of schedule. The Typhoon-class ballistic missile submarine was launched. The Backfire and Blackjack bombers emerged. The Soviet surface navy began to make its presence known. The SS-20s were deployed. Afghanistan was taken. Poland was invaded. Two apparently *new* ICBMs, the PL-4 and PL-5, appeared in testing. And the Soviets began to flex their muscle in Latin America.

Americans seemed almost to sag in their traces. The Soviets no longer had a cumbersome second-rate military with crass third-rate technology. They were big time, moving fast, with resolve. So we entered the 1980s with "bargaining chips" as our watchwords. We have gone through five rounds of START talks in good faith, offering substantial reductions in strategic forces, with special emphasis on the ICBM, and we have been turned down flat. It is most instructive to note that in every case the Soviet objection has centered around a requirement that preserves a Soviet advantage of almost eight-to-one in prompt, hard-target kill capability—that is, in ballistic missile forces.

A number of fundamental issues continue to block the path to meaningful arms control. One is preemptive capability, which the Soviets are determined to retain. And because preemptive capability has now become more a matter of technical quality of missiles (that is, their accuracy and payload flexibility) than of sheer numbers, it is not a property one can necessarily control by fiat.

Another issue is trust. Because the Soviets do not understand us, they do not trust us any more than we trust them. The Soviets suffered staggering losses following the German sneak offensive in June 1941. They have reserved a special place in their preparations for the "surprise" ever since.

In addition, as John Collins says, the Politburo assigns a low priority to sophisticated concepts of limited nuclear war. The Soviets take few risks, and they prefer to employ mass wherever possible to reduce that risk. In Russian methodology, attempts to reduce arms under current circumstances not only raise the risk to them, but compromise their prospects for prompt and conclusive victory as well.

VI

How, then, do we agree on any arms control measures that *matter*? As Admiral Noel Gayler recently commented on Braden and Buchanan's *Cross-Fire* program, today's arsenals are such that one side's strategic advantage of a thousand weapons or so is really lost in the noise. Going further, Carl Sagan postulates that the detonation of just a few hundred weapons would, in his opinion, trigger nuclear winter. Admittedly, Sagan's thesis is undergoing heavy scrutiny and criticism. Both his phenomenology and threshold levels, as well as the winter, or perhaps summer, effect have come under question. But in the end the precise numbers really are not the issue. It is clear that a large portion of the earth's population—perhaps a quarter billion people or considerably more—could die as the result of a global thermonuclear war involving even a fraction of present-day arsenals.

Sagan is probably close to being correct when he says the only real answer is to disarm. But he forgets that retaliatory deterrence is not a phenomenon of the nuclear age. In one form or another, it has been man's primary international stabilizer for all of recorded history.

And as I have described, in deterrent theory the punishment must fit the crime. In our nuclear age, both crime and punishment have accelerated to the point of suicide. The reason for this escalatory spiral—the reason why real arms control has been unable to take hold—is the continually improving ability, real *or* perceived, of each country to disarm the other.

In reality, the possibility of a disarming first strike is the subject of considerable debate. As Brent Scowcroft pointed out, the U.S. Triad structure mitigates the preemptive aspect of most Soviet attack options—at least for today. The Soviets cannot be sure of completely destroying the U.S. bomber fleet, which carries nearly half our megatonnage, with their ICBMs because the 25- to 30-minute missile flight allows time to get some of our bombers off the ground. While Soviet submarine-launched ballistic missiles

(SLBM) might have a good bolt-from-the-blue chance at most of our bombers, they are not now accurate enough to destroy ICBM silos. Moreover, any early SLBM launch to catch the bombers would provide the United States with unmistakable attack confirmation with which to release our ICBMs. In addition, neither Soviet weapons system can now attack U.S. submarines.

Similarly, it is our assessment that U.S. land- and sea-based ballistic missiles are currently unable to completely destroy the Soviet ICBM force; Soviet silos are very hard and our weapons have inadequate accuracy and yield. Our bombers give at least six to eight hours warning time, and like ours, Soviet submarines are presently secure.

But the reader should note two crucial points. First, although the situation may be stable, it is very fragile. Second, the situation will change. Both sides already have the technologies and have initiated the necessary developments for hard-target kill of even the most advanced silos. And while Admiral Gayler advises us to bank on the fact that "our submarines are invulnerable," I would hasten to point out that survivability of our nuclear submarines is a function of how well they can hide. This, in turn, is a function of signal-to-noise in detection devices and also of data processing. Data processing is our most rapidly accelerating technology, the one most sought by the Soviets, and the one most easily researched, developed, tested, and deployed without our knowledge. What's more, the Soviets need not know our exact submarine locations, just their general operating areas. Submarines operating within 100 square miles of a one-megaton underwater explosion would be effectively neutralized. In short, although we retain a viable submarine force now, change is inevitable.

The era of survivability through passive measures, such as hardening of underground facilities, is rapidly drawing to a close. That the offense will always triumph over the defense is debatable, but it is a sure bet that it will if the defense does nothing. One might also consider that, unchecked, these improvements in offensive weapons could foretell the end to arms control because under the measure-countermeasure theory of deterrence, mutually vulnerable offensive forces would have to undergo escalation at an unprecedented rate.

VII

It is time to pursue the technological options for active defense. Significant technological advances have occurred since the last serious debate on ballistic missile defense in the late 1960s. We have before us the prospect of advanced defenses that can provide crisis stability and slam the lid on the MIRV. James Fletcher's Defensive Technology Study team spent over 100,000 man-hours in the summer of 1983 reviewing the state of the relevant technology. They called in several hundred technical and industrial experts, which probably brings the total man-hours up to a half million. I really could not improve upon their summary of the differences two decades have brought:

In the 1960s, there were no credible concepts for boost-phase intercept. Today there are multiple approaches based upon directed energy concepts and kinetic kill mechanisms. Midcourse intercept was hampered in the 1960s by the lack of credible approaches for decoy discrimination, unmanageable signal and data processing loads, the cost per intercept, and the undesirable collateral effects of nuclear weapons used for the interceptor warheads. Today, multispectral sensing of discriminants, birth-to-death tracking in midcourse, and small hit-to-kill vehicles that have promise as inexpensive interceptors appear to offer capabilities that overcome the limitations in midcourse.

In the 1960s, the inability to discriminate against penetration aids at high altitudes and limited interceptor performance resulted in very small defended areas for each terminal defense site and gave the offense unacceptable leverage over the number of interceptors needed. Today, technology provides the potential to discriminate at high altitudes, and improved interceptor technologies should allow intercepts at these higher altitudes. When these improvements are coupled with the potential for boost-phase and midcourse intercepts to disrupt pattern attacks, robust terminal defenses seem attainable. Finally, 1960s technology in computer hardware and software and signal processing was incapable of supporting battle management for a multilayered defense. Today, the rapid advancement of these technologies is believed to permit realization of the complex command and control systems needed.

We are already in an era when warning and decision times are becoming extremely short. As technology advances during the next decade, those intervals may be reduced to the point at which in times of crisis—or mechanical or human error—a policy of shoot-first-and-ask-questions-later may become an option, a terribly dangerous option, for both sides. At the very least, active defenses can conceivably give us precious time to make those decisions. At best, they can reduce the consequences of an accidental or erroneous launch, nuclear adventures by Third-World countries or madmen, and massive retaliation and the loss of hundreds of thousands of lives. Of possibly greater import, once having made a mistake, the offending country would not automatically have to deal with what I'll call the "failsafe" dilemma—that is, a decision on whether to immediately follow the mistake with a complete nuclear attack rather than face retaliation. Experts, of course, dismiss this possibility. The ordinary citizen has a deep-rooted fear of it.

The prospect of boost-phase defense nullifies MIRV technology as it has now evolved. For the first time, the large Soviet heavy-lift booster, the SS-18, becomes an albatross instead of a work-horse. Fully half the payload of the Soviet fleet becomes obsolete, not overnight, but by-and-by.

Believers in the "ten-foot-tall Russian" quickly counter this argument by trotting out the Soviets' "easily attainable" next generation of the fast-burn, protectively coated, quick-spin booster that cuts the SS-18's 500-second burn time by an order of magnitude. Never mind that the Fletcher study team looked at these same Soviet countermeasures and projected that defense technologies could defeat them. Never mind that their proposed 40- to 50-second burn times still leave the reentry vehicle well inside the atmosphere—thereby requiring a post-boost vehicle that is vulnerable to boost-phase defenses. Never mind that there are a number of directed-energy wavelengths that can reach into the atmosphere just as far as the booster dares burn out. Never mind that if the fast-burn boost is possible at all, it is probably three to five generations away from those ICBMs the Soviets already have in the works. Never mind that it causes the Soviets to completely change directions with a 15-year investment in 75 percent of their strategic force. Never mind that it significantly reduces payload and MIRV capacity.

Strategic defenses of the type we can reasonably project—even in their early modes—can be vital catalysts for arms control. Critics are quick to point out that if any defense system is not perfect, some weapons will unquestionably leak through. In fact, early and intermediate defenses will undoubtedly be imperfect, and any nuclear weapon that makes it through to its target will be devastating. While hardened military assets can be very successfully defended by these transition systems, civilian population centers will still be hostage to a determined adversary. Critics cite this as a major failing. In fact, it is crucial to stability during those transition years because as long as there is some leakage in those transition defense technologies, there remains a retaliatory deterrent against first strike.

We will have effectively turned the clock back 20 years. Some will accuse us of returning to an era when weapons were safe but people were not. Perhaps so. But we will once again have a common ground for negotiating real weapons reductions. After all, realistic, survivable, retaliatory arsenals do not have to be enormous, not nearly as large as the arsenals we now require to survive preemptive strikes (or in the Soviet case, to launch them). With the preemptive option clouded, or even removed, we would have an opportunity to negotiate major arms reductions that would still leave each side with a strong retaliatory deterrent.

At that point we would have accomplished two things, two goals that have eluded us for 20 years. We would have reduced both nations' perceptions that the other could launch a successful disarming first strike, and we would have drastically reduced the size of the arsenals.

Achieving these goals could introduce a new transition period during which conventional military technologies and forces would be rebuilt. This will be the price we pay for moving out from under the nuclear umbrella. At the same time, second- and third-generation defensive technologies would become available. This could further reduce the effectiveness of strategic nuclear weapons to the point that civilian targets could become truly viable candidates for defense.

These options will probably become available when the strategic nuclear forces we must build today to maintain our near-term deterrence reach the limits of their operational lifetimes. We then have a new option: rather than replace them, let each side retain only token nuclear forces for their sole remaining purpose—restricted retaliation.

It is only at this point, in the presence of near-zero arsenals, that arms control begins to have any real meaning in the minds of ordinary people. Only when the prospect of final world holocaust reverts to "mere" catastrophe—that is, when the stockpiles can be measured in the dozens, rather than in the tens of thousands—can we once again depend on the sun coming up the next day.

As Colin Gray has said, this can only happen in the presence of defense; treaties that attempt to draw offensive forces to very low levels are impractical without an insurance policy. Although some policymakers, both liberal or conservative, may publicly espouse truly deep, near-zero reductions in the world's nuclear arsenals, they know these reductions to be impossible, even irresponsible, in a world wherein nations dare not trust one another. A world disarmed would be at the mercy of any state or faction that had concealed only a handful of weapons. In the land of the blind, the one-eyed man is king.

Gray notes that it would be naive to tie comprehensive nuclear disarmament to our adversaries' evolution into trusted democracies. Soviet habits, attitudes, and policies are the product of a thousand years of brutal historical experience. There is no reason to believe that the Soviet Union will suddenly become a country that we would trust to respect the legal requirements of a near-total disarmament treaty. And even were a very un-Soviet U.S.S.R. to emerge, I would still worry about the nonaligned Third World.

One might conclude that there is absolutely no prospect for the superpowers to negotiate any treaty that would reduce their nuclear arsenals below the uncertain threshold that could cause almost certain annihilation. This reality drives many longtime arms control proponents to an almost "schizophrenic frenzy," in Gray's words. They loudly endorse nuclear disarmament, but then explain that it is necessary to retain massive retaliatory deterrence.

Strategic defense provides the option to break this cycle. Although we cannot disinvent nuclear weapons, and although nations will continue to distrust one another, heavily defended countries could nonetheless realistically enter into treaties to reduce nuclear forces to near zero. The scale of cheating necessary to provide an arsenal capable of successfully engaging several layers of active defenses would be so large as to be impractical within the context of normal intelligence-gathering capabilities.

Strategic defense therefore provides an option for a world effectively disarmed of nuclear weapons, yet still retaining national sovereignty and security. In fact, deployment of strategic defense is the only way in which the superpowers will be able to achieve these very deep arms reductions. It now becomes extremely important to recognize that the ballistic missile and air defenses that might look less than 100 percent perfect in the context of an offensive exchange involving tens of thousands of warheads could be expected to perform magnificently against an attack by only tens, or at the most hundreds, of weapons.

I do not offer this scenario lightly. Moving out from under the nuclear umbrella under any circumstance is a serious, sobering, and expensive proposition. Neither our military structure, organization, nor technology is prepared for it now—not strategically or tactically.

Moreover, I must issue one caution. Strategic defense must never be perceived as a technological panacea. It is a tool, a catalyst, nothing more. The roots of our security problems are political. However, pending a benign transformation in the ways of the world, it behooves us to invest in a military capability that increases the prospects for meaningful arms control and gives hope to those that follow us.

Admittedly, there are many "if's" in the prospects for strategic defense. But the president proposed that we use our ingenuity to pursue these defensive technologies, and outstanding scientists substantiate his faith. It is our obligation—our responsibility—to provide new options for our political leaders.

We cannot look down each other's gun barrels indefinitely, regardless of the rational balance we think we can maintain. Rational men have rarely started history's wars. Nor can we play into the Soviets' strong suit—men and materiel. Instead, we must start to play our trump—technological leverage. We must move rapidly to develop the means to both reduce our own reliance on tactical and strategic nuclear weapons and the Soviets' perception that either side could use them to advantage. And we must couple these technical moves with negotiations for deep reductions in nuclear weapons. We must begin our transition from the 1950s to the year 2000. And we must offer hope that we can achieve a world free of the fear of nuclear war.

IS THE ADMINISTRATION'S "STAR WARS" STRATEGIC DEFENSE INITIATIVE SOUND NATIONAL POLICY?—PRO[2]

Almost a year ago, President Reagan offered a hopeful vision of the future, based on a program to "counter the awesome Soviet missile threat with measures that are defensive." Many Americans welcomed this initiative, sensing that it could provide a road to escape from the confrontation of ever-more destructive missile forces. But there were others who had doubts about the initiative, and some who are still strongly opposed to it.

Several developments have come together at this time that have made the President's initiative timely:

First, the continuing growth of the ballistic missile threat from the Soviet Union that could force upon us ever more difficult improvements in our offensive forces for second-strike deterrence.

Second, advances in technologies relevant for ballistic missile defense that require us to reassess the feasibility of various defensive systems.

Third, the substantial, ongoing Soviet efforts for ballistic missile and air defense, in particular the Soviet research and development programs for ballistic missile defenses and the fact that the Soviet Union has now deployed a large radar in Central Siberia which almost certainly violates the ABM Treaty.

Clearly, the role of ballistic missile defenses must be viewed in the context of the overall military and political requirements of the United States. A decision to deploy ballistic missile defenses would have major implications for nuclear strategy, the preven-

[2]From a statement by Fred C. Ikle, U. S. Under Secretary of Defense for Policy, before the Senate Armed Services Committee on March 8, 1984. Reprinted from *Congressional Digest.* 63:76+. Mr. '85.

tion of nuclear war, deterrence of aggression, and arms reduction. Our policy on missile defenses must be shaped with this broad context in mind. To permit informed and prudent decisions we have to conduct research on many aspects of the relevant technology and develop a range of specific choices.

It seems plausible that components of a multi-layered defense could become deployed earlier than a complete system. Such intermediate versions of a ballistic missile defense system, while unable to provide the protection available from a completed multi-tiered system, may nevertheless offer useful capabilities. A research and development program that provides options to deploy such intermediate capabilities would be an important hedge against an acceleration in the Soviet strategic buildup. And if such intermediate systems were actually deployed, they could play a useful role in defeating limited nuclear attacks and in enhancing deterrence against large attacks.

One of the criticisms that has been levelled against ballistic missile defense is the allegation that such defenses would overturn principles of deterrence that have worked throughout the nuclear age. This criticism is based on amnesia—forgetting the true history of the nuclear age.

We recognize full well that there are many important uncertainties that will not be resolved until more is known about the technical characteristics of defensive systems, the future arms policies of the Soviet Union, the prospects for arms reduction agreements, and the Soviet response to U.S. initiatives. Important questions to be addressed are: (1) the absolute and relative effectiveness of future U.S. and Soviet defensive systems and how this effectiveness is perceived by each side; (2) the vulnerabilities of the defensive systems (both real and perceived); (3) the size, composition, and vulnerabilities of each side's offensive forces; and (4) the overall U.S.-Soviet military balance. While these uncertainties cannot be fully resolved, we will learn more about them with the passage of time. Our assessment of these issues should, of course, affect our design and deployment decisions.

Despite these uncertainties, a vigorous R&D program is essential to assess and provide options for future ballistic missile defenses. At a minimum, such a program is necessary to ensure that the United States will not be faced in the future with a one-sided Soviet deployment of highly effective ballistic missile defenses to which the only U.S. answer would be a further expansion of our offensive forces, such as the addition of penetration aids and more launchers. Such a situation would be fraught with extremely grave consequences for our security and that of our allies.

There is no basis for assuming that decisions on the deployment of defensive systems rest solely with the United States. On the contrary, Soviet history, doctrine, and programs (including an active program to modernize the existing Moscow defense, the only operational ballistic missile defense in existence) all indicate that the Soviets are more likely and better prepared than we to deploy ballistic missile defenses whenever they deem it to their advantage.

Since long-term Soviet behavior cannot reliably be predicted, we must be prepared to respond flexibly. A U.S. research and development program on ballistic missile defense that provides a variety of deployment options will help resolve the many uncertainties we now confront, and over time offers us flexibility to respond to new opportunities. By contrast, without the research and development program, we condemn future U.S. Presidents—and future Congresses—to remain locked into the present exclusive emphasis on deterrence through offensive systems alone.

Over time, our research and development on ballistic missile defense might induce a shift in Soviet emphasis from ballistic missiles, with the problems they pose for stability, in favor of air-breathing forces with slower flight times. By constraining Soviet efforts to maintain offensive forces (and making them more costly), U.S. options to deploy ballistic missile defenses might increase our leverage in inducing the Soviets to agree to mutual reductions in offensive nuclear forces. In turn, such reductions could reinforce the potential of defensive systems to stabilize deterrence. Reductions of the magnitude proposed by the United States in the Strategic Arms Reduction Talks (START) would be effective in this regard.

In its initial stages, a U.S. ballistic missile defense research and development program would be consistent with existing U.S. treaty obligations. Were we later to decide on deployment of a widespread defense of the United States, the ABM Treaty would have to be revised. If the results of the research and development program warranted such a decision in the future, it would be appropriate to address it in the context of a joint consideration of offensive and defensive systems. This was the context contemplated at the outset of the SALT negotiations; but while we reached an agreement in limiting defenses, our anticipations of associated limitations on offensive forces have not been realized.

Both the Soviet national interest and traditional themes in Soviet strategic thought give reason to expect that the Soviets will respond with an increased shift toward defensive forces relative to offensive forces. The nature of a cooperative U.S.-Soviet transition to defensive forces would depend on many factors, including the technical aspects of each side's defensive systems, their degree of similarity or dissimilarity, and whether U.S. and Soviet systems would be ready for deployment in the same period. Because of the present uncertainties, no detailed blueprint for arms control in such a transition period can be drawn at this time. A list of arms control measures might include agreed schedules for introducing the defensive systems of both sides, and associated schedules for reduction in ballistic missiles and other nuclear forces. Confidence-building measures and controls on devices designed specifically to attack or degrade the other side's defensive systems are other potential arms control provisions.

If both the United States and the Soviet Union deployed defensive systems against a range of nuclear threats, it would not diminish the need to strengthen U.S. and allied conventional military capabilities. Moreover, if the United States in such a future period decided to realize the protection offered by a fully effective strategic defense, we would also require air defenses. The integration of defenses against air-breathing vehicles with defenses against ballistic missiles requires further study.

Defense against ballistic missiles offers new possibilities for enhanced deterrence of deliberate attack, greater safety against accidental use of nuclear weapons or unintended nuclear escalation, and new opportunities and scope for arms control. The extent to which these possibilities can be realized will depend on how our present uncertainties about technical feasibility, costs, and Soviet response are resolved.

The essential purpose of the U.S. strategic defense initiative is to diminish the risk of nuclear destruction. In contrast with continued, sole reliance on the threat of nuclear retaliation, the purpose is to provide for a safer, less menacing way of preventing nuclear war in the decades to come.

Some of the most fervent opposition to ballistic missile defenses is ideological. That is to say, it is not based on facts, but on fixed beliefs. Any proposed revision of this belief is attacked as heresy, any internal inconsistencies of the belief are ignored. Thus, you may have one and the same person:

One, applaud the Biological Weapons Convention because it prohibits offensive use of biological weapons, while defenses are permitted;

Two, oppose binary chemical weapons for deterrence, but support defensive chemical warfare equipment; and

Three, turn these rules upside down for nuclear arms, by supporting offensive arms but opposing defensive ones. The ideological opponents to nuclear defense also seem to forget that the basic premise of banning missile defenses has been disproven. The premise was that the prohibition of such defenses would permit us to curb the growth in offensive arms. But after the ABM Treaty the Soviet offensive build-up continued as if there had been no change.

A curious aspect of the ideology against missile defenses is the notion that outer space must be reserved for offensive missiles, so that they can travel without obstruction to create holocaust on earth. The ideology demands a sanctuary in outer space that excludes any protection for the cities we live in, but offers a free ride for the missiles that could destroy our cities.

The American people, in reacting to the President's initiative, and in various opinion polls, have already shown that they do not agree with these ideologues. They are more pragmatic. They support an initiative that offers hope for the future. They do not wish to preserve for the next generation the present nightmare of huge and unimpeded missile forces, constantly poised for mass destruction.

IS THE ADMINISTRATION'S "STAR WARS" STRATEGIC DEFENSE INITIATIVE SOUND NATIONAL POLICY?—CON[3]

The two hottest concerns of the American people at this moment are the threat of nuclear war and the colossal deficits that threaten to cripple our economy. We in the Congress will be called upon to decide a little later this year whether or not to spend $2 billion next year and $24 billion over the next 5 years for research on an antiballistic missile defense. Obviously, we should spend whatever it takes to protect this country against the ultimate tragedy of a nuclear attack. But there is every reason to believe that the following disastrous results will follow a decision to fund this part of the administration's military budget. First, we would increase, not decrease, the danger of nuclear war. Second, we would end up spending not $24 billion but hundreds of billions, perhaps more than $1 trillion, on such a system. Third, it would almost certainly fail to work. Fourth, to the extent that it did somehow succeed, it would greatly reduce our deterrent capability.

This "Star Wars" defense is dead wrong on two counts. First, it makes a profound military mistake. It assumes that a superpower today can prevent or even win a nuclear war by relying on defensive military measures. It ignores the obvious fact that ever since World War I, more than 65 years ago, technology has overwhelmed the most elaborate military defenses. In the 1930's the French built their "impregnable" Maginot Line with the firm assurance that that elaborate series of heavily armed pill boxes, organized to maximize crossfire and defeat the most determined onslaught, would frustrate the most determined kind of German assault. But what happened? The Germans hit the defenses with blinding speed in a blitzkrieg attack and simply waltzed around the famed Maginot Line.

[3]From addresses by Sen. William Proxmire of Wisconsin to the Senate on April 26, June 20, and June 26, 1984. Reprinted from *Congressional Digest*. 63:77+. Mr. '85.

Again, 12 or 14 years ago, both the United States and the Soviet Union seemed well on their way to the construction of antiballistic missile systems very similar to the antimissile defenses the Reagan Administration now wants to fund. I vividly recall the Senate floor debate on funding that antiballistic missile system. Critics of the system at that time contended that any ABM system we could construct, no matter how brilliantly conceived, deployed, and operated, could be easily defeated at a fraction of the cost of the defensive ABM system. At that time the going estimate was the expenditure of $1 on offense could overwhelm $10 spent on any defensive weapon designed to stop nuclear missiles. The surprise, the mobility, the choice of timing for attack, the level of attack—whether from a high altitude or hugging the ground or even from ground transported weapons—all of these elements would favor the offense. Furthermore, the offense could pour in successive waves of missiles in an endless series until the defense was exhausted. In addition, in a military milieu in which technology changes swiftly and drastically, even the most elaborate kind of defense against nuclear attack could be overcome at any time with an equally elaborate offense and at a fraction of the cost.

Second, the "Star Wars" defense is wrong because it strives to achieve peace by extending an arms race that simply cannot be won. What is worse, it accelerates an arms race that not only fails to build national security but literally contributes to insecurity. We will end up spending hundreds of billions of dollars and find ourselves less safe.

At the beginning of this speech, I warned that any success this expenditure achieved would simply reduce and maybe destroy deterrence—the basis of our security in this nuclear world for the past 30 years. How could this happen? Here is how: Suppose we found that the Russians were on the verge of some kind of magical breakthrough that would render our massive nuclear deterrent capability useless. What would we do? Would we quietly accept world domination by the Soviet Union and an end to our freedom? What do you think? Put it the other way. Suppose the Soviet Union found that the United States was succeeding in building a truly effective antimissile system that made all their missiles useless. What would they do? Would they seriously consider a preemptive strike before we had put the final touches on our "Star Wars" defense? Of course, they would.

Above all, if this nation mistakenly proceeds down this path, we would obviously violate the Anti-Ballistic Missile Treaty of 1972. We would greatly dim the prospect of effective arms control agreements any time in the foreseeable future. We would be taking a long and tragic step toward a nuclear holocaust.

The first reason this Congress should not accept the President's recommendation and appropriate $2 billion for 1985 and commit ourselves to $25 billion over the next five years is because it will not work.

The Congressional Office of Technology Assessment issued a report saying "that a comprehensive antiballistic missile system should not serve as the basis of public expectation or national policy."

If we can win an arms control agreement on which we can rely that will limit and reduce nuclear weapons on both sides, we will not need to spend billions of dollars on this dreamy Star Wars defense.

Offensive arms control is dead in the water. Frankly, it is hard to construct a scenario more likely to keep it dead than for the Congress to comply with the Presidential request to fund the President's Star Wars program.

Why would funding the Star Wars defensive ABM program gut any real prospect of limiting offensive nuclear arms? Just put yourself in the position of the Russians. The only way we can expect to frustrate a Soviet missile attack is for the Soviets to agree to limit their offensive nuclear force in an arms control agreement with us.

Would they do this? Are they crazy? Why in the world would the Soviet Union agree to limit their nuclear arsenals in a mutual agreement with the United States when such an accommodation with the Soviet Union is the only way we can stop their missiles and destroy their deterrent capability? It is what has made them a superpower. Are they going to enter into an arms control agreement that will kill their deterrence? Of course not.

What a ridiculous dilemma this whole Star Wars gambit has driven this country into. The Soviet Union has vigorously protested the U.S. intention of building an elaborate antiballistic missile system. They see it as a very serious threat to their painfully constructed nuclear deterrent. Now we are told that for the program to work, we need to secure an arms control agreement with the Soviet Union to limit and reduce offensive nuclear weapons. So we cannot make this fabulously expensive defensive system operate effectively unless the Soviets agree—that is right, the Soviets agree—to limit their offensive missiles so we can gain this super advantage over them.

In my 27 years in this body I have seen some ridiculous proposals for spending the public's money. Indeed, I have given well over 100 Golden Fleeces to various agencies for throwing the public's money away over the past 9 years, but this baby takes the cake. We are asked to spend $2 billion in 1985 and $25 billion over the next 5 years just for the research on this program. The program itself will obviously cost hundreds of billions of dollars. There is no way it can work unless the Soviet Union decides to accommodate us by agreeing to limit their offensive missiles so that we can destroy whatever deterrent power their nuclear arsenal now possesses. Does anyone believe the Soviet Union will make President Reagan's Star Wars a big success by agreeing that it will not build the offensive missiles to overcome it?

As a program for defending this country, the Reagan proposal is so ridiculously bad that I cannot believe the President seriously expected to win with it. This program, if carried out, will not defend this country. But it will accomplish something else. It will kill nuclear arms control. It drives a spike right through the heart of any basis for United States–Soviet agreement on limiting offensive missiles. It leaves nuclear arms control dead. Far more is riding on whether or not the Congress agrees to fund this antiballistic missile system than a disagreement on nuclear weapons policy. If the Congress goes ahead, nuclear arms control will be dead for a very long time. There would be no way the Russians could agree to it—not ever.

The Star Wars proponents have two arguments designed to appeal to peace advocates. First, they claim that their antiballistic missile defense is exactly that: a defense. It would not attack. It would defend. It would not initiate war. It would reduce or prevent the casualties of war. Even if it should be used first it would be used to anticipate an enemy attack. And second, these nuclear weapons would never be used against people, always lethal nuclear weapons on the other side. These Star Wars proponents argue that nuclear war has previously been viewed as an offensive operation. A weapons program designed to wreak the total destruction of an enemy. Now, with the Star Wars, here come the boys with the white hats: the good guys—the A Team—Lifesavers not life destroyers. Guardians of peace because missile defense would stop missile attack.

And that's not all. The proponents of Star Wars contend that defensive antimissile activity can supplement arms control, not kill it. They argue that Star Wars can operate in the interest of both the Soviet Union and the United States. They argue it can provide either side or both sides the assurance that there is an option other than massive civilization-ending retaliation; that is, intercepting and destroying the incoming missiles of the other side. Presumably a President warned that the Russians had launched an ICBM attack would not be faced with a choice between doing nothing and pressing a button that would set the world on fire. He would have the option of putting out the fire by intercepting and destroying most, and perhaps all, of the incoming missiles.

What validity does this argument have? Is it conceivably possible that we could develop a defensive missile system that would work? Could we intercept and shoot down enough offensive enemy missiles to prevent total destruction? Is it possible that both sides could agree to a balance that would make nuclear war less instead of more likely? Is all this just a happy—maybe a slaphappy—dream? How about it? Is it possible? Well, anything is possible.

After all if we could put an American on the moon for $25 billion with the technology of the 1960's why could we not shoot down moving missiles with technology of the 1980's or 1990's for 10 or 20 times that much, say $250 billion or $500 billion. Maybe we can succeed with Star Wars, maybe we cannot. But why not try? Certainly there is no price we could pay, no burden we could bear that would be too great to prevent the total devastation of a nuclear attack on our country.

So what is wrong with "Star Wars"? What is wrong is that there is no real prospect that a defensive antimissile system would work. None. None. It will not work. Why not? Because whatever dynamic progress we can expect from a defense against missiles, we can surely anticipate an equally potent and opposite reaction from offensive missiles. At this moment where does the advantage lie? Clearly and obviously with the offensive. Even the staunchest proponents of Star Wars agree that offensive missiles have a massive advantage over any kind of a defensive antimissile system using presently researched and deployed weapons. But they say give us time; give us time; the Star Wars people plead, and we will construct a defense that will knock out all or almost all offensive incoming missiles.

At this point I have a confession. I believe that on this limited point, they are right. Yes, indeed, 20 years or maybe even 10 or 5 years from now with our lasers and other advanced technology, we will have the defensive technology to intercept and destroy incoming missiles that are deployed today. Then why not go ahead? There is an easy answer: If we do proceed, the other side will proceed too, but not with today's offensive missile technology and not with an antimissile technology that simply matched the defensive system missile for missile but with a highly intensified offensive missile program. The proponents of Star Wars have loaded the dice in this argument. They hand us a phony scenario. They make the patently ridiculous assumption that only the defense will be dynamic and progressive. They assume the offense will stand still, frozen, paralyzed. Armed with that utterly unrealistic assumption they predict victory for the defense. Of course, this is nonsense. Certainly without a negotiated mutual nuclear freeze both superpowers will continue to refine, modernize, and improve their offensive nuclear weapons. Whatever technological advantage might be temporarily with antiballistic missile defense, the offense will swiftly move to overcome. Will the offense succeed? Of course, they will. Why will they not? The offense can take its own initiative. After all the offense will always have the advantage of selecting the time of attack and the place. It can concentrate its resources on the targets it selects.

For example, Star Wars proponents do not even try to defend against such offensive nuclear weapons as groundhugging cruise missiles. So what is to prevent a superpower frustrated by antimissile defense from simply sliding under the defensive screen with cruise missiles? The answer—nothing. Nothing.

Several times I have asked the proponents of Star Wars when they have appeared before our Appropriations Committee what they would do about cruise missiles. They say they do not have an answer to that. They are not trying to defend against cruise missiles, only trying to defend against the missiles they can defend against which is the intercontinental ballistic missiles.

The Star Wars proponents contend that we have to move into a massive strategic defense because the Russians are already deeply into it. But the SDI advocates' demands are based on the usual Pentagon approach to selling expensive hardware to Congress—that the Russians are 10 feet tall. Russia, indeed, has a long record of stressing defense, but there is little or no significant evidence that the Russians are spending substantial sums on antimissile defense. If we proceed with Star Wars, it will become a trillion-dollar boondoggle.

So how do we defend against nuclear war? One way: Stop the arms race. Stop it cold. Stop it now with a negotiated, mutual, verifiable, and comprehensive nuclear freeze.

CAMPUSES' ROLE IN ARMS DEBATED AS 'STAR WARS' FUNDS ARE SOUGHT[4]

Spurred by the Reagan Administration's project to develop a shield against nuclear missiles, military research is returning in force to top universities, reviving a heated debate over the universities' proper role in developing weapons systems.

[4]Reprint of an article by reporter David E. Sanger. *New York Times.* p. A1+. Jl. 22, '85. © 1985 by The New York Times Company. Reprinted by permission.

But even as the debate is waged, hundreds of researchers are racing to claim a share of more than $600 million that the Strategic Defense Initiative, informally called "Star Wars," is expected to spend at American universities over the next five years. At the downtown Washington headquarters for the project, proposals from campus scientists seeking research money are piled high against a back wall—more than 1,000 applications in all.

'EVERYONE WANTS TO GET INVOLVED'

"Virtually everyone, on every campus, wants to get involved," said James A. Ionson, the ebullient Administration official in charge of organizing universities into about a dozen research consortiums to tackle specific problems for the project. "There will be many, many Manhattan projects in this."

Comparisons with the supersecret Manhattan Project that developed the atomic bomb 40 years ago have only fueled the debate on many campuses. At the University of Illinois at Champaign-Urbana, one of the nation's top research centers, 57 professors in the physics department signed a petition last week to boycott the program, calling it "deeply misguided, dangerous, and enormously expensive." Similar movements are afoot at the University of California at Berkeley, Cornell University and the Massachusetts Institute of Technology.

Some academics concede that their opposition to the project is primarily political. But even scientists and university officials who say they have no ideological objections to the Administration's plan wonder whether, over the long term, participating in the project and other military programs could jeopardize their academic freedom and ultimately harm basic research efforts.

Among the concerns are these:

• Researchers are increasingly worried that key elements of their work for the antimissile project will ultimately be classified, thus threatening their rights to publish research findings and exchange those findings with colleagues around the world. Reagan Administration officials dismiss those worries as unfounded, insisting that little of the work will be subject to publication controls and that sensitive projects will be quickly moved off campus.

• Several top academic officials have accused Administration officials of misrepresenting university participation in an effort to sell the project to Congress. The strongest attack came last month, when Paul E. Gray, president of the Massachusetts Institute of Technology, charged that the involvement of some M.I.T. professors in the research, though limited, was being cited by the Administration in a "manipulative effort to garner implicit institutional endorsement" of the project.

• Other academics are afraid that drawing such a large part of the nation's leading scientific talent into a single military project could lead to neglect of other important research. "The infusion of such a large amount of money," said Marvin L. Goldberger, president of the California Institute of Technology, "can distort activities within the university. It can draw people into research areas they might not otherwise pursue." Others worry that universities will overcommit resources to the project, only to find themselves in trouble as support for it waxes and wanes on Capitol Hill.

LEGACY OF VIETNAM WAR

Military research, of course, is hardly new to university laboratories. But much of it, including nearly all classified work, was chased off many campuses during the Vietnam War. Pentagon officials say that in the years since, research in critical military technologies suffered.

Now, they say, the Pentagon is again a welcome research sponsor. Officials of the antimissile project have already formed a half-dozen research consortiums, pooling academic talents in the design of super-fast computers, the development of enormously complex battle management software and the construction of compact, lightweight power supplies for laser stations in space.

But academia's embrace of military research is hardly limited to the antimissile project. Scores of universities have delved into a variety of other key Pentagon projects. In the shield research and the other programs, scientists say they are drawn partly by the availability of funds, but also by the chance to tackle some of the most pressing scientific projects of the decade.

At Carnegie-Mellon University, the computer science faculty is deeply involved in the $100 million Software Engineering Institute, being financed by the Air Force to solve critical problems in the writing of computer programs. And at the Georgia Institute of Technology in Atlanta, one of the few major research institutions still willing to perform classified work on campus, Department of Defense financing for a number of projects accelerated so fast that researchers moved into a six-story laboratory that was still under construction.

"There are still people at some universities who will tell you that the presence of a D.O.D. dollar is evil," said George A. Keyworth 2d, President Reagan's science adviser, who is a strong advocate of a tighter link between the military and academia, adding, "You still see vestiges of that in anachronistic corners of the country, like Cambridge," the Massachusetts city, home to Harvard and M.I.T., where citizens tried unsuccessfully two years ago to ban all nuclear research.

"But," he said, "I don't think that the majority feels that way."

Classification of Work and Effect on Discourse

If the current debate about campus military research had a starting place, it was a large hotel ballroom in New Carrollton, Md., a suburb of Washington, on a warm day at the end of March. Almost 300 college deans and scientists gathered for the first formal description of the remarkably varied antimissile research projects open to university laboratories.

Dr. Keyworth remembers the day as a turning point in government-university relations. "I was astonished when I went out to talk to those people," he recalled in a recent interview. "I was not prepared for the size and breadth of the representation, or for the enthusiasm and depth of interest those deans brought to the project."

Some participants, however, recall emerging with more questions than answers, particularly on classified research. On most campuses, classified work is either banned or relegated to off-campus institutes, like M.I.T.'s Lincoln Laboratories. Most of the work the Defense Department has traditionally sponsored on campuses is for basic research: fundamental work in pure or theoretical science that has no direct relationship to the development of weapons systems. Almost none of it carries restrictions on publication of results or discussion of ideas with colleagues and students, considered a cornerstone of academic freedom.

Would these freedoms apply to the shield project's "mission oriented" research on campus? "We are treating this just like basic research," Mr. Ionson said in an interview soon after the meeting. "There is no intent for any of this work to be classified."

But other statements made by Mr. Ionson and his colleagues have left academics unsure. Project officials have urged scientists involved in the research consortiums, who are called "principal investigators," to hold security clearances, so that they understand what research areas are classified and should be avoided, particularly by graduate students. In April, Mr. Ionson said that in some cases the Government might restrict the publication of such details on performance as descriptions of the exact accuracy or power of a laser beam used to destroy an enemy missile.

"Any principal investigator knows how to slant a paper to make it unclassified," Mr. Ionson said, explaining how university researchers could avoid running afoul of Defense Department censors. "Anyone can publish on how something works," he added. "How well it works, that's the only classified part." He said scientists would not object to those ground rules.

But he said in an interview last week that university work would be limited to fundamental research and that performance details would go "beyond their contract."

Many scientists argue that basic findings and performance details are often inseparable. Some of those applying for the research grants, who insisted on anonymity so as not to jeopardize their chances of getting them, express fear that the project officials may be enticing them into the research with promises of complete academic freedom that the officials will later be unable to fulfill.

"It may be unclassified right now," said Dorothy Nelkin, a professor of science, technology and society at Cornell who has examined the rush for Pentagon funds. "But when the work becomes interesting, I can't imagine classification won't be imposed. And then it is too late for the institutions to back out." Others cite the Pentagon's recent efforts to bar some unclassified papers from presentation at a Washington conference.

"This all has the potential of becoming exceedingly awkward for the universities," said Kenneth A. Smith, the associate provost and vice president for research at M.I.T. "Unfortunately, so far the Pentagon and the S.D.I. office has done nothing to allay our fears."

Reagan Administration officials counter that university researchers misunderstand their role in the project. "The vast majority of S.D.I. *in toto* is not classified," said Dr. Keyworth. "In any case, the components that we look to universities to provide are new ideas, new concepts, fundamental research." As soon as the work takes a sensitive turn, he said, it will be turned over to a private contractor or a Federal laboratory. Universities, with their tradition of openness and a plethora of foreign students, "are hardly an appropriate environment" for classified work, he said.

University officials question whether researchers can be changed midstream so easily.

Administration officials point to a Pentagon directive issued last summer instructing that "no restrictions may be placed upon the conduct or reporting of fundamental research that has not received national security classification." Some academics note, however, that this does not prevent the Defense Department from classifying research once it begins to yield results.

The Pentagon has been treading lightly in other fields, however. "I think the Defense Department understands that it cannot develop a history of marching in on successful research and classifying after the fact," said Donald Kennedy, president of Stanford University, who is co-chairman of a panel of Pentagon and academic officials that deals with such issues. "Obviously, if that happened, we would quickly develop antibodies to that kind of research."

Some See a Threat to
Other Research

Another fear is that universities will quickly grow overdependent on research funds provided through the project.

"The problem is that it throws the balance of science research all out of whack," said Mr. Kennedy, who has also voiced similar concerns about university ties to industry. The danger with the relatively abundant Defense Department grants is twofold, he and others maintain, in that they can lure scientists away from both basic research and research in other fields.

The largest underwriter of university research is the Department of Health and Human Services, which accounts for nearly half the Government-sponsored research and development at universities. Its work includes all research financed by the National Institutes of Health.

But statistics from the National Science Foundation appear to support assertions that universities are growing increasingly dependent on the Defense Department. Financing from other agencies that were mainstays of scientific research in the 1970's—the Department of Energy, the National Aeronautics and Space Administration, and the Department of Agriculture—has leveled off or declined. Meanwhile, Pentagon spending on campuses has grown to $930 million in the 1985 fiscal year, an 89 percent increase over the $495 million the Pentagon spent in 1980, while Health and Human Services' increase over that period was 34 percent.

Counting approximately $230 million spent off-campus at M.I.T.'s Lincoln Laboratories, Pentagon university spending now exceeds that of the National Science Foundation, traditionally the largest underwriter for nonmedical research.

Most of the Pentagon's research and development money goes to the development of specific weapons systems, mostly done by industry, and this year it expects to spend about $2.7 billion, more than triple the $898 million of 1983. By the Pentagon's own estimate, basic research, which was 6 percent of the total research and development budget two decades ago, accounts for less than 3 percent today. Thus, scientists say it is clear that their projects have a far better chance of Pentagon contracts if the work is likely to lead to a specific weapons system.

"Is it worrisome?" asked Leo Young, who directs the Pentagon's campus spending. "Absolutely. But we need weapons, and it is hardly surprising that at a time you are building up for weapons systems, basic research gets short shrift."

Already, Mr. Young added, the Defense Department is moving to counter the trend. In its current budget, it has proposed a "University Research Initiative," totaling $175 million over three years, to pay for special fellowships and strengthen fundamental research. But academics say the program will be swamped by the huge influx of Strategic Defense Initiative funds.

The project's funds for university research fall under the budget category for highly applied research. But Mr. Ionson says that it is really "mission-oriented basic research," which is close to pure basic research.

"The difference is this," he said recently. "A basic researcher can get in his car and drive wherever he wants. A mission-oriented researcher gets in his car and goes to Florida—because we need to get to Florida. Whether he takes Interstate 95 or U.S. 1 is his choice."

Universities' Worries on Politics of Plan

Even before Congress began serious deliberations on the budget for the antimissile project this spring, project officials were already seeking proposals from scientists, reversing the usual sequence of events. "It's probably something that's never been done," Mr. Ionson was quoted as saying in the journal *Science*, which is widely read in academia. "But this office is trying to sell something to Congress. If we can say that this fellow at M.I.T. will get money to do such and such research, it's something real to sell. That in and of itself is innovative."

That comment, officials on several campuses say, touched off perhaps the hottest debate surrounding university participation in the project: whether doing antimissile research constitutes an endorsement of the project.

Universities "have been entrusted with certain resources by society, and we should not be using them to influence social policy," Mr. Gray, the M.I.T. president, said recently. He said Mr. Ionson's comments showed that the Administration was "trying to nudge us out of the middle."

Mr. Ionson, who is an astrophysicist, said last week, "I could care less about institutional endorsement," explaining that he was simply trying to show Congress that many researchers had "good ideas for good science" that deserved financial support.

In announcing the first university consortiums in April, the Defense Department listed a host of "participating institutions," although only one or two researchers were involved on many campuses. That led to the charges that the universities were being manipulated for political purposes. "It was a case of poor wording on our part," said Col. Lee De Lorme, a project spokesman. "It gave the impression that the consortium was larger than it was. But that has been corrected."

University officials say their decisions whether to accept money for any research are made on scientific grounds, regardless of the sponsor. But both academics and project officials admit privately that politics may play a large role in the shield project. Scientists on several campuses say that the shield is essentially a weapons system, with offensive capabilities as well as defensive ones, and assert that universities are no place to design instruments of destruction. Mr. Ionson counters that the shield is different because it seeks to eliminate the threat of nuclear weaponry, and that scientists who share that goal will embrace the project.

"This whole bit that university scientists are against S.D.I. is a lot of propaganda," he said. Much of the opposition, he said, has come from "Nobel laureates who say S.D.I. is impossible." But, he said, "a Nobel laureate in molecular genetics knows nothing about problems of plasma physics. Nothing. Nothing at all."

The Union of Concerned Scientists, long a critic of the defensive shield project, asserts that universities are not critical enough. Howard Riss, the group's executive director, said "you can basically see the universities becoming another Congressional district" as the Administration seeks support for the program. "When scientists discover that S.D.I. is not such a good idea," he said, "it will be difficult to turn off the faucet."

Campus-Pentagon Ties beyond
Antimissile Plan

The shield project is the biggest but hardly the only example of the Pentagon's tightening link with university researchers. The Georgia Tech Research Institute, on the campus of the Georgia Institute of Technology, is to carry out about $60 million in sponsored research this year, 80 percent of it Government financed. The flow of Defense Department research funds to the campus has increased ninefold since 1976, spurred greatly by the institute's willingness to take on classified work. Unlike most universities, it even lets students obtain security clearances to participate in the work. "It's just another union card," said James C. Wiltse, associate director of the institute.

The university takes few foreign students, in part, officials say, so that its classified work is not jeopardized. Joseph M. Pettit, the university president, says the school's role in academia is unusual. "We have career-oriented students here—they tend to be less ivory tower," he said, with a "different view of the world" than those in the humanities and social sciences. "They don't worry about what is the academy and what is pure research," he said. And in time even classified research will enter the public domain, he said, noting that radar technology was classified until the end of World War II.

Other schools are pushing harder than ever for Pentagon contracts. Universities that sought the $100 million Software Engineering Institute hired lobbyists and made elaborate presentations at the Pentagon.

At Carnegie-Mellon, which won the institute, officials say it will be separate from the university, but on the central campus. While school officials say they will do almost no classified work, they say some professors will hold security clearances "at the highest levels" so that they can review the Pentagon's most pressing software problems.

"It would be nice, of course, if we could avoid all classified data," said Angel Jordan, the school's provost, who himself will hold one of the top clearances. "But that would mean not being able to see some of the data that is on the cutting edge." The school took pains to assure that there were no restrictions on its publication rights, he said.

But a copy of Carnegie-Mellon's contract, made public by the Air Force, raises questions about the extent of that freedom. It specifies that "distribution will not be made of technical data" that either the contractor or the Government find "to have classified or potentially classified military end-item applications." In case of doubt, it continues, Carnegie-Mellon must obtain Pentagon permission for publication.

"That is a very, very dangerous clause," said Prof. Lincoln Wolfenstein of Carnegie-Mellon. "The general freedom of this campus will not be aided," he said, expressing fears that the Pentagon will be determining the school's research agenda, while teaching will be neglected.

Professor Jordan responded, "The majority of the faculty support this, and so do the students." He said Professor Wolfenstein and others really objected to the institute "on moral grounds, and this is not a moral issue."

STAR WARS: THE FINAL SOLUTION[5]

I call upon the scientific community in our country, those who gave us nuclear weapons, to turn their great talents now to the cause of mankind and world peace, to give us the means of rendering these nuclear weapons impotent and obsolete.

—Ronald Reagan
March 23, 1983

With these words, President Reagan ushered in a new arms race and brought the world closer to atomic war. His Strategic Defense Initiative, popularly known as Star Wars, can no longer be dismissed as a cockeyed fantasy, for it has assumed central im-

[5]Reprint of an article by Matthew Rothschild and Keenen Peck, associate editors of *The Progressive*. *Progressive*. 49:20+. Jl. '85. © 1985 by The Progressive, Inc. Reprinted by permission from *The Progressive*, 409 East Main Street, Madison, WI 53703.

portance in the nuclear strategy of the Reagan Administration. The dream of rendering nuclear weapons "obsolete" is turning into a nightmarish threat to global peace.

"It is difficult to imagine a system more likely to induce catastrophe," nuclear scientists Hans A.. Bethe, Richard L. Garwin, Kurt Gottfried, and Henry W. Kendall have asserted.

The planned Star Wars research program will require the effort of eight Manhattan Projects, in the estimate of one Pentagon official. The end price tag could be enormous—perhaps as much as $1 trillion for deployment, according to former Defense Secretary James Schlesinger. The social costs, harder to tabulate, are likely to be just as heavy: We may be entering the Star Wars Society, where key aspects of our lives—where we work, what we study, how we engage in politics—will be touched and twisted by this gargantuan project.

Yet space weapons are not inevitable. The Strategic Defense Initiative, now in its third year, can still be stopped, though opportunities for doing so are diminishing each day as weapons companies line up at the trough. Star Wars may soon have the commitment of such powerful interests that it will take on a momentum all its own.

Caught off guard by the President's initiative, the U.S. peace movement is only now beginning to fashion a program to defeat Star Wars. The movement's task is formidable: Ronald Reagan had taken the moral high ground by calling for the abolition of nuclear weapons. Star Wars poses as much of a challenge to peace activists as it does to the Soviet Union, and the risks of not meeting the challenge are great.

The idea of Star Wars is ostensibly defensive. The United States would build a shield above the Earth, using satellites, lasers, super-high-speed projectiles, and other threshold technologies. Though Reagan likes to call it a non-nuclear defense, a substantial portion of the Strategic Defense Initiative involves development of beam weapons powered by nuclear explosions.

The President originally sketched out a technological breakthrough that would, he said, "free the world from the threat of nuclear war." Secretary of Defense Caspar Weinberger has been similarly unequivocal about the goal of Star Wars. "The defensive systems that the President is talking about are not designed to be partial," he said a few days after Reagan's landmark speech. "What we want to try is to get a system which will develop a defense that is thoroughly reliable and total." Weinberger has repeatedly reaffirmed his faith. In May 1985, he said the Strategic Defense Initiative would "make nuclear weapons obsolete."

A perfect defense would also render obsolete the strategic doctrine that has governed the arms race for forty years: Mutually Assured Destruction (MAD). The MAD theory holds that neither superpower will risk launching a first strike against the other because each could survive an attack and retaliate with enough force to inflict unacceptable damage.

Reagan openly broke with MAD in his March 1983 address to the nation. "I have become more and more deeply convinced," he said, "that the human spirit must be capable of rising above dealing with other nations and human beings by threatening their existence." He asked, "Would it not be better to save lives than to avenge them? . . . What if free people could live secure in the knowledge that their security did not rest upon the threat of instant U.S. retaliation to deter a Soviet attack . . . ?"

Edward Teller, often called the father of the hydrogen bomb, is an enthusiastic promoter of Star Wars. He met with Reagan four times in the fourteen months leading up to the President's speech, and told him in a letter that the Strategic Defense Initiative "would end the MAD era and commence a period of assured survival on terms favorable to the Western alliance."

But an impenetrable defense is no longer the Administration's actual goal, despite Reagan's and Weinberger's continuing protestations to the contrary. It has become apparent to the Government's scientists that no technology can provide an absolute shield. "A perfect astrodome defense is not a realistic thing," Lieutenant General James Abrahamson, head of the Strategic Defense Initiative Organization, acknowledged last year.

Because of the destructive power of nuclear weapons, millions of Americans would perish if even a few warheads could penetrate the shield. Furthermore, Star Wars is designed only to stop intercontinental ballistic missiles (ICBMs); it would not be a defense against jet bombers, low-flying cruise missiles, or suitcase bombs.

The Administration has, in fact, quietly scrapped the notion of protecting the population. Instead, at least in the minds of every policymaker except Reagan and Weinberger, the Star Wars program is aimed at assuring the survival of missile silos and important military posts—not cities and people. Instead of superseding deterrence, Star Wars would actually reinforce the MAD doctrine.

"Providing a better, more stable basis for enhanced deterrence is the central purpose of the SDI program," the White House acknowledged in a recent pamphlet. A 1985 Pentagon report to Congress made the same point: "The U.S. goal has never been to eventually give'up the policy of deterrence. With defenses, the United States seeks not to replace deterrence, but to enhance it."

Though the Star Wars shield could not prevent all ICBMs from smashing into the United States, it could conceivably stop some of them from destroying U.S. missile silos. "It's not likely to be perfect," says Gerold Yonas, chief scientist of the Star Wars program, "but it will give us a better deterrent posture." Republican Representative Jim Courter, a member of the Armed Services Committee, is even more blunt: He recommends Star Wars as "a point-defense system to protect the MX missile." This is, of course, a far cry from rendering nuclear weapons "impotent and obsolete."

"It is not a protection of the people," observes Herbert "Pete" Scoville, president of the Arms Control Association and a former deputy director of the CIA. "What it is doing is essentially defending missiles and command-and-control centers. That is lesson number one."

The Reagan Administration has downplayed its shift in emphasis, probably because it realizes how difficult it would be to persuade Americans to buy an enormously costly program simply to protect missiles. But that is what Star Wars is now about, and high officials are openly talking about "early" deployment of a "leaky shield."

The implications are frightening.

"I clearly recognize that defensive systems have limitations and raise certain problems and ambiguities," Reagan said in his

March 1983 speech. "If paired with offensive systems, they can be viewed as fostering an aggressive policy. . . . "

On this point, he was right on target. To the extent that Star Wars would work, it would give the United States the ability to launch a first strike against the Soviet Union without being wiped out in a counterattack. Having a defense—or believing that you have a defense, even if it is not complete—makes it easier to consider attacking.

Merely installing the system would be perceived as a threat by the Soviet Union, and would give it an incentive to strike preemptively. At the very least, the Soviets would have a reason to shoot down the Star Wars satellites—an act of war that former CIA Director Stansfield Turner has predicted will occur as soon as components are placed in space.

"Although the American people are led to believe that [Star Wars] is defensive, that is far from the case," says Robert C. Aldridge, a former Trident missile designer turned military critic. "If Soviet missiles which survive a first-strike attack could be intercepted in flight, that would remove any threat of retaliation and there would be no restraining force on U.S. aggressive behavior. The concept of deterrence, for all its faults and ambiguities, would be nullified and the United States could attack the Soviet Union with impunity."

Even if the defensive system were to prove only partially effective, it still might be useful in waging nuclear war. "Such a system makes much more sense as an adjunct to a first-strike capability than as a shield from a first strike," Frank von Hippel, physicist and Princeton professor, pointed out in a recent issue of the *Bulletin of the Atomic Scientists*. "Because of its inevitable vulnerability, a Star Wars–type system would be fairly easy to neutralize at the beginning of a highly orchestrated first strike. But, in the face of a disorganized retaliatory strike by an unprepared *victim* of a surprise attack, it might be more effective."

The Soviet Union has about 6,000 land-based ICBMs. If a surprise U.S. nuclear attack on Soviet missiles were 95 per cent effective, the Soviets would have 300 missiles remaining—more than enough to retaliate against the United States. But if the United States also had a Star Wars shield in place and it was 90 per cent effective, only thirty Soviet ICBMs could penetrate. Since the U.S. first strike would also diminish Soviet command-and-control functions, it seems likely that fewer than thirty missiles—and perhaps only a handful—would get through. Such diminished capacity to retaliate might make the waging of nuclear war attractive to U.S. military strategists.

Obviously, a Star Wars defense would place the Soviet Union at a strategic disadvantage and frighten the Kremlin. "The Soviet Union, fearing that it would be effectively disarmed by a U.S. attack, might be tempted in a crisis to launch a preemptive strike against the United States rather than risk losing its ability to retaliate," points out the citizens' group Common Cause.

Take the example of the 6,000 Soviet land-based ICBMs. If the United States attacks the Soviet Union, the Soviet Union would hypothetically lose all but thirty or so of its missiles. But if the Soviets struck first, they could get 600 of their missiles through. This assumes the Star Wars defense is 90 per cent effective; the Soviets would lose 5,400 of their ICBMs in their own first strike, but 600 of their ICBMs would be able to hit the United States.

If both the United States and the Soviet Union had Star Wars shields in place, the situation would not be more stable; in fact, it would be more threatening. Each side would want to launch its missiles first for fear that it would lose them later.

"The incentive to cut one's losses by striking first in a crisis will be even greater than it is now," scientists Bethe, Garwin, Gottfried, and Kendall wrote in *Scientific American*.

That would be "the worst crisis-instability situation," says missile designer Charles A. Zraket, executive vice president of the Mitre Corporation. "It'd be like having two gunfighters in space armed to the teeth with quick-fire capabilities."

The gunfighters might, incidentally, find a way to use their space systems to shoot at each other, as well as at each other's missiles. The Pentagon is currently testing devices that it hopes will be able to destroy ground targets from space. One "well-connected source with years of experience in military space projects" told *The Christian Science Monitor* that this is "probably one of the most sensitive aspects" of the space shuttle program.

Even before we get to high noon, however, the Strategic Defense Initiative will heat the arms race to the boiling point. The Soviet Union will respond to Star Wars by developing offensive measures to frustrate the system and by constructing its own defense. Our Government expects as much, so it will spend about $200 million this year devising measures to penetrate any Soviet defensive shield.

(The Reagan Administration no longer talks about sharing Star Wars technology with the Kremlin. Reagan's rhetorical flourish in the second Presidential election debate served its purpose; today, the Pentagon says it is "unlikely" to let the Soviets in on the deal.)

"If the United States starts militarization of outer space and thereby undermines the existing military-strategic equilibrium," said Soviet Defense Minister Sergei Sokolov in May, "the Soviet Union will have no other choice but to take reply measures to restore the position."

Initially, the Soviets would respond by increasing their stockpile of strategic missiles as a way of overwhelming the Star Wars shield. The more ICBMs they produce, the more of their missiles will survive a first strike and get by the U.S. defense. They will also bolster their arsenal of bombers and cruise missiles.

The Soviets' first response, the Defense Department predicted in an April report, would be "increasing missiles, warheads, and penetration aids in an attempt to saturate the defense."

Such a build-up would greatly reduce the chances of reaching an arms limitation agreement on offensive weapons. "As a practical matter," noted retired Air Force General Brent Scowcroft, who headed the President's Commission on Strategic Forces, "it would be very difficult to induce the Soviets to reduce their offensive forces if they faced the prospect of a strategic defense for which they might need those offensive forces to penetrate."

In addition to increasing their offensive weapons and building decoys to confuse our defensive system, the Soviets can be expected to try to build their own strategic defense and to make new weapons that could knock out the U.S. Star Wars complex. The late Soviet leader Yuri V. Andropov asserted four days after Reagan's March 1983 speech that Star Wars will "open the floodgates to a runaway race of all types, both offensive and defensive." The chief U.S. arms negotiator, Paul Nitze, has made a similar point: "The defensive systems could encourage a proliferation of countermeasures and additional offensive weapons to overcome deployed defenses."

In such a climate, the entire concept of arms control will go out the window. The first item to be lost will be the 1972 Anti-Ballistic Missile Treaty between the United States and the Soviet Union. That treaty states: "Each party undertakes not to develop, test, or deploy ABM systems or components which are sea-based, air-based, space-based, or mobile land-based." Star Wars, a space-based antiballistic missile defense, would clearly violate the treaty.

Reagan Administration officials admit this, and the only question is when the United States will abrogate the treaty. "We would have to depart from the treaty" at some point, General Abrahamson has told Congress, suggesting that the time would come in the early 1990s. The National Campaign to Save the ABM Treaty says the violation may come as early as 1988.

In that year, the Reagan Administration plans to demonstrate an airborne optical surveillance system—a Boeing passenger plane with the roof sawed off and heat-sensitive telescopes placed inside. John Pike, associate director of space policy for the Federation of American Scientists, calls the scheduled test "a near-term, unambiguous violation of the treaty."

Breaking the ABM treaty, considered one of the few accomplishments of arms control negotiations, would signal the revival of superpower competition in both defensive and offensive weaponry. If the ABM treaty is scuttled, says the peace organization SANE, "both sides will feel tremendous pressure to 'break out' of the SALT I and II restrictions on offensive nuclear weapons." Indeed, it appears that the most hawkish members of the Reagan Administration support Star Wars as a surefire way of overcoming SALT limits.

Star Wars would not only undermine the tenuous peace, it would distort the society in which we live. "It will alter the political, social, and economic fabric" says Michael T. Klare, professor of peace and world security studies at the five-college consortium in Amherst, Massachusetts. "Our society will become a Space Wars, a Star Wars, society."

The sheer size of the enterprise will divert resources from civilian science and absorb funds that could go toward social spending. The venture will fatten the pockets of military contractors and increase the dependency of a few states on military largesse.

"It is the equivalent of a war, in terms of the mobilization of Americans and the potential commitment of resources," Klare says.

Reagan intends to spend $3.7 billion on Star Wars research and development in fiscal 1986—up from $1.4 billion the year before. The Administration says the entire research phase of the program will cost $32.2 billion through 1990.

But this estimate does not include the costs of personnel and maintenance, nor does it take into account strategic defense work being conducted outside the Star Wars program. The Pentagon is seeking about $500 million for such research in 1986 alone. According to the Federation of American Scientists, the Department of Energy and other agencies will spend $8 billion over the next five years on laser and particle beam research related to Star Wars.

The $32.2 billion estimate also makes no provision for cost overruns, which are routine and all but inevitable for military projects. The official assumption that Star Wars research will be completed by 1990 makes little sense, given the technical obstacles that must be overcome in developing a missile defense. Richard Garwin, IBM fellow at the Thomas J. Watson Research Center and a Pentagon consultant, predicts that five more years of research will follow the first five, at an additional cost of $50 billion.

Beyond research, the price tag for deployment—the amount of money needed to put up the kind of full-scale defense envisioned by the President—would be astronomical. Former Defense Secretaries Harold Brown and James Schlesinger put the figure at $1 trillion (for an ineffective system, they add). Richard DeLauer, former Under Secretary of Defense for Research and Engineering in the Reagan Administration, told Congress that deployment would cost at least $500 billion. "When the time comes that you deploy any of these technologies," DeLauer said, "you'll be staggered at the cost they will involve."

A partial Star Wars defense would, of course, be less expensive than the unattainable "leakproof" version. But even a partial system would have to defeat countermeasures; defend itself from attack in space and on Earth; operate automatically; destroy attacking missiles before they release their multiple warheads (for maximum effectiveness); and process vast amounts of data in split seconds. Billions of dollars would still be required, and politicians would be hard-pressed to justify spending so much to protect missile silos but not people.

For now, the House and Senate Armed Services Committees are moving more cautiously than Reagan would like. They recently trimmed his 1986 Star Wars request from $3.7 billion to $2.5 billion in the House and $2.97 billion in the Senate. The full Congress will take up the budget this fall.

The Council on Economic Priorities, a private research organization, recently examined the economic effects of the Pentagon's planned outlays for Star Wars. In a report issued in May, the Council found:

• "Strategic defense research could represent as much as 4.5 per cent of the nation's research and development expenditures in 1986, up from 2.2 per cent in 1984."

• "While strategic defense research will require only a small amount of total national research and development, growth is so rapid that it may well 'crowd out' other Federal research and development efforts with less political clout."

• "In a market projected to be tight, the Strategic Defense Initiative will take up a significant portion of the growth in scientific, engineering, and technical personnel. It could require roughly 4 per cent of all new engineers between 1984 and 1987; the Defense Department will take up a third of all new engineers, and the Strategic Defense Initiative will require more than 12 per cent of the Defense Department total."

• "If strategic defense technologies reach full-scale development, the macroeconomic impact could be substantially greater."

Rosy Nimroody, co-author of the Council study, points out that the proposed increase in the Star Wars budget between 1985 and 1986 could pay for AMTRACK, rural development agencies, the Job Corps, and a host of other social programs the President has targeted for elimination.

"All the technical genius and talent which would be used for rebuilding cities and modernizing industries will be diverted away," says Michael Klare. "You can't have Star Wars and a welfare state. To finance Star Wars, they will have to dismantle the welfare state."

The Council warned that Star Wars may soon acquire "an economic and institutional life of its own." Companies now assessing the feasibility and advisability of a strategic defense are the same ones that would ultimately construct the system. "The danger lies in the program being launched on the basis of economic benefits to key contractors and constituencies whether or not it is proven worthwhile on national security grounds," the Council observed.

In 1983 and 1984, more than 90 per cent of the major space weapons contracts were awarded in four states already heavily dependent on Pentagon dollars: California (45 per cent), Washington (22 per cent), Texas (13 per cent), and Alabama (10 per cent). Elected representatives from those states will be working overtime to make Star Wars a reality.

At the same time, the private sector is stampeding to get a piece of the Star Wars action. "It is the business opportunity of a generation," *The Wall Street Journal* reported in May, "a chance to cash in on billions of dollars in Federal contracts." The Pentagon's Strategic Defense Initiative Organization has conducted a number of briefings for businesses, and the response has been overwhelming—"like a fish-feeding frenzy," one industry analyst told the *Journal*.

Many of the major Star Wars contractors—Boeing, McDonnell Douglas, Lockheed, and Rockwell—also manufacture nuclear weapons. For them, the President's scheme promises more than a new pot of gold: His plan may quiet calls for arms reductions, thereby letting the nuclear assembly lines continue to roll.

A strategic defense trade association has already been formed with the "sprinkling of holy water" from the Pentagon, according to the group's founder, aerospace consultant Jack Coakley. "The Strategic Defense Initiative isn't going to go any place if it isn't pulled along by industry," he says.

"What we see happening today is the rapid conversion of the President's Star Wars proposal from stardust and moonbeams to that great pork barrel in the sky," commented Paul Warnke, former U.S. arms control negotiator, in the report from the Council on Economic Priorities.

Since the American people would reject Star Wars if they perceived it as a pork barrel, proponents of the Strategic Defense Initiative claim it will bring vast benefits to the economy as a whole. High Frontier, an organization fanatically devoted to space-based defense, touts Star Wars as "A High Technology Answer to the Economic Challenge." General Abrahamson has claimed that "relative to SDI, computer, communications, propulsion, and laser technologies have attractive and significant spinoff possibilities. Clearly they could help the SDI program pay for itself." One of the most vociferous Congressional supporters of Star Wars, Representative Kenneth Kramer, Colorado Republican, says space ventures "will lay the foundation for an educational-vocational renaissance for the American labor force, particularly the unemployed in the 'smokestack industries.'" "It is the WPA program of the 1980s," jokes Kramer's Colorado colleague, Democrat Patricia Schroeder, an outspoken critic of Star Wars.

The economic promise will probably never be fulfilled. "Benefits of military research and development to the civilian economy have been small and are declining as military technology becomes increasingly specialized and exotic," concludes a study completed earlier this year by the Center for Defense Information, an independent watchdog organization. The space wars technology will be the most exotic yet developed by the Pentagon.

The Council on Economic Priorities, too, doubts that Star Wars will spur the overall economy. Not only will it drain talent from the civilian sector, the group noted in its report, but the applied nature of the research will lead to few general uses. Moreover, "the cloud of secrecy surrounding the Strategic Defense Initiative . . . tends to reduce the possibility of commercial spinoffs."

Secrecy will necessarily cloak Star Wars research, with dramatic effects on one junior partner in the crusade: the nation's academic community. Though university administrators are publicly committed to the open exchange of ideas, they long for the big bucks available in the strategic defense program, especially since the nonmilitary share of the Federal research and development budget plummeted by 30 per cent between 1980 and 1984.

The President's science adviser, George Keyworth II, says the Administration wants to repair ties between academia and the Pentagon that were damaged during the Vietnam war. He fondly recalls "a time in the decades after World War II when that relationship was very close and very productive."

Already, a consortium of four universities has received a $9 million, three-year Pentagon contract to develop computer technologies for Star Wars. Defense Department officials told *The New York Times* that "many of the researchers will need security clearances and that some specific details of how well equipment performs may be blocked from publication."

In the field of laser research, too, the Pentagon has an interest in subverting academic freedom. Last March, at a conference of the Society of Photo-Optical Instrumentation Engineers, military officials restricted access to several sessions in which unclassified scientific papers were discussed. The papers described lasers bouncing off satellites.

James Ionson, who coordinates university projects for the Strategic Defense Initiative Organization, told *The Times* that cooperating researchers will often be compelled to publish classified and unclassified versions of their work. (This is not mentioned in the twenty-nine-page booklet that Ionson distributed to universities last March. There, he boasts of "a new and exciting time for us in the science and engineering community.")

Censorship obviously pollutes the academic atmosphere—to say nothing of this nation's principles—and it is scientifically and economically counterproductive in the short run, as even Edward Teller, the best-known advocate of Star Wars, concedes. "Secrecy is a measure that hurts our opponents a little and us a great deal," he remarked a few months ago.

But secrecy will be only one element of a new repressive climate that is sure to be encouraged by Star Wars. In the same way that the start of the nuclear arms race sparked national paranoia—witchhunts and pressure to conform—so will the space weapons race bring out America's "dark side" (to borrow the phrase made popular by the movie *Star Wars*).

"Star Wars has become a test of loyalty to the Government," says Klare. "Those who criticize Star Wars are themselves the target of criticism. If you resist, you're going to be attacked."

A retired Army general, Henry Mohr, recently wrote in the *St. Louis Globe-Democrat*, "Whether they realize it or not, quibblers in Washington, like former Secretary of Defense Robert S. McNamara and Carl Sagan, through their bickering, are giving aid and comfort to the Soviet Union. On matters such as this, what normally might be considered as mere dissent and exercise of freedom of speech goes too far. They may actually be endangering the lives of the American people, and our allies."

In its March newsletter, High Frontier published a report asserting that the Council on Economic Priorities is "part of the domestic surrender lobby. It's closely connected with the left-wing Institute for Policy Studies, which sounds like Polly (of wanna cracker fame) when it comes to parroting the Soviet line."

At the White House, science adviser Keyworth says opposition to Star Wars is "trash." Critics in the media, he adds, seem "to be drawn from a relatively narrow fringe element on the far Left of our society."

The U.S. peace movement confronts all these challenges in Star Wars: a new arms race; a greater danger of war; a scheme that will take Federal money from the needy and bloat the military-industrial complex; increased secrecy and heightened repression.

But Star Wars can be stopped. "Politicians still don't know whether they're likely to win support or lose support by voting for Star Wars," says John Isaacs, legislative director of the Council for a Livable World. Public opinion polls show that a majority of Americans oppose the Strategic Defense Initiative; however, those same polls reveal that 30 to 50 per cent of the population is unfamiliar with Star Wars. Education must be a high priority for opponents of the program.

The first task is to strip bare Reagan's rhetoric. The President exploits the public's fear of atomic war when he calls for an effort to make nuclear weapons "obsolete." Similarly, his repudiation of the policy of Mutually Assured Destruction sounds comforting. (He even has begun to express concern about "nuclear winter.")

"It makes our work more difficult," says Jane Gruenebaum, executive director of the Nuclear Weapons Freeze Campaign. "He's using our rhetoric to usurp our issue. He's claiming the high ground we thought we had all to ourselves. It's part of a concerted effort to co-opt the peace movement."

The ideology of Star Wars is tailor-made to the American psyche. In addition to tapping into the public's anxiety, Reagan has proffered a plan to restore U.S. supremacy simply by building a better mousetrap. "We are technology junkies," says Representative Schroeder. "People think if we spend enough money, we can go back to 1945, when we were Number One."

A return to innocence—to being the most powerful nation, by virtue of either a nuclear monopoly or a defensive shield—appeals to popular instincts and corresponds with official hopes. This is how those hopes are summed up by Colin Gray, an arms control adviser to the Reagan Administration: "In the event that the United States succeeded in deploying a population defense that was technically robust, a considerable measure of U.S. freedom of political action should be restored as a logical consequence."

The domestic goal of Star Wars has been articulated in an equally crude fashion by High Frontier. "It constitutes an effective counter to the nuclear freeze movement," wrote High Frontier's director, "around which the Left has been rallying and reviving the old McGovern coalition."

Whether the President's plan does turn out to be "an effective counter" to the peace movement will depend, to a large extent, on the peace movement's own strategy. If the movement opposes Star Wars merely by lending its support to Mutually Assured Destruction, it leaves itself open to the charge of endorsing an immoral and potentially suicidal doctrine—a charge that critics of the arms race have themselves leveled against past Administrations.

This dilemma was addressed at a convention of peace activists in May—a gathering entitled Stop the Arms Race in Space, or STARS, that drew about 400 grass-roots organizers and lobbyists from some twenty states. They assembled in Colorado Springs, site of several major Air Force installations and the future home of the Government's $1.15 billion Consolidated Space Operations Center.

At the convention's opening session, Patricia Mische, author of *Star Wars and the State of Our Souls,* urged participants to devise "security alternatives" to the Strategic Defense Initiative. Failure to provide the public with alternatives to Star Wars and MAD would mean "we contribute by default to the policy we are against," she said. Mische mentioned "the need for strengthened international structures to arbitrate international conflict," but her main interest was in redirecting Star Wars funds toward peaceful uses of outer space. Several other speakers—including Representative Schroeder—echoed the call for an expanded civilian space effort.

Unfortunately, the peaceful potential of the heavens is beside the point. Star Wars was designed to give the United States more power in the world by obtaining a military advantage over the Soviet Union; this country's interventionist policies (and the Soviet Union's, for that matter) will remain intact even if cosmonauts and astronauts shake hands on the moon.

Physicist Richard Garwin and Herbert Scoville, president of the Arms Control Association, offered an even less palatable alternative. They criticized Star Wars and endorsed MAD.

"I know mutual deterrence is not a very popular concept," said Scoville. "On the other hand, nuclear weapons are here and they're not going to go away overnight. So one must fall back on the umbrella of mutual deterrence." Garwin argued that the "threat of retaliation" ensures superpower stability.

But the fact remains that MAD, as Reagan says, holds Soviet and American citizens hostage to each other's nuclear bombs. Since 1945, the arms race between the superpowers has sped ahead in the name of deterrence, increasing rather than decreasing the likelihood of war. Several times in the MAD era, the United States has come within a hair's breadth of initiating tactical nuclear war.

The peace movement has to "tackle the MAD problem," says Michael Klare. "The peace movement has been saying, 'MAD is immoral.' Reagan says, 'I agree with that.' This has created a split within the movement on MAD—a very serious one."

"There are some in the peace movement who don't see any alternative to MAD," says Matthew Goodman, public information director of the Institute for Defense and Disarmament Studies in Cambridge, Massachusetts. "For a lot of people, MAD seems like the safest alternative to Star Wars."

The peace movement must break clearly and unequivocally with the doctrine of Mutually Assured Destruction. This is no time to retreat, to accept the pernicious notion that we must possess nuclear weapons to avert nuclear war. It is MAD that has spurred the arms race, and the arms race has brought us Star Wars.

Just as MAD is no alternative, neither is the arms control process. For four decades, that process has produced steadily higher "ceilings" on weapons stockpiles. Stabilizing the nuclear balance would, in any event, leave each superpower with a huge and dangerous arsenal.

Once that reality begins to sink in, people will be well on their way to embracing the only sensible way out of the nuclear bind: disarmament. E. P. Thompson, the British author and antinuclear leader, made this point while describing Star Wars in a recent issue of *The Guardian* of London: "At astronomic cost, an astral venture will be set in motion to achieve an end—the blocking of each others' missiles—which could be achieved tomorrow, at no cost at all, by a rational agreement by both parties to disarm."

Disarmament—not MAD—undermines the case for Star Wars. Disarmament—not the arms control process—can ensure the survival of the planet and the stars.

IV. WORLD OPINION

EDITOR'S INTRODUCTION

Star Wars will not be built in a vacuum. America's allies and the Soviet Union will be following the progress of the Strategic Defense Initiative closely. So far, the Allies have been quite skeptical. Clumsy U. S. efforts to involve European governments in Star Wars have met with a lukewarm reception at best, as John Newhouse reports in an article from *The New Yorker*. But European businesses are anxious to grab some of the $26 billion in grants and contracts scheduled to be spent by the SDI through 1989. Thus, according to *Business Week* staff reporters in the second selection, the Reagan Administration has launched a "selling blitz" aimed directly at overseas industries to bypass political opposition. The viewpoint of the nonaligned nations is represented in the article by K. Subrahmanyam for the *Times* of India. Massive spending by both superpowers on Star Wars is incompatible with the need for third-world economic development, he believes.

It is Moscow's reaction, however, that is crucial. The concept of Star Wars is after all predicated on the assumption that the Russians will *allow* us to do it, that they will not launch a preemptive strike before the system is in place. A switch to defensive systems in which the Soviets collaborate is likely the only workable plan. So far, however, they have been unrelenting in their opposition to the SDI, perhaps because they see their own research efforts rapidly falling behind those of the United States, especially in computer technology. (During the preelection presidential debates President Reagan offered to share Star Wars technology with the Russians, but this idea was quickly withdrawn.) Academician G. Arbatov expresses the official Soviet view in his article, condensed from *Pravda*. In the final selection, David B. Rivkin, Jr., a defense analyst, points to the lack of rigorous analysis of the Soviet reactions to Star Wars. Without a determined effort to design a defensive strategy that the Russians can accept, he warns, the pursuit of Star Wars will be dangerous indeed.

TEST[1]

"Obsessive" is a fair description of the state of mind into which the Star Wars project—President Reagan's plan for taming the nuclear genie—has maneuvered European governments. Reagan's commitment to his strategic defense initiative, or S.D.I., as diplomats and soldiers call it, is reliably said to be total and unshakable; the project is meant to be his enduring legacy to the cause of keeping the planet Earth in one piece. But other governments, along with most people in official Washington, strongly doubt whether the plan is feasible; nor will it be, they say, for as far into the future as most imaginations can stretch. Also, every European capital is deeply apprehensive about the near-term consequences of the initiative, which is known to be very much Reagan's own. In mid-May, just after the economic summit meeting in Bonn, I visited Bonn, Paris, and London to find out what people were thinking and saying about Star Wars and how they were responding to heavy American pressure to endorse the project and take on a part of the immense research, much of it recondite, that underlies the largest spending program this or any other country has ever proposed. In all three capitals, people seemed to be talking of little else; Star Wars has become a consuming topic. Even though the press coverage of the summit meeting dwelt largely on Reagan's visit to the Bitburg cemetery, Star Wars, I learned, was really the dominant, if generally offstage, topic of the conference. In Bonn, some of my appointments were postponed because emergency meetings on Star Wars popped up. One official cancelled an appointment because he was abruptly hauled off to Washington for an unexpected meeting on the subject. The issue has pushed the Germans into what is for them the most uncomfortable of positions—having to choose between America, their protector,

[1]Reprint of an article by John Newhouse. *New Yorker.* p 37+. Jl. '85. © 1985 by John Newhouse. Originally in *The New Yorker.*

and France, an old enemy but now the other half of a partnership that anchors Europe's political and economic stability. The contesting pressures from Paris, which is openly hostile to Star Wars, and Washington are heavy, and may become intolerable; a choice between the two places isn't one the Germans can make. They need both. A European ambassador based in Bonn says, in describing the effects of Star Wars, "The Foreign Ministry is *Ratlosigkeit*"—a condition somewhere between stumped and bewildered.

In Paris, the government of President François Mitterrand has been maneuvered or tempted—or in part both—into playing *cavalier seul*, a role that General Charles de Gaulle exalted in the nineteen-sixties. In matters affecting French security, de Gaulle incarnated France's strong preference for free hands and self-sufficiency. "However large may be the glass offered to us, we prefer to drink from our own, while touching glasses round about," he said. Actually, most French, British, and German officials and diplomats are roughly in agreement about Star Wars. But each of their leaders is dealing with the problem largely in terms of political self-interest—hence differently from each of the others. [The British government signed an agreement to participate in Star Wars research in December 1985. Ed.] Mitterrand wants to cut the losses he is expected to suffer in parliamentary elections next year, and he reckons that he can gain politically by saying what he and his people think about Star Wars; he is probably right. His colleagues in Bonn and London, Chancellor Helmut Kohl and Prime Minister Margaret Thatcher, confront a more complicated situation. Kohl's is especially difficult; like Mrs. Thatcher, he wants to avoid getting into a row with Washington over Star Wars, or even getting very far afield from its eminent patron. Kohl's political stock is falling. A member of his government, Interior Minister Friedrich Zimmermann, has openly criticized him for lack of leadership. And on Sunday, May 12th, Kohl personally and his Christian Democratic Party experienced an unexpected and shattering political defeat in North Rhine–Westphalia, where about a third of the electorate lives. Although Star Wars wasn't an issue, German diplomats worry that it will become one—perhaps the pivotal issue in federal elections to be held in April of 1987. The Social Democratic Party is unalterably opposed to it, and some of Kohl's political advisers are already envisioning a campaign in which Germans will be asked whether they are for or against America and the Atlantic alliance, with Star Wars becoming the test of continued German support for both. German officials and diplomats, most of whom are as appalled by Star Wars as the French, also worry that their Chancellor, because of his heavy-handed insistence that Reagan go through with the ceremony at Bitburg, is deeply indebted to him and will be asked to make good with open support of Star Wars. After Bitburg, Kohl was apparently overheard to say, "Ron, I will personally never forget what you did." The Administration isn't letting him forget. Stories about Kohl's having damaged his standing with the White House began to appear just after the summit. "Reagan's trust and confidence in Kohl have been impaired, perhaps permanently, by the controversial wreath-laying ceremony," a story in the Washington *Post* said. And the French government has used the press almost unceasingly to register its unhappiness with Kohl's summit performance—especially his quite unexpected expression of support for Star Wars, which seemed to undercut Mitterrand's efforts to rally support behind a European alternative. The French campaign appears to be working. "We are hearing tones out of France that we have not heard in a long time," a German official told the *Times*.

Although Margaret Thatcher shares the concern of her ministers and civil servants about Star Wars, there is her somewhat special relationship with Reagan to be protected; and it is said that, being a scientist (a chemist) herself, she is generally sympathetic to efforts to cross distant frontiers. Still, since she plans to spend well over ten billion pounds sterling to improve Britain's nuclear deterrent she can hardly join the Reagan claque in extolling missile defense and denouncing nuclear deterrence as immoral. Then, there is the anti-ballistic-missile, or A.B.M., treaty, which some of the Reagan people would like to scrap, partly because it forbids putting devices into space that are supposed to destroy offensive missiles—and Star Wars is built around the notion of using lasers and other "directed-energy" weapons for just that purpose. All Europeans hope that the A.B.M. treaty will be kept intact. They and most orthodox American thinkers on the subject are sure that any sizable defensive system would have the perverse effect of creating an enormous spiral in offensive nuclear arms—a situation in which there would be far less stability, and so less security for all. The British and the French have another reason for cherishing the A.B.M. treaty: without it their own modest nuclear-missile forces might have trouble reaching Russian cities, because the Soviets could in theory erect strong defenses around them. European governments are also strenuously in favor of continued compliance by Washington and Moscow with the second strategic-arms-limitation accord—SALT II—which was signed in June of 1979 and, although it has never been submitted to the Senate for ratification, has been adhered to; the treaty expires at the end of this year, and the Reagan people have been bitterly divided over whether to continue accepting its restrictions.

While what is said about Star Wars in Bonn, Paris, and London varies somewhat, it amounts to a variation on the same basic themes. Germans stress their concern about predictable Soviet countermeasures and the over-all military effects. "If the strategic defense initiative goes forward, we will be in difficult times," says a German general who is closely involved. "Our leaders would have to ask the people for more money for defense. And the Americans, we think, would have to improve nuclear weapons across the entire spectrum: short-range and long-range ballistic missiles, cruise missiles—all weapons."

Suppose Star Wars comes to nothing, I said.

"You can't spend twenty-six billion dollars"—the Administration's five-year spending goal—"and not have something," the general replied. "That something may be improved offensive weapons, possibly a new family of them, or a mixture of new offensive and defensive weapons. We can't say now what it will be. But all that money will buy something." He and most other Europeans strongly doubt, however, whether the something will resemble the Reagan vision.

The French are the most abusively critical and seem to be the most deeply offended by what they regard as the arbitrary and impulsive manner in which Star Wars was thrust upon them. Washington, they say, is trying to impose an entire new strategy on the

Western alliance without any consultation. "Our first objection is to the Reagan presentation," a French diplomat says. "We regard nuclear deterrence as indispensable. We cannot all go to the ends of the earth persuading Europeans that they should accept deployment of missiles, and then call them immoral and about to become obsolete. This is a great contradiction. The Germans and the British share our precise concerns, and their analyses correspond to our own." The British, Mrs. Thatcher included, emphasize the importance of protecting the accepted arrangements concerning deterrence. "All this is terra incognita, and everyone puts his own particular gloss on it," one of her advisers says of Star Wars. "But what is most important to her is the inviolability of existing treaties and the SALT II constraints."

What, I asked, did he hear from the Administration about its intentions on that score?

"Washington is a Tower of Babel on this," he said.

In all three European capitals, various officials speak of Star Wars as one of those political tests which West Europeans confront every decade or so and can pass only by acting jointly. Acting jointly comes harder to them than just about anything, so the test is usually, though not invariably, flunked. Some Europeans are saying that the test, although clearly there, is more economic or technological than political. Star Wars won't budge very far from Square One militarily, they think—and some Americans agree— but the commercial spinoff from all that money spent on the most awesome technologies could be immense; phrases like "third industrial revolution" are bandied about. "In the end, the spinoff may be all there is of S.D.I.," an American diplomat says. "I mean the artificial intelligence, space telecommunications, miniaturized computers, and the rest. Directed-energy devices have uses other than destroying objects. You can communicate information with them. Commercial projects in space will be far more feasible, because the program should drastically reduce the price per kilo of space vehicles." One is told that Star Wars will have an even greater impact on high-technology commerce in the years ahead than the Apollo program had in the nineteen-sixties and seventies. "Apollo had to be made fail-safe, because people were being sent to the moon and had to be returned safely," says a French expert on high technology. "The unproved, cutting-edge technologies couldn't be risked. S.D.I. is creating a demand for the cutting-edge technologies that wouldn't otherwise exist. It will mean no less than a revolution in software, and will have very direct impact on industry in general." A technology gap with the United States and Japan is felt by some Europeans to be their most serious problem. Others among them demur, saying that what is laggard isn't European technology but, rather, Europe's ability to exploit its attainments commercially—a problem that returns conversation to Europe's lack of cohesion and its failure to convert national markets into one huge single market. "America and Japan make money with high technology, and Europe loses money with it," a French diplomat says. Mitterrand talks sombrely about "the Balkanization of European technology." And all Europeans seem to agree on the need either to plug their countries into Star Wars in some way or to create comparable demand in Europe for the cutting-edge technologies. A concern about missing the boat is general. "Europeans can't be sold, but they may be bought" is an allusion to their dilemma over Star Wars that one hears in Washington. It means that the attractions of taking part in the program will overcome doubt and aversion. Perhaps. But the comment overlooks some reasons for Europeans to be polite yet essentially noncommittal about Star Wars. First of all, there is the so-called brain drain; America already attracts a share of the bright young lights in European science and technology. The Apollo program made deep inroads, especially into British talent, and the impact of Star Wars could be greater still—unless, that is, Europe can create an alternative. An even larger reservation arises from the widely held doubts of Europeans that their companies will be offered more than crumbs by the people running Star Wars. The more alluring projects are in most cases likely to be highly sensitive, and thus classified and off limits to non-American firms. Europeans also know that Congress can exclude them—and often has excluded them—from projects in which their involvement had been approved by other areas of the federal government. The most skeptical of the Europeans are the British and the French—the ones with the most experience in cooperating with Americans on advanced weapons. Washington's real interest, they think, lies not in recruiting their companies but in drawing teams of especially accomplished Europeans away from companies. "The trade will be brains for crumbs," a Whitehall civil servant says.

Few Europeans, however hostile they may be to Star Wars, oppose American research in space weaponry, if only because they know that the Soviet Union has a similar program. Both programs have been under way for some time—probably since the late nineteen-sixties. Each is a hedge against the other, but it is thought that, given the forbidding nature of the technologies, neither has progressed much. The assumption has been that directed-energy weapons might be an option in the distant future, and that at some point—probably well into the next millennium—these devices could be phased into the deterrence scheme and nuclear weapons could perhaps be phased out. In brief, none of Reagan's predecessors have questioned the wisdom of sustaining research in this family of weapons, which includes lasers, beams of charged particles travelling at nearly the speed of light, and ultra-high-speed missiles, along with an array of daunting support technologies for them. What to do about "exotics," as they used to be called, was an issue during the negotiations on the A.B.M. treaty. Late in 1971, the parties agreed to ban testing and deployment of such systems and their components; no restrictions were placed on research, if only because it isn't possible to monitor, and so verify, the extent of research. But the ripple effect of the Reagan proposal would include moving research out of the laboratories and into space—starting probably in the early nineteen-nineties—and carrying out tests that would violate the A.B.M. treaty. Since the planning for all this is under way, the treaty—the backbone of the arms-control regime—is in jeopardy, and a common anxiety is uniting America's allies.

Reality in the nuclear age tends to become what people whose voices carry say it is. Competent technicians are available to shore up any side of any argument. A given point of view may be vulnerable to ridicule but not to being disproved by facts; these are obscured by unknowns and abstractions arising from the nature, the role, the destructive potential, and the reliability of nuclear weapons. Probably no one other than a politically secure American

President could have imposed upon his own country and others—
allies and adversary alike—a notion as farfetched as most experienced scientists and technicians consider the Star Wars proposal
to be. In one short passage of a speech delivered in March of 1983,
the President proposed creating a defense that would "give us the
means of rendering . . . nuclear weapons impotent and
obsolete." Virtually no one beyond a remarkably tiny circle in the
White House had been aware that he would make such a proposal, or even that he was contemplating it. Within the government,
the idea hadn't been examined, let alone "staffed out," as Presidential initiatives invariably are. Secretary of Defense Caspar
Weinberger may have been forewarned, although it is far from
clear that he was, but Secretary of State George Shultz was blind-
sided. On the evening before the speech was delivered, Shultz was
meeting in his office with three aides when a copy of the speech
arrived from the White House—not for comment but for Shultz's
information. One of the aides described their reaction as "stunned,
flabbergasted." Nuclear deterrence, it appeared, was out, and defense—not just partial defense but a seamless, perfect astrodome—was in. Many people in the Administration were
appalled, and most were skeptical, to put it mildly. The true believers and the advocates were a small group—as they still are—
including the President's science adviser, George Keyworth, and
Edward Teller, who pioneered the development of the hydrogen
bomb. The advocates have tended to equate technically competent
opponents of Star Wars with the scientists who questioned the feasibility of the Manhattan Project and the Apollo program. Predictable breakthroughs in computers and data processing, they
argue, will allow lasers and particle beams to destroy ballistic missiles during the four minutes or so of their boost phase, which is
when they are most vulnerable: in this phase they are rising slowly; their hot exhaust plumes make them easy to detect with infrared sensors; and each missile constitutes one target instead of
many, because its numerous warheads and decoys are still lodged
in the nose cone awaiting release. And what about attacking vehicles that may survive the boost phase? It is said that these, too, can
be knocked out—in a "layered" space defense—but Star Wars advocates concede that destroying them becomes progressively

more difficult during the twenty minutes of flight remaining.

Reagan, in his remarkable speech, said that society should be defended against a nuclear attack instead of merely avenged. No one disputes his preference. And he isn't the first Chief Executive to believe, quite genuinely, that if an idea he likes plays well as a speech it will play as policy. Nor do the many Star Wars critics—space scientists, weapons experts, and numerous others—dispute the proposition that objects on earth (or in space) can be readily destroyed by devices in space. The issue, they say, is whether a defense—either the leakproof astrodome envisioned by Reagan or something just partly effective—can be built on the Star Wars concept. It can't, they say, because a good offense will always beat any defense. And they strongly dispute the analogy that is made with splitting the atom and with putting people on the moon. These accomplishments, they observe, were strictly scientific projects, with only the barriers to knowledge and insight to be overcome. The moon, which is unarmed, has little in common with Russia, which is heavily armed with an array of nuclear forces, some portion of which would be unaffected by a Star Wars defense even if it could be made reliable against ballistic missiles. The point, the critics say, is that the Soviets won't sit by idly while the other superpower cobbles together a defense against a major component of their strategic forces. First, they can be counted on to neutralize a defense, or try to, by swamping it with more offensive weapons or decoys. Second, they could deploy beam weapons of their own against orbiting Star Wars battle stations. Some of these weapons might be ground-based, with mirrors directing the beams; others would be space-based themselves. It turns out to be much easier to destroy space-based devices than it is for space-based devices to survive long enough to destroy missiles launched from the ground. In any case, a Star Wars defense, if one is ever built, will vindicate the name, because its orbiting battle stations will be pitted against similar Soviet battle stations intended to counter them. The mise en scène could be enriched by the positioning of explosive mines in space. As yet another hedge against Star Wars, the Soviets might adopt techniques that would enable them to reduce the vulnerable boost stage of their missiles from four minutes to one. Two European Foreign Ministers—one

British, one French—have used the term "Maginot Line" in talking about space-based defense.

Star Wars is hard on American diplomats, who have to explain and justify whatever their leaders serve up. The advocacy role in this case is especially difficult, partly because other governments are aware that much of the American support for Star Wars comes from people who don't believe in it at all but do see it as a vehicle for quietly pushing land-based nuclear defense. These are people who want to replay the debate on A.B.M.s that occurred in the late nineteen-sixties and early seventies, and went against A.B.M.s. They intend to win the debate this time. Star Wars, they reckon, will sooner or later enter an irreversible decline, and at that point A.B.M.s—ground-based—will come into their own. Among these people are some whose first priority is sidetracking the arms-control process altogether and getting on with the job of building not just a major A.B.M. system but many more offensive-weapons systems as well. Their goal is strategic superiority. A less ambitious lot, including some who really don't want a replay of the debate but see a need for some compromise, would like to try persuading the Soviets to amend the treaty to leave room for a few more A.B.M. sites than the single site it currently allows. Weinberger, a staunch advocate of Star Wars, which he has called "an inspired vision," told Mitterrand last March that his job was to strengthen deterrence but that Reagan wanted something better, so the research on Star Wars was going forward. And a senior figure in the Élysée Palace says that Assistant Secretary of Defense Richard Perle, who is the chief influence on Weinberger in these matters and the Administration's most resourceful advocate of scuttling arms control, told him that the idea of space-based defense was absurd and wouldn't work but that he and others wanted the money to protect missile silos. Yet in a speech to the National Space Club on March 29th Reagan said that Star Wars "is not, and should never be misconstrued as, just another method of protecting missile silos."

Briefly, the public advocacy of Star Wars now contains two potentially contesting viewpoints. In one group are people who echo the President's line and say that the project actually will eliminate nuclear missiles. The other, more modest contention is that Star Wars won't do that but will strengthen nuclear deterrence, because it will complicate Soviet planning for a first strike. An American diplomat compares the selling of Star Wars to a light-beer commercial on television. "Some people say it's less filling, others that it tastes great," he says.

Not until late last year did Europeans start to take Star Wars seriously. For nearly eighteen months, their governments largely ignored it, seeing no reason to do otherwise, since most people in Washington, including many of Reagan's, didn't seem to take it altogether seriously. "The strangest thing about the strategic defense initiative is how long it took us to react," a senior French diplomat says. "For a long time, we treated it as unserious—as *la cowboyerie.*" All that changed in November and December. The scale of Reagan's reelection meant that for some time to come—at least until he entered his lame-duck phase—his people, other people, and other governments would be obliged to take any of his proposals, however notional, very seriously. In mid-December, Mikhail Gorbachev, who at the time was judged the probable successor to Konstantin Chernenko as General Secretary of the Communist Party of the Soviet Union, visited London. It was Gorbachev's first significant visit to a Western capital, and it was a great success. He made a strong impression on Margaret Thatcher—who after several hours of conversation described him as someone she could work with—and on other political figures as well. He cut a *bella figura* in the British press, as did his attractive and stylish wife. The main topic of the Thatcher-Gorbachev talk was Star Wars, to which the Soviet government had not reacted slowly. Mrs. Thatcher and her entourage were struck by the single-minded force of Gorbachev's case against what his government had for several months been calling the militarization of space. "He made it clear at every stage of the conversation that they were afraid of S.D.I. and saw it as inevitably escalating the arms race," one of her advisers says. And a senior American diplomat says, "Gorbachev woke up Europeans with his heavy emphasis on Star Wars."

Actually, the British Foreign Office was quicker off the mark than the others, and had developed deep reservations about Star

Wars—many of which Mrs. Thatcher largely shared—well before Gorbachev's visit. His argument was rather disconcerting, because some of it matched British worries about extending the arms race into space and possibly killing off arms control in the bargain. Also, the British want no replay of the harsh East-West political struggle that was provoked by the decision taken in 1979 to deploy medium-range American missiles in Europe. The uncompromising Soviet line about space weaponry seemed to portend just such a struggle. Gorbachev's success in London—especially with Mrs. Thatcher—was much more than a media event, because the Reagan Administration was flustered by it and hasn't yet recovered. The mere prospect of the old Kremlin guard's being displaced by Gorbachev had already been a bit unsettling: a younger, more vigorous, and possibly more capable figure than any predecessor in the post-Stalin era would be dealing with the oldest of American Presidents, and in his second term—always a time of ebbing power. Washington was ready to be thrown off stride by the Gorbachev triumph in London.

America's major allies handle almost any serious disagreements with Washington, when they have them, in different ways. The French tend to go public, since open disagreement with Washington isn't a bad thing politically in France. The Germans criticize Washington in private talks with other governments, but they generally shrink from direct argument with the Americans. (Helmut Schmidt, the former Chancellor, was an exception.) The British preference is for arguing out the divergent views directly but always privately. And that is what Mrs. Thatcher did at Camp David last December 22nd—six days after her meeting with Gorbachev. She is probably the only person who has told Reagan to his face what is wrong with Star Wars—from a European viewpoint, at least—and she may be the only one who could do so without creating friction, because their relationship is such a strong one. For about an hour and a half, she explained why a Star Wars defense might not be attainable. Thus it seemed to her unwise to go on saying that it was attainable, and nuclear weapons could be made obsolete, or that nuclear deterrence is immoral. It would be especially helpful, she said, if that part of the rhetoric could be dropped. Most of the ensuing discussion was on the first point—the feasibility of a Star Wars defense. First, Reagan addressed it, then Shultz, and then Robert C. McFarlane, Reagan's national-security adviser. Still, the Americans were reacting to what one of her advisers calls "a great Thatcher performance."

Before breaking for lunch, everyone agreed on the need for a public line, and a few minutes later a member of the Thatcher entourage produced a statement containing four points; it was accepted, and it has become, next to Reagan's speech, the best-known document in the Star Wars literature, and one that many European diplomats can quote verbatim. The first point disavows any aim on the Western side to achieve strategic superiority; the second says that the potential deployment of Star Wars–related systems would be a matter for negotiation; the third says that the goal is to "enhance, not undercut, deterrence"; and the fourth is a bow to the arms-control talks in Geneva. Mrs. Thatcher had arrived seeking to protect the principle of deterrence based on parity, or equivalence, in nuclear arms, and she also wanted a commitment that Star Wars would be negotiable with Moscow. The four points covered this ground. The meeting at Camp David was useful not just because the intensity of British feeling about Star Wars was borne in on Reagan directly but also because the depth of his commitment to the idea was borne in on the British. "He seemed to think that once she glimpsed the beauty of the concept she, too, would scramble aboard Star Wars," one of her advisers recalls. Weinberger wasn't there, and he lost no time in making clear to Reagan and others his aversion to the four points. His own point was, in effect, that you can't ask Congress for twenty-six billion dollars to develop a system you say you may never deploy. A few days later, the State Department drafted a telegram for American missions quoting the four points as policy guidance. The Defense Department refused to clear the telegram, even though it contained language approved by the President, and it wasn't sent.

In February, eyebrows shot up all over when Paul Nitze, who is now a special assistant to Shultz in these matters and a wielder of substantial power, said in a speech that "new defensive technologies" should be both "cost-effective" and "survivable." Not many people in Europe or in Washington think that Star

Wars can meet those criteria. Then the ides of March became the occasion for the hardest blow yet struck against Star Wars, and it came from an unlikely assailant: Sir Geoffrey Howe, Britain's discreet and widely respected Foreign Secretary. In a speech that raised many serious questions about the system, Howe asked whether it could be deployed "without generating dangerous uncertainty." He said, "There would be no advantage in creating a new Maginot Line of the twenty-first century, liable to be out-flanked by relatively simpler and demonstrably cheaper countermeasures." Howe cited Nitze's criteria, and also worried aloud about whether political leaders would be able to control any such new system or would be yielding control to "computers and automatic decision-making." Richard Perle, who chanced to be in London a few days later, delivered a broadside against Howe's ad-dress in a speech of his own; it may have been the first time that a sub-Cabinet-level official of one government attacked a minister of another, and on the minister's turf. The State Department was annoyed, because Howe hadn't warned Shultz of what was com-ing, even though they had conferred two days before, at Chernenko's funeral, in Moscow. But if Howe had done that, Shultz would certainly have alerted Reagan, who would very probably have called Mrs. Thatcher and asked her to tell Howe to talk about something else. Howe's speech reverberated far and wide, even giving a frisson of pleasure to the Quai d'Orsay and the Élysée Palace; he must be the only British minister in modern memory to have accomplished that. No. 10 Downing Street also felt a frisson, but not one of pleasure. Mrs. Thatcher had seen ear-ly drafts of the Howe speech, and must have approved its thrust. But, for reasons that no one fully understands, given the meticu-lous clearance procedures of the British system, she didn't see the final version, and seems to have been taken aback by the tone of certain passages, and by the "Maginot Line" reference in particu-lar. Her relationship with Howe was not affected by the episode, but she wrote Reagan a letter expressing regret about the tone of the speech.

A few days later, Weinberger and Perle were in Luxembourg for a semiannual meeting of the Nuclear Planning Group—a body consisting of most of the Defense Ministers of the Western alliance. There Weinberger presented each of his colleagues with a letter inviting participation in the Star Wars research program and giving their governments sixty days to respond. (Japan, Australia, and Israel were also invited to participate.) Most capitals were surprised; they hadn't had any warning from their embassies in Washington about such an initiative, which would normally have been preceded by some diplomatic probing. The sixty-day deadline was more than a little surprising, as was Weinberger's signature on the letter. "That was a bungle," a European ambassador in Washington says. "Such a letter should have been signed by the President or the Secretary of State. Having it signed by the Secretary of Defense allowed governments to assume that this was more of a technical than a political matter." What he was unaware of is that no one in Washington outside the Weinberger circle had known about the letter; it hadn't been cleared by the normal interagency process. Weinberger was already en route to Luxembourg when the State Department was shown a copy and asked to clear it—a meaningless gesture in the circumstances. "That's how business is being done in this town," a State Department official said.

A few weeks later, a second letter went out to allied capitals; it withdrew the deadline and said, in effect, that Washington wanted only to see if there was any interest in participation in the research. At that point, teams of official people from the various capitals began visiting Washington and meeting with Lieutenant-General James Abrahamson, who is in charge of the Star Wars program, and with State and Defense Department officials, to find out what lay behind the letters. Some of them asked political and military questions, trying to see if the four points were intact and how they were being interpreted. All the teams wanted to learn what participation would mean—whether Washington envisioned government-to-government agreements or agreements with companies. These meetings haven't gone well. "We are telling them they don't have to sign on to the program's philosophy— the political part—but just to the technology itself," says an American who is closely involved in promoting the fortunes of Star Wars.

I asked an American diplomat who is also involved how much he could tell Europeans about what was in this for them.

"Very little," he said. "We aren't asking them to do anything. We say instead, 'What would you like to do? We'll discuss it.' We have no idea what we actually want them to do."

A senior British official says, "No one is asking the really dirty question: How can you envision changing the rules without having the least idea of whether any of this can work? The Americans we see invite the participation question. But how can you talk about that if no one can say what is supposed to come of all this?"

I asked a British diplomat what the Americans said when he asked hard questions.

"The answer is always 'We don't have the answers now,'" he said. "They say the purpose of the research is to find the answers. 'Well, wouldn't the money be better spent on projects of a less uncertain nature?' we ask. There is usually no response to that. Sometimes they say that what may come out of all this is defense of hard targets"—missile silos. "But when we say, 'If it's hard targets you want to defend, why do it in space, where it won't work and where the systems will be vulnerable? Why not do it on the ground, where it might work?,' they say, 'We won't get the money unless we do it in space.' It's all circular. No one other than the President has made a clear statement, but no one among the Americans whom Europeans talk to thinks his concept is anything other than nonsense and fantasy."

I also put the question about American intentions to a French diplomat, who said that he got different answers to his questions on different sides of the Potomac.

"This is a gimmick," he said. "There is no dossier. We don't yet know whether it is to be a company-to-company or government-to-government agreement. We don't know whether the exotic technologies will be involved, or the pedestrian ones."

A senior Belgian official answered my question with a question: "What is S.D.I.? I don't know. I haven't the least idea."

According to some European officials, companies interested in Star Wars have been pushing for their governments' official endorsement of the project, reasoning that the Americans will offer very little without solid political support. But current signs are that the real situation isn't that simple. In some countries—Italy, for example—the commercial interest appears to be unambiguously strong. In others, the picture is mixed, with some companies beginning to question whether research in Star Wars will create business afterward and—more important—whether the expected spinoff will really be there. At a conference in Maastricht, in the Netherlands, on June 6th, Lewis Branscomb, vice-president and chief scientist of I.B.M., said he thought that Star Wars would be largely irrelevant for the civil side and that the supposed spinoff would more likely be "dripoff." Dieter von Sanden, until recently head of the communications division of Siemens, Germany's largest electronics company, said at the conference, "We agree with Branscomb."

The British have been sounding out the Japanese on the subject, and I was told—in both Britain's Foreign Office and its Ministry of Defense—that the attitude in Tokyo was mainly skeptical, not just at the official level but on the industrial side as well. "Their officials want benign neutrality on S.D.I.," a Whitehall diplomat says of the Japanese. "They are afraid their people will see it as Japan's being drawn into a major project leading to a war in space. Public opinion there wants no part of it." And Japanese industry, I was told in various Whitehall offices, has become very cautious about Star Wars and frankly skeptical about the commercial spinoff. Japan's commercial success in the high-technology sector has, of course, been tied to strictly nonmilitary research.

I asked a senior official in Whitehall what was going to happen.

"We have to live with S.D.I.," he said. "It isn't enough to say it's rubbish." And an American diplomat, replying to a question about the Europeans, said, "Their support can't be bought. Their acquiescence can be managed."

Acquiescence may not be enough for the Reagan people. They want an endorsement. They feel that they need it, if only because of the Soviet pressure on Europeans to resist Star Wars. Still, acquiescence may be as much as Washington can reasonably expect. Mrs. Thatcher won't go beyond the four points, which are confining. "Perle and Cap Weinberger think they can bully us into giving them a blank check," one of her people says, and he made it clear that they won't get it. Most of the other capitals have also anchored themselves to the four points, while in Bonn the struggle for the heart and mind of Helmut Kohl continues. When I was in Bonn, I tried to find out how much pressure the Soviets were putting on the Germans. I wondered whether they might have drawn a lesson from their unsuccessful campaign against the decision to deploy medium-range American missiles in Europe. By overplaying a hand that wasn't strong to begin with—putting extraordinary pressure on the Germans, and crudely, at that—the Soviets annoyed Western Europe and harmed their own cause. They loathe the prospect of an arms race in space at least as much as they do the new American missiles, partly because the effort to catch up or stay even would be depleting and perhaps all but impossible for them. Yet with the apparent conflict between Star Wars and arms control, plus other European concerns about it, the Soviets have a better hand now; Star Wars may actually be the best political weapon vis-à-vis the West they have ever had. It isn't clear that they have learned from the past, however. In talks with Kohl and his Foreign Minister, Hans-Dietrich Genscher, Soviet officials have intimated that support for Star Wars would mean a decline in economic relations. "They never said that during the missile dispute," a senior German diplomat said. He added, though, that F. Wilhelm Christians, a prominent German banker, had a two-hour conversation with Gorbachev during a recent visit to Moscow. At that time, Christians was the only German who had seen Gorbachev since Kohl met with him at the Chernenko funeral. According to Christians, Gorbachev was fairly relaxed about the possibility of German companies' taking part in Star Wars research. What he stressed was unyielding Soviet opposition to German political support—a German endorsement—of the program.

So far, the endorsement hasn't been within Washington's reach. Mitterrand took the lead in heading off American pressure to have something close to it emerge from the Bonn summit meeting; he succeeded. During the meeting, Mitterrand rejected the American invitation to participate, and his spokesman, Michel Vauzelle, described the offer as "a vague advertising circular." Besides lobbying against Star Wars, the French are pushing a research proposal of their own, called Eureka, which was unveiled a few weeks before the summit and is aimed at attracting European countries that seek self-improvement in the high-technology sector. So far, Eureka is more of a gleam in the eye than a fully formed proposal; what does seem clear is that while it would involve most of the same technologies as Star Wars, it would be mainly a civil program with some military spinoff—the opposite of Star Wars. If Eureka is to prosper, however, it must become a plausible and attractive program in its own right—not simply a contrived alternative to Star Wars. After a shaky start before a gallery of highly skeptical European capitals, Eureka is now being treated somewhat more seriously by most of them. The Germans have endorsed the idea, and a British official was recently quoted as saying, "We expect that Eureka will become a reality. But it will become a reality as its concrete nature evolves. Right now, it is a cluster of ideas focussing on the concept that industry in Britain, France, Germany, and other countries can do better if their cooperation is enhanced."

Diplomatic maneuvering during the month following the summit was even more intense than it had been before the meeting. Washington and, especially, Paris put Kohl under heavy pressure—heavier, probably, than any he had previously known. "Poor Kohl," said a German diplomat. "The French have the enviable position, because S.D.I. is so obviously undesirable and they have managed to maintain some distance from it." Helmut Schmidt took the usual step of sending Kohl a letter in which he warned about the impact of West German support for Star Wars. "Our close relationship with France has an extraordinarily high priority," he told his successor. "An isolated participation in the United States research-and-development program would endanger the inner cohesion of the European-alliance partners." A senior political figure in the German opposition says, "Bitburg—its price—is being equated with every move being made. The question being asked here in Bonn is: Who has more leverage with Kohl—Reagan or his own constituency? He is more committed to S.D.I. now than his government is, and after yesterday"—a reference to Kohl's political setback in North Rhine–Westphalia last May—"he may not be able to deliver his government." The three most directly concerned of his ministers are Genscher; Heinz

Riesenhuber, Minister of Research and Technology; and Manfred Wörner, Minister of Defense. All three are anti–Star Wars. Wörner, who once said that Star Wars would lead "not to stability but just the opposite," has since moderated his public line—at times sounding like a quasi-advocate; but his private view continues to be negative.

A meeting of the Foreign Ministers of the North Atlantic Treaty Organization was scheduled for early June in Estoril, near Lisbon, and Washington hoped to obtain there the pro–Star Wars language that it had been denied at Bonn. The resistance was already manifest, but Washington thought that in order to avoid an open dispute within the alliance on Star Wars the Europeans might agree among themselves to give something. They didn't. Again, it was the French who took the lead, refusing to yield even an inch on Star Wars, and Shultz had to give up. Also, by then the situation had abruptly changed, and it was Shultz who was under pressure from the Europeans rather than the reverse. Europe's preoccupation with Star Wars had for a moment been displaced by a new issue: America's continued compliance with the provisions of the unratified SALT II treaty. It was clear when the Lisbon meeting began, on June 5th, that Reagan would be announcing a decision on the issue the following Monday, June 10th. Weinberger, Perle, and their ultra-right allies in the Senate were publicly urging Reagan to banish SALT II once and for all, on the ground that the Soviets were violating some of its provisions as well as some of those of the A.B.M. treaty. In January of this year, shortly before coming to the White House as Reagan's director of communications, Patrick Buchanan wrote a newspaper column in which he said that to continue complying with SALT II would be "an act of strategic folly and appeasement that invites not Moscow's appreciation but Moscow's contempt." Leaks to the press had disclosed Reagan's options, which, boiled down, were: continued full compliance; selective, or partial, compliance; and scrubbing SALT II altogether. Neither in Washington nor in Europe was the President expected to decide in favor of continued full compliance, if only because he had called the SALT II treaty "fatally flawed." The choice was universally judged to lie between partial compliance—flouting various provisions in a kind of tit for tat with the Soviets—and gratifying the hard-liners' strong preference for abolition.

On this issue, the British, not the French, had become the point of Europe's spear. London's position was no different from any other capital's, but it was more pronounced, partly because the British were better informed on the merits of the key issue—alleged Soviet violations of the agreements. British Intelligence works closely with America's; the two sides exchange information, and they often compare their assessments of a situation. In the case of supposed Soviet violations, there is a long list, which insiders do not take seriously, and there is a short list, which they do take seriously. It includes, most notably, a large radar station at Krasnoyarsk, in central Siberia, which Washington says is a violation because it is of a type that, according to the A.B.M. treaty, may be located only on the periphery, not inland, where it could be used to track incoming ballistic missiles. According to the Soviets, the radar is there only for tracking space vehicles—a function allowed by the treaty. Several American analysts also contend that the Soviets are developing two new land-based missile systems, although the SALT II treaty permits only one. Moscow says that one of the two—the SSX-25—isn't new but, rather, an improved version of an old system, and that the modification falls within limits set by the agreement.

The British do not regard either of these cases as a proved violation. The data, they say, do not decisively support the argument of either party to the dispute. The British are working with data supplied by the Americans. It isn't the first time the two governments have reached different interpretations of the same data, but no previous argument has attained the intensity of this one. At a meeting of NATO Defense Ministers in Luxembourg in late March, Michael Heseltine, a stalwart of the Thatcher Cabinet, simply told off Weinberger. Britain, he said, wouldn't be badgered into supporting America on the compliance issues; the evidence, he said, wasn't there. According to a British diplomat, he went on at some length, and "with great heat and passion." A senior colleague of Heseltine's now says, "Our concern is not so much compliance as whether there is an approach in Washington that is designed to justify retreat from the A.B.M. treaty. We need to find a solution to Krasnoyarsk. Everyone in Washington is more interested in using the issue than in resolving it."

At Estoril, it was clear that none of the European ministers would accept the American position on Soviet violations. They hoped Reagan would decide on a so-called middle option—continuing to comply with the essentials of SALT II while reserving the right to match the Soviets in going around some provisions. Everyone urged something of the kind on Shultz, who turned out to be a sympathetic ear and actually incorporated the allies' views in a message to Reagan. On his way back to Washington, Shultz had a private session on Friday evening, June 7th, with Mrs. Thatcher, and she thereupon sent a strong message to her good friend in the White House urging full compliance with the treaty. By then, Reagan was getting a number of messages, both private and public. On Wednesday, June 5th, the Senate voted ninety to five for a resolution urging Reagan to continue abiding by the treaty, although the language did allow him reciprocity in the event of alleged Soviet violations.

On June 10th, Reagan astonished everyone, including, with the exception of McFarlane, his most senior people. Neither Shultz, Weinberger, nor anyone else had expected him to favor full compliance. McFarlane knew because the decision memorandum, which is normally drafted by the President's own staff, was actually written at Camp David on Saturday, June 8th, two days before the Monday meeting. Reagan alone knows what lay behind his decision. Pressure from allies—especially the Thatcher message—is assumed by diplomats to have had some effect. Yet he couldn't have seen that message before Saturday, when he made the decision, if, indeed, he hadn't made it even earlier. The moderate preferences of a bloc of Senate Republicans, twenty-two of whom must run for reelection next year, may have been a factor. My guess is that the Joint Chiefs of Staff were a key influence, and possibly the decisive one. On June 4th, six days before the National Security Council's meeting, they leaked word of a split between them and Weinberger on the compliance issue. At least three of the five, according to a page-one story in the *Times,* judged that without the limits of SALT II the Soviets would build many more strategic weapons than the United States, which would be held back by budgetary and perhaps political restraints. The Chiefs' well-known aversion to allowing funds for conventional weaponry—usable military power—to be funnelled instead into more nuclear weapons was also noted. In the meeting on June 10th, the Chairman of the Joint Chiefs, General John W. Vessey, Jr., didn't take a position for or against any of the options; he didn't have to. By declining to endorse the Weinberger line and—more important—displaying charts projecting a perverse effect on the strategic balance if the SALT II limits were shelved, Vessey was reflecting a viewpoint of which Reagan was already aware and that must have influenced his thinking. During the week before the meeting, some of the Chiefs had met individually with McFarlane, who would have reported the gist of what was said to Reagan.

Reagan's decision didn't exactly propel SALT II into open water. His announcement was somewhat hedged, by including a threat to do in the future what for the moment he was declining to do—take "proportionate response" to Soviet violations. He asked the Defense Department to submit a report in mid-November recommending steps that the United States might take to modernize its strategic arsenal in response to Soviet treaty violations. Disappointed hard-liners are saying that the decision has little meaning—that Reagan is only mollifying allies and other doves for a time, during which he will give the Soviets enough rope. Neither American nor most European diplomats are buying that line. Although wary, they think that Reagan probably made a historic decision and will stay with it, unless, of course, the Soviets do something foolishly provocative—a possibility that cannot be ruled out. For the first time in the Reagan era, the issue of arms control was posed on a yes-or-no basis. Until now, the President had been able to have it both ways; he could continue calling the treaty fatally flawed while informally observing its provisions. But because it was due to expire this year and Congress had required a statement of his intentions Reagan had to choose. And he ruled clearly and unambiguously in favor of the moderates and against the nay-sayers of his administration—another first. Those who think that he will reverse all this after the mid-November report from Weinberger are probably whistling in the dark. The con-

gressional elections in 1986 will be that much nearer then. And
Reagan will be on the eve of his meeting with Gorbachev, now
scheduled for November 19th and 20th. The correspondence between the White House and the Kremlin has been livelier than
it has been in at least a decade, according to one State Department
official who sees it. Reagan isn't likely to do anything that would
jeopardize a meeting to which he has devoted so much effort.

A British diplomat recently described the Star Wars project
as "a Kabuki doll behind a glass that no one is allowed to touch."
He was referring to Reagan's stout commitment to it. In May,
however, Reagan signed a so-called decision memorandum, in
which he instructed all government agencies to observe as formal
policy the four points he had agreed to in his meeting with Mrs.
Thatcher at Camp David last December. Until then, the Defense
Department had continued to withhold its clearance on telegrams
and other statements that sought to make that point. And Star
Wars, quite evidently, has put the United States in what one experienced negotiator calls "the best negotiating position we've ever
had." He and others say that in return for reaffirming the A.B.M.
treaty and agreeing to a moratorium on testing space weapons the
United States could, within reason, obtain just about everything
it wanted from the Soviets in the Geneva arms talks. But unless
there is a significant American concession on Star Wars the talks
won't go anywhere. That, at least, is the opinion of most diplomats. Reagan, they reckon, has a choice: he can decide in favor
of an agreement during his second term or he can hope that some
distant President will bag the elusive birds in the bush—a perfect
missile defense.

In the end, some people think, Reagan will listen to the Europeans—certainly to Mrs. Thatcher and the beleaguered Kohl, if
only because he wants to see their hands strengthened, and dislikes
the prospect of dealing with alternative British and German re-
gimes, either of which would be to the left of its predecessor and
much more adamant on Star Wars. Others doubt whether Reagan
cares much about successor governments in Europe. (He wouldn't
have long to deal with them, in any case.) If he is turned around
on Star Wars, they say, it will be not because of external influ-

ences but, rather, because of domestic pressures. Congress is already paring his budgetary request for Star Wars in the coming fiscal year. "The S.D.I. budget is critical," a European diplomat says. "It is an objective fact, not an abstraction." The State Department would like to see S.D.I. put on the back burner, and is urging that view on the rest of the government. Whatever does or doesn't happen in the year or so ahead, Europeans are saying and, in some cases, hoping that Star Wars won't outlast the Reagan Presidency. In most capitals, the strategy will be to play for time.

THE SELLING OF STAR WARS TO BUSINESSES ABROAD[2]

Fiat executives insist they have no idea how it happened. "Somehow," says one, an internal 17-page report found its way into the hands of U. S. officials. But Fiat isn't terribly upset. Conveniently, the leaked document covers the technologies that the Italian industrial giant wants to contribute to the U. S. plan to develop a Star Wars missile defense system. It boasts of strengths in laser weapons, hypervelocity guns, rocketry, and robots.

Fiat may be taking a less-than-straightforward approach to getting its message to Washington, but it is far from the only European company enticed by the prospect of getting a piece of the $26 billion scheduled to pour out of President Reagan's Strategic Defense Initiative through 1989. With the first round of contracts slated to be awarded by yearend, a steady stream of international defense contractors is flowing through the SDI office in Washington. Since January, at least seven countries—Britain, France, Israel, Italy, the Netherlands, Norway, and West Germany—have sent delegations. And more are coming this summer.

The companies nosing around Washington are doing so even though their governments have yet to decide whether they will

[2]Article by Dave Griffiths, Ronald Taggiasco, Thane Peterson, and Frederic A. Miller, reporters for *Business Week*. Reprinted from the July 15, 1985 issue of *Business Week* by special permission. © 1985 by McGraw-Hill, Inc.

participate in the Star Wars program. In Europe, SDI is even more controversial than it is at home. Efforts by the U. S. to win the support of its allies have met opposition from many Europeans who believe SDI could precipitate, rather than prevent, a nuclear war.

'Eureka.' Clouding the picture further are ambitious research programs proposed by the Europeans themselves. French President François Mitterrand wants to create a European space program called Eureka. It would involve Europe's high-tech companies in a mainly civilian effort to develop space technology. West German Chancellor Helmut Kohl has rolled out a military scheme of his own—a European Defense Initiative to develop a shield against the short- and medium-range Soviet missiles that are aimed at Europe.

Eureka is rapidly gaining support. The West German Cabinet has voted to back it, and the research ministers of Germany and France have set up a working group to study such potential Eureka projects as supercomputers and advanced integrated circuits. And Eureka won endorsement at the Milan summit of the European Community that ended on June 29. A high-level meeting is set for July 14 to begin nailing down details.

Four of Europe's biggest high-tech players—Siemens, Philips, Thomson, and Britain's General Electric Co.—say that given a green light from their governments, they could have a proposal by yearend for research on large data processing systems under the Eureka umbrella. Norsk Data, a fast-growing Norwegian computer company, and France's Matra have already agreed to jointly develop a "near supercomputer."

The outlook for a European Defense Initiative is still tenuous, however, partly because of worries that it also might upset the strategic balance. But if it does catch on, some European companies might back away from SDI to concentrate on technologies for defending Europe. Since funding is uncertain, though, few companies are apt to turn their backs on the billions that the Pentagon is ready to spend.

The foreign companies see SDI funds—a third of which could be spent overseas, according to one Star Wars expert—as a bonanza of badly needed research money. Moreover, they fear that if the

U. S. goes it alone, the inevitable spinoffs into commercial technology will leave them in the dust. "We could well find we are no longer at the leading edge of technology," says Val O'Donovan, president of Com Dev Ltd., a Canadian producer of signal processing systems for satellites.

Laundry list. To pull in foreign companies, the U. S. has launched a selling blitz. Lieutenant General James A. Abrahamson, who heads SDI, wrote to European officials asking which companies could contribute. Defense Secretary Caspar W. Weinberger has also sent letters soliciting help. Since January, Abrahamson, Weinberger, and, most recently, Vice-President George Bush have stumped Europe to drum up support.

Washington's hard sell has ruffled the feathers of European officials, who see it as a diplomatic end run, an attempt to use the companies' desire to cash in on SDI to influence policy. Some pressure, in fact, is being brought to bear by companies. Umberto Agnelli, vice-chairman of Fiat, recently told top Italian government officials that unless Europe gets on the SDI bandwagon soon, pressure groups in the U. S. might begin working to exclude foreign participation.

The political brouhaha has caused many companies to back off from publicly expressing a desire for SDI work. "We must not jeopardize public funding by taking up independent discussions," says an official of Germany's Dornier. But privately, many companies continue laying the groundwork for SDI contracts.

In May the chairman of Germany's huge Messerschmitt-Bölkow-Blohm defense empire, tired of waiting for a green light from Bonn, flew to Washington for talks with SDI. Logica PLC, a London computer software and systems company, has discussed an SDI contract. And France's Matra and Britain's Plessey Co. have hired Richard D. DeLauer, who recently resigned as Defense Under Secretary for research, to represent them on SDI matters.

European universities also are getting into the act, and the first contract is about to be awarded. At SDI's request, Edinburgh's Heriot-Watt University has submitted a bid for a $150,000 grant to continue work on superfast optical computers. And this is just the start. In 1986 alone, SDI hopes to distribute about $50 million for scholarly research overseas. "I'm hoping the scientific community will drive the international collaboration," says James A. Ionson, who heads SDI's effort to develop new technology.

Unlike the Europeans, Japanese companies won't even discuss participating in SDI until their government agrees. SDI officials hope that the agreement reached in June to exchange radar and missile guidance technology is a positive sign. In fact, on June 26, Defense Minister Koichi Kato said that "the Japanese government standpoint on SDI is that we're interested."

But international interest is tempered. Since long before SDI entered the Administration's jargon, foreigners have been cynical about American promises of a "two-way street" in weaponry. The balance of U. S.–European arms sales, for example, has heavily favored the U. S. Now, despite assurances to the contrary, many Europeans fear they will get small contracts and function as subcontractors. "It's hard to imagine a U. S. company contracting a major portion of a project to a European company," says Gérard Payelle, an executive with the French aerospace firm Aerospatiale.

Foreign executives also have a tough time reconciling the U. S. drive to check high-tech exports with its willingness to cut foreign companies in on sensitive SDI research. They worry that export controls will limit the commercial application of anything they develop. Pentagon officials say they want to keep only certain technologies out of Soviet hands—especially computers. "It's essentially a mechanical, administrative problem of making sure that information is passed to nonporous recipients," says Assistant Defense Secretary Richard N. Perle.

If the Allies accept that, the next few years could see an international effort that dwarfs the Apollo and Manhattan projects. But if America goes it alone, the Allies may enter the 21st century at such a technological disadvantage that severe diplomatic damage results. Warns a West German industrialist: "If SDI is solely a U. S. enterprise, it will be the end of NATO as we know it."

THE 'STAR WARS' DELUSION[3]

President Reagan's March 23 address unfolding his plans for a new defense strategy that will alter the basic concepts of nuclear war developed over the past three decades will rank in history with Winston Churchill's 1946 speech ushering in the Cold War, and with President Kennedy's proclamation of U.S. determination to land a man on the moon. Neither of the earlier speeches, however, had the ominous implications for humanity that the present presidential announcement has.

The process of shifting from a doctrine of mutual deterrence, based on the idea of mutual assured destruction, to one of actually fighting a nuclear war began with U.S. Defense Secretary James Schlesinger in 1974. During the Carter period this was carried forward to developing a capability to fight a protracted nuclear war.

Up to this point fighting capability was predicated on the accuracy of missiles, and on the ability to get information on enemy targets and to destroy the enemy's arsenal by striking first. Now President Reagan is further reinforcing the concept of nuclear fighting by an attempt to develop a capability to destroy the enemy's warheads after they are launched. Until now both sides had only swords to fight with, but now one side is proclaiming its intention to acquire a shield.

Ironically, President Reagan's ideas are neither new nor original. His rhetorical question, "Would it not be better to save lives than to avenge them?" was voiced in 1967 by Soviet Premier Aleksei Kosygin to defend the Soviet development of an antiballistic missile system.

The U.S. argued that the uncertainties involved in a certain number of warheads being stopped in midflight were more destabilizing than the mutual assured destruction of two superpowers, leaving their cities hostages to one another. The U.S. strategic community finally persuaded the Soviet leaders to accept their

[3]Excerpted from an article by K. Subrahmanyam in the *Times* of India. Reprinted by permission from *World Press Review.* 30:21+. Je. '83.

view. The result was the antiballistic missile treaty of 1972, hailed in its day as a breakthrough in arms control.

The plan that President Reagan announced on March 23 had been advocated in a monograph, "High Frontier: A New National Strategy," published in February, 1982, by the Heritage Foundation, a right-wing think tank. The director of the study was Lt. Gen. Daniel O. Graham, former director of the Pentagon's Defense Intelligence Agency.

The study declares, "If both East and West can free themselves from the threat of disarming nuclear first strikes, both sides will have little compulsions to amass ever larger arsenals of nuclear weapons. And it will allow us to avoid leaving to future generations the horrendous legacy of a perpetual balance of terror." These ideas were repeated by the U.S. President in his speech.

The "High Frontier" study says its objectives are to "nullify the present and growing threat to the U.S. and its allies which is posed by Soviet military power; replace the dangerous doctrine of mutual assured destruction (MAD) with a strategy of assured survival; and provide security and incentive for realizing the enormous industrial and commercial potential of space."

These are unexceptionable objectives even if one does not share the official U.S. view of the Soviet military threat, but their implications induce apprehension. The study says, "Cruise missiles become a more attractive option in a new strategic setting that includes defenses against ballistic [missiles]."

The authors of the study contend that the strategy they advocate—which has now been adopted by President Reagan—will "confront the U.S.S.R. with precisely the sort of armaments competition that the Soviet leadership most fears." Secondly, it will "severely tax, perhaps to the point of disruption, the already strained Soviet technological and industrial resources." And thirdly, it will "seriously threaten the very foundations of the strategic structure the U.S.S.R. has built at great cost over the past twenty years."

Clearly the proposed system is not meant to defend the U.S. but to engage the Soviet Union in an arms race of sophisticated technology and at a cost the Russians will not easily be able to afford. In a *Pravda* interview on March 27 Soviet leader Yuri V.

Andropov said, "This would set in motion a runaway strategic arms race. . . . All attempts at achieving military superiority over the U.S.S.R. are futile. The Soviet Union will never be caught defenseless. Let there be no mistake about this in Washington."

Proponents of the "High Frontier" estimate the cost of the new system at $24 billion in the next five or six years, and $40 billion through 1990. They argue that these costs compare favorably with programs like the Apollo moon landing. The Reagan administration has proposed $1 billion for research and development in the budget for 1984.

The first issue arising out of the "High Frontier" proposal was whether it constitutes a violation of the 1972 antiballistic missile treaty. The Soviet news agency Tass says that it does. Advocates maintain that the new system will not violate the treaty.

The philosophy and approach to ballistic missile defense has undergone a change. During the late 1960s and early 1970s the argument centered on the impossibility of preventing an attack from getting through that persuaded the superpowers to agree to the antiballistic missile treaty.

It is now argued that the purpose of any defense is not to make an attack impossible but to make it difficult and costly. If through ballistic missile defense a significant proportion of enemy warheads can be destroyed and the enemy cannot be certain of destroying the entire retaliatory force, that uncertainty will constitute deterrence.

This perception of the U.S. strategic community is linked to its obsession with the Soviet landbased missile force and its perceived ability to take out the U.S. landbased force in a first strike because of the multiple warheads. The U.S. has 1,052 landbased missiles with about 2,100 warheads. The Soviets have some 1,400 landbased missiles with more than 5,000 warheads.

The Americans argue that the Soviets could disarm their entire landbased missile force by using about 3,000 warheads at the rate of three per silo to assure destruction of each missile, and still be left with 2,000 warheads in landbased missiles. This is what the Americans call their window of vulnerability. But it is not the whole picture.

Only one fourth of the U.S. arsenal is in landbased missiles. If the Soviets were to carry out a first strike they would expend nearly 40 per cent of their somewhat smaller strategic arsenal to take out 25 per cent of the U.S. arsenal. That would leave the U.S. with three fourths of its larger arsenal (50 per cent in submarine-based missiles and 25 per cent on bombers), while the Soviet Union would have 20 per cent of its arsenal in submarine-borne missiles, 5 per cent on its bombers, and 35 per cent on land. This is not advantageous to the Soviet Union, especially when its submarines have to pass through narrow sea passages that are continuously monitored by the U.S.

While the Americans emphasize that landbased missiles are more accurate, they try to obfuscate the point that their bombers carrying 25 per cent of their arsenal are equipped with exceedingly accurate air-launched cruise missiles. Even the accuracy of their seabased missiles will improve with the commissioning of NAVSTAR navigation system. On the basis of a self-induced paranoid fear that their landbased missiles would be disarmed in a first strike, the Americans justify the buildup of the proposed ABM system, and oppose the freeze proposal. But this situation is mostly of America's own making. In 1972, when SALT I was being negotiated, the Soviet Union proposed that multiple warheads for strategic missiles should be prohibited. The Americans rejected that idea.

Henry Kissinger, who negotiated SALT I, recently reported that the American stand was based on the assessment that the Soviets would need at least ten years to catch up with the technology. Having created this Frankenstein, Dr. Kissinger now advocates that both sides renegotiate a new strategic arms treaty to replace all multiple warhead missiles with single warhead missiles.

This technological overconfidence on the part of Americans has been the main engine of the arms race. It is evident in the latest speech of President Reagan when he calls upon the scientific community to turn its great talents to rendering the nuclear weapons impotent and obsolete.

In 1946 the Americans refused to destroy their nuclear weapons before bringing the Soviet nuclear effort under international control under the Baruch Plan. They felt that the Soviets, who did not even make good door bolts, would not be able to make nuclear weapons for the next twenty years. In fact, they did so in three years. The same thing happened with the hydrogen bomb, the intercontinental bomber, the nuclear submarine, the neutron bomb, and the cruise missile.

The Soviets tend to follow the American lead in the arms race, but they always catch up. Because the U.S. is generally ahead technologically, the Soviets tended to fear that they might be surprised with some breakthrough in weapons technology. As a weaker power, they are extremely secretive about their preparations. The Americans cite this secrecy as justification for pushing their arms race.

In the light of its history one can safely assume that the Soviet Union will develop an ABM system of its own. The most dangerous period is the one during which one nation is able to deploy its system and the other is still catching up. The former may decide that it can eliminate the missile force of the other in a first strike and protect its own force. President Reagan is taking the world toward this perilous situation. A world with two superpower ABM systems will be most dangerous.

The new ABM system is intended to protect the U.S. mainland from attack by intercontinental ballistic missiles. It cannot offer any protection against low-flying cruise missiles. In a world where intercontinental missile attacks can be warded off, the cruise missile becomes more attractive.

Even if the Soviet Union were to protect itself with the ABM it would be vulnerable to cruise missiles. That accounts for the "High Frontier" study's contention that this new weapon system will confront the U.S.S.R. with precisely the sort of armaments competition that Soviet leadership most fears. No ABM protection can save Europe—Western or Eastern—from the devastation of a nuclear war in which low-flying cruise missiles, short-range missiles, free-fall bombs from tactical aircraft, and artillery with nuclear explosives will be used.

With the installation of the new ABM, President Reagan's statement that limited nuclear war in Europe need not escalate into a strategic nuclear exchange can be translated into reality. Behind the safety of its ABM shield the U.S.—and possibly the Sovi-

et Union if it develops a similar shield—will be able to fight a
nuclear war on European soil without undue worry that such a
war might engulf their own territories. The "High Frontier"
study ignores this aspect and assumes that the change in U.S.
strategy from MAD to a mix of offense and defense will be welcomed in Europe.

Under the circumstances the Soviet Union will be strongly
tempted to subject the U.S. to the same degree of risk to which it
is exposed by the combination of ABM and cruise missiles. This
would mean the U.S.S.R. would have to secure facilities from
which it could launch low-flying nuclear cruise missiles against
the U.S. The missiles are compact and could easily be introduced
into the Western Hemisphere.

There are reports that the Soviet Union is building a 30,000-
ton submarine capable of long endurance. Such submarines could
carry cruise missiles. In view of the compactness of the cruise missile there is no reason why even ships not normally designated as
warships should not carry nuclear cruise missiles.

Radar, antiaircraft guns, and surface-to-air missiles have not
rendered aircraft obsolete as a weapon. They only made the aircraft fly lower, utilize standoff weapons, adopt stealth technology
that eludes radar, and equip themselves with electronic measures.
Given the spacewar scenario outlined by "High Frontier" technol-
ogists, one wonders when similar countermeasures to evade detection during space transit will be developed.

An ABM system will downgrade all other nuclear weapon
powers and establish a strategic bipolarity of the world, with the
technological hegemony of the superpowers. With Europe the potential battlefield for nuclear war, Western Europe and Japan
will be reduced to a security dependence reminiscent of the 1950s
that translates into political and economic gains for the protecting
power. This is likely to have an impact on economic and technological competition now offered by West Germany and Japan to
the U.S.

Moreover, if Europe is to be a potential nuclear battlefield using various categories of low-flying nuclear weapons with the two
superpowers protected by ABMs, then the Soviet Union cannot
afford to relax its hold on Eastern Europe.

The U.S. calculation may be that the Soviet Union will not be able to compete technologically or economically in the arms race in space, and therefore America is bound to emerge as the supreme power in the world. Alternatively, if the Soviet Union were to succeed in keeping up with the U.S., then the international system would revert to the bipolarity of the 1950s, when the U.S. had to face the military challenge of the Soviet Union but not the economic and technological challenge of West Europe and Japan or the political challenge of the nonaligned.

According to a classified study of the U.S. General Accounting Office, the laser weapon can be readied for deployment by 1993 at a cost of $30 billion. That is the cost of only one component of the system envisaged. At the same time, five former Treasury Secretaries and one former Commerce Secretary have warned the U.S. administration in a joint letter against excessive defense spending.

The proponents of "High Frontier" argue that the new ABM will lead to industrialization of space, along with its militarization—and in this area of high technology the U.S. is in a position to lead the world. They also enumerate many industrial and commercial activities that would generate two to four million jobs in the U.S. by the year 2010 and an annual tax revenue of $20 to $40 billion.

Yet another school argues that with militarization of space, wars will be initiated, fought, and terminated in space. According to these strategists if one side finds that its command, control, communications, and intelligence framework in space has been destroyed or severely damaged, it will have to terminate hostilities because it would know that continuance of hostilities would mean nuclear destruction of its territory and people.

A globe enveloped by two sets of 300 satellites armed with laser weapons and infrared sensors is not likely to be tension-free. As the Nonaligned Movement seeks to collaborate with peace movements in the industrialized world, a massive blow is being struck to perpetuate the cold-war bifurcation of the entire globe.

A UN study on the relationship between disarmament and development warns, "The world can either continue to pursue the arms race . . . or move consciously and with deliberate speed toward a more stable and balanced social and economic development within a more sustainable international economic and political order. It cannot do both."

The arms race implied in President Reagan's ABM proposal means a bid by the U.S. to regain its supremacy in international relations through military technology at the expense of political and economic considerations. The arms race and development are in a competitive relationship—particularly for resources. When the new ABM gathers its full momentum, it will be incompatible with the attitudes and perceptions that are requisite to promoting the North-South dialogue, global negotiations, or the new international economic order.

PLAYING WITH FIRE[4]

A report that the US Congress has allocated enormous appropriations for "research" under the so-called Strategic Defense Initiative program (commonly known as "star wars") went almost unnoticed in the United States. The apparent reason is that both American Congressmen and the public have long since become accustomed to this program. And, as always, many lies went with it. Sometimes, it must be said, the lying has been clever. And so it happened that this action slipped through Congress virtually without debate. However, from the standpoint of the arms race and the threat of war this is perhaps the most dangerous action in many years.

It has long been evident to those who follow US policy that the Reagan Administration has embarked on a course aimed at dismantling the regime established by signed arms limitations agreements and treaties and at wrecking the talks on these questions, which are of overriding importance. . . .

On the one hand, the Strategic Defense Initiative (SDI) is called upon to serve as the main weapon for wrecking the whole arms

[4]Condensed from an article by Academician G. Arbatov in *Pravda*, p 6, Jl. 1, '85. Reprinted from *The Current Digest of the Soviet Press*. 37:7+. Jl. 24, '85.

limitation process, and on the other hand it is supposed to be a means of obtaining a "first-strike" capability (needless to say, in combination with other weapons systems—missiles that are being developed for a preemptive strike against the Soviet Union's strategic retribution forces and its command and communications centers).

All this is being hushed up or concealed, of course. On the contrary, the US President is presenting the "star wars" project to the public as a weapon that will put an end to the nuclear threat and will lead mankind to a paradise for all. . . .

What President Reagan promises to gain by the "star wars" program is impossible in principle. One can imagine, of course, that with the aid of new types of weapons—mysterious beams, super-super computers, etc.—in time (even enthusiasts promise to do this no sooner than several decades from now) a system can be created that may be rather effective in downing now-existing missiles. But will they be "now-existing" by that time? The US President has ignored a perfectly obvious truth: The same human brains, the same research capacities and the same instruments that will be put to use developing "defensive" weapons will at the same time be working on weapons designed to destroy these "defensive" weapons, to overcome or evade them, or will even be finding something new against which these weapons will be powerless. In this sense, there can be no absolute weapons as promised by the President—it's really impossible to stop technical progress, science and technology. . . .

The impracticability of the project in the form in which an attempt is being made to "sell" it to American legislators, as well as to the American public and the US's allies, does not, however, make it any less dangerous. Besides, it will not just be dangerous some time in the future, it is dangerous right now, at the stage that is being hypocritically called "research." . . .

What is actually behind what is being called "research and development" is plans for the unprecedented mobilization of money, scientific potential and all conceivable resources for a new qualitative jump forward in military technology. A jump forward in all areas: defensive and offensive arms, nuclear and conventional arms, space, beam, kinetic and all other kinds of weapons. A jump forward to new and hitherto unknown dangers that would surpass by far the dangers of military nuclear technology, although mankind has not yet been able to cope with them, either. Is the world community ready for such a leap into the unknown, into danger, into uncertainty? And does it want it? No one has yet asked this question: the problem has, to all intents and purposes, not even been discussed on this level.

Moreover, the essence of this problem is being concealed in every way; an effort is being made to reduce it to something much safer and simpler. "Why not try to rid ourselves of the nuclear threat with the aid of new defensive systems?" they say. "Let us at least study this problem, and then decide what to do."

But "then" it will be too late to decide anything—too late for a whole series of reasons. One of them is the fact that, besides the $70 billion, an enormous political price will also have to be paid for the program of so-called "research" that, so to speak, is already "in the works." Probably one of the first casualties of this program would be the Soviet-American talks on arms limitation. Their goal was defined in January 1985, by an accord between A. A. Gromyko and G. Shultz, as preventing an arms race in space and terminating it on earth. But now Washington declares that the US, despite this accord, will in any event be working on the development of an antiballistic missile defense, in order, it is said, to ascertain whether this system works or not. When this is ascertained (according to current plans, no earlier than 1993), a decision will be made as to whether an antiballistic missile defense should be deployed or not. If the decision is to deploy, only then will the time come to make the following decision: to either break the ABM Treaty unilaterally or try to persuade the Soviet Union to agree to emasculate this treaty to such an extent that it will not interfere with the implementation of American plans.

A startling approach! But, in this case, on what will the USSR and the US conduct talks in Geneva over the next eight or more years? That is, until the moment when the US itself, depending on the success of work in the field of military technology, decides what to do next? When the question is stated in this way, space weapons will not be subject to discussion at all in the next few years. And if this is so, there is no reason to discuss arms on earth either. After all, back in the late 1960s and early 1970s the USSR and the US reached the common decision that the limitation, and especially the reduction, of offensive arms is impossible without the limitation of defensive arms. The "star wars" project does not abrogate this inescapable strategic logic in the slightest. This suggests the conclusion that in the next eight or more years the US is not even planning to conduct talks in earnest but regards them as a propaganda trick, as an instrument—pardon me for this free expression—for cheating everyone. I assume that Washington wants this. But do officials there really think that the Soviet Union will participate in these unseemly and dangerous games? A few days ago, Comrade M. S. Gorbachev expressed the Soviet viewpoint on this question perfectly clearly: If the US continues to merely procrastinate, this will force us to reevaluate the whole situation.

What has been said above makes it possible to draw the conclusion that "star wars" is a destructive mine under the entire process of arms limitation and reduction, destructive even at the current stage of work on this project. Another conclusion: "Star wars" is a powerful generator of the arms race, one that is destabilizing the military-political situation in the world, despite the utter bankruptcy and impracticability of the very idea of creating an "impenetrable shield." The whole point is that even a not very perfect antiballistic missile defense of US territory may become a component of what is conceived of as a "first-strike" arsenal. . . .

This is why, with the development of work on SDI, the nuclear threat will not disappear but will increase.

For President Reagan himself, "star wars" perhaps has indeed, as they say, become an object of faith, an insane, fanatical faith that knows no doubts. But, as far as one can judge, even among his close entourage the number of the faithful who unreservedly support SDI can be counted on one's fingers. The pragmatic calculations of the rest have nothing in common with what the President promises. It seems to me that these calculations consist in the following.

The present administration represents an extremely conservative part of the US political spectrum and is under the very strong influence of extremist circles and the military-industrial complex, for which the White House incumbent is a stooge. In the President's entourage, among those who share these extreme views, there are certainly a good many people who understand that the right-wing, and especially the extremist, wave cannot last long. Therefore, in both US domestic and foreign policy deliberate attempts to consolidate the policy of the extreme rightists, to impose it on the country for years to come, and thus to impose it on Reagan's successors, no matter who wins the next election—and, I should add, on the American allies—are now becoming increasingly obvious. People in Washington are in a feverish hurry precisely because they want to make a new and very dangerous round of the arms race irreversible while the current administration is still in office—through using the inertia of systems once put into motion and the creation around these systems of significant economic and political pressure groups with selfish interests. . . .

WHAT DOES MOSCOW THINK?[5]

What will the Soviets do about strategic defense and arms control? Even those who analyze President Ronald Reagan's Strategic Defense Initiative (SDI) from a strictly technological angle recognize that this query will determine the program's future as surely as the question, "Will it work?" Thus James Fletcher, chairman of the Pentagon's SDI feasibility study team, told the House Armed Services Committee in March 1984 of his panel's conclusion that "the ultimate utility, effectiveness, cost, complexity and degree of technical risk in this system will depend not only on the technology, but also on the extent to which the Soviet Union either agrees to mutual defense arrangements or offensive limitations."

Unfortunately, a rigorous assessment of likely Soviet responses to the SDI has largely been lacking. To date, two extreme viewpoints have dominated the skimpy discussion of Soviet attitudes.

[5]Reprint of an article by David B. Rivkin, Jr., a Washington-based defense analyst. *Foreign Policy.* p 85+. Sum. '85. © 1985 by the Carnegie Endowment for International Peace. Reprinted by permission.

SDI advocates hold that Washington can either educate or pressure Moscow to rely more on defensive systems and less on its current strategy, which stresses large intercontinental ballistic missiles (ICBMs) topped with multiple independently targetable re-entry vehicles (MIRVs). Some SDI supporters cite as evidence for such a future change in Moscow's position the USSR's own active defense programs.

Conversely, many SDI opponents maintain that repeated Soviet criticisms of Reagan's SDI speech and Moscow's continuing rhetorical endorsement of mutual deterrence ensure that any U.S. deployment of ballistic missile defenses (BMDs) will generate an equalizing Soviet force build-up and cause a spiraling arms race.

The truth is probably more complex than either view. The best available evidence—Soviet strategic writings and official policy statements crosschecked with actual Soviet military decisions—shows the Soviets to be agnostics when it comes to strategic defense. Their views on the desirability of large-scale operational deployments have changed as the strategic situation they perceive has changed. Despite their support of the 1972 Anti-Ballistic Missile (ABM) Treaty, which sharply curtails defensive deployments, the Soviets consider strategic defenses neither inherently good nor inherently bad.

Thus the USSR's opposition to the SDI reflects simply a conviction that deploying the kinds of defenses envisioned by the SDI would not serve its interests in the strategic environment Moscow sees existing today and continuing for the future. The Soviets have changed their minds before and will surely do so again if they believe that circumstances so warrant. In fact, an analysis of Moscow's long-term strategic options suggests that the defense-dominated world that American planners profess to envision would provide the Soviet Union with many important political and military benefits.

But this Soviet flexibility does not yet vindicate SDI supporters. For Soviet statements on strategic defense clearly reveal that Moscow does not at this time see how the transition to this defense-dominated world could be undertaken without creating what it sees as unacceptable risks along the way. The Soviets appreciate the scientific and technological obstacles to building highly effective ballistic missile defenses. But they are haunted by a nightmare scenario in which the United States beats them to the defensive punch and combines these new systems with ongoing offensive improvements to gain real nuclear superiority.

It is theoretically possible, therefore, to pull Moscow onto the defense bandwagon. The only way to accomplish this goal, however, is to present a plan for the transition that the Soviets will find convincing. Specifically, Washington must persuade the Soviets that it is indeed aiming to diminish the nuclear threat in general, and not striving for nuclear superiority.

The Kremlin's Nuclear Objectives

The Soviet Union's record in strategic defense and its decisions on offense-defense tradeoffs derive from Moscow's overall strategic nuclear objectives and from its assessment of the foreign-policy and arms control impacts of Soviet nuclear deployments. Since the 1950s, three major strategic goals have shaped the evolution of Soviet nuclear forces. First, they are supposed to provide, at a minimum, robust deterrence with respect to Western and Chinese nuclear weapons and, at a maximum, extended deterrence of any hostile military operations against the USSR and its allies. Second, the Soviets have sought options that theoretically enable them to prevail in any type of nuclear conflict and under any conceivable scenario. Although the Soviets have never been able to develop nuclear-war-fighting options that give them great confidence in their ability to win a meaningful victory, this has not discouraged them from trying. Finally, Moscow is determined to prevent any adversary from acquiring political leverage over Soviet policy by dint of its nuclear forces and, if possible, to gain political leverage from its own arsenal.

In addition, Soviet nuclear weapons policy has been influenced by arms control and overall foreign-policy factors. The Kremlin has seen arms control as a key element of its détente policy with the West. Therefore, although the Soviets have steadfastly refused to accept a fundamental restructuring of their nuclear forces, as the United States sought during the 1970s, they have been prepared to consider certain modest alterations in their nuclear force developments. For example, Moscow abandoned the SS-16 ICBM in order to stay within the SALT II limits.

Parochial considerations and interservice rivalries have no doubt also affected Soviet policy. At the same time, logic indicates that these factors were most influential when reinforced by other, more rational, considerations. The existence of a strong Soviet General Staff also helps mitigate the interservice rivalry. And civilian involvement in Soviet weapons decisions is much lower than it is in the West. The result is a nuclear weapons policy that, whatever its substantive merits, is much more unified and consistent than America's.

The Soviets maintain that robust deterrence ultimately flows from high-quality strategic forces and credible options to use them. Yet they also appear to believe that the quality of deterrence at any given time is not solely a function of the existing nuclear balance. Such intangible factors as the perceived resolve of one's own leadership, the attitudes and inclinations of the adversary, existing alliances, and the world's potential for conflict also are critical.

Consequently, Soviet strategists tend to view specific deterrence postures as robust under most circumstances, but possibly fragile in a major crisis. Indeed, in certain situations deterrence might fail even though the aggressor is militarily inferior, since the costs of inaction may loom larger than the risks and costs associated with attacking. Such thinking apparently prompted the Japanese attack on Pearl Harbor. And the Soviets believe that the advent of nuclear weapons has not entirely removed the possibility of deterrence failure.

Moreover, the Soviets have long believed that although superior strategic capabilities, all other things being equal, provide higher-quality deterrence, BMD can strengthen deterrence in a unique way. Soviet doctrine through the mid-1960s was expressed in a famous October 1964 article in *International Affairs* by N. A. Talensky, a former editor of *Military Thought*, a classified journal of the Soviet General Staff. He claimed that deterrence based solely on offensive forces was inherently unstable, since it was "dependent chiefly . . . on the good will of the other side."

Talensky rejected the Western argument that BMD deployments would undermine mutual deterrence. He argued that "the creation of an effective antimissile defense system by a country which is a potential target for aggression merely serves to increase the deterrent effect [of its retaliatory forces] and so helps to avert aggression." Defensive systems, he added, were also highly desirable, since they were certain to be used in case of an attack and yet did not directly threaten one's adversary.

Further, Soviet strategists have noted that BMD systems can serve as a hedge against an all-out nuclear war caused by an accidental or unauthorized nuclear launch. And at times they have justified their relatively greater efforts in strategic defense by citing the unique third-country nuclear threats they face.

Indeed, the Soviets, in contrast to certain U.S. strategists, have never claimed that a situation in which each superpower's territory is largely invulnerable to strategic attack necessarily upsets deterrence. As late as 1967, while indicating their willingness in principle to discuss limits on both offensive and defensive systems, the Soviets—notably at the Pugwash conference that September—continued to praise the virtues of strategic defense.

The Soviets claimed that in addition to buttressing deterrence, strategic defenses helped negate the leverage of hostile nuclear forces and enhanced Soviet war-fighting options. Nor did Moscow view strategic defenses as incompatible with arms control. Thus, Moscow established an independent BMD organization within its air defense command in 1958; by 1961, a vigorous BMD research and development program was under way, focusing on radars, interceptors, and data processing facilities. The Soviets also began to endow existing and projected air defense systems with BMD capability. By the mid-1960s, primitive BMD systems had sprung up around Moscow and Leningrad.

The Soviets were even more active on the rhetorical front. On several occasions, then Soviet leader Nikita Khrushchev boasted that Soviet defensive missiles could hit "a fly in outer space." And then Soviet Defense Minister Marshal Rodion Malinovsky claimed that "the problem of destroying ballistic missiles in flight has been successfully solved." These statements vastly exaggerated existing Soviet capabilities, but they probably reflected a Soviet belief that progress on strategic defenses would eventually justify large-scale deployment.

During the 1964–1965 period, however, the Soviets faced their first critical choice relating to the proper balance between offensive and defensive systems. The strategic build-up launched by the Kennedy administration not only presented Moscow's offensive forces with a huge increase in U.S. targets but also greatly multiplied the challenges to Soviet defenses. The Soviets could have responded by developing a defense-dominated force mix, creating a balanced offense-defense posture, or accelerating deployment of new offensive weapons while postponing defensive deployments. Influenced by the deficiencies of BMD technology, the Soviets chose the last option.

Yet in no way did the Soviets give up on strategic defenses. In fact, Talensky's 1964 article argued that a balanced offense-defense mix would result in high-quality deterrence and that the deployment even of defensive systems might negate some of the offensive edge America had built by then. The impression generated by this and other Soviet statements was that large BMD deployments would begin in the late 1960s or early 1970s, once the technological problems had been solved and the deployment of new, third-generation offensive missiles completed.

In 1967 and 1968, however, Soviet writings and pronouncements indicated that differing expectations of the effectiveness of strategic defense had begun to split Soviet military leaders. This apparent debate was inextricably tied to the ongoing Soviet internal discussions on how to respond to U.S. SALT initiatives. By 1969, the prevailing Soviet view was that for the time being BMD would remain only marginally effective against a responsive offensive threat. Moscow also began to reassess its views on BMD's contribution to deterrence and strategic stability. As a result, Soviet deployments of defensive systems began to slow down.

By 1970–1971, Moscow evidently decided to forgo large-scale operational BMD deployments that might have resulted in a balanced offense-defense posture. The Soviets concluded that defensive technology would for years lag behind the offense, making it difficult to devise stable offense-defense configurations and reducing Soviet confidence that BMDs could appreciably shore up deterrence. And the U.S. Safeguard ABM system, although plagued by many technical problems, was vastly superior to any Soviet counterpart.

Moreover, by 1969–1970 the Soviets must have realized that American domestic opposition to strategic defense created the opportunity to negotiate an arms control regime that might succeed in virtually crippling the U.S. BMD program. For the first time in history, Moscow seemed to be on the verge of acquiring real leverage on U.S. nuclear force development. Since the Soviets expected to press ahead vigorously with their own BMD research and development, they could anticipate erasing the U.S. technological lead one day. Meanwhile, the Soviets intended to maintain a large air defense system with residual BMD capabilities, and an extensive civil defense network.

Further, by the late 1960s the Soviets had few reasons to expect any sudden growth in West European and Chinese nuclear forces. In particular, Bonn's ratification of the Treaty on the Non-Proliferation of Nuclear Weapons in July 1968 considerably diminished Soviet anxiety about the emergence of a nuclear-armed West Germany. The Soviets also believed that low ceilings on defensive forces would inject predictability into offensive-force planning and would help slow the growth in U.S. offensive capabilities. Conversely, the failure to establish such a ceiling, it was feared, could lead to the rapid growth of U.S. offensive forces.

The advent of MIRVs was another key factor in the Soviet decision to forgo deployment of strategic defenses and reveals how war-fighting considerations have shaped Soviet attitudes toward defense. By 1968, once their MIRV program was on track, Soviet planners realized that MIRVing could provide a much more cost-effective way than their primitive BMDs of achieving a major strategic goal: the neutralization of U.S. leverage.

Soviet writings reveal a long-standing belief that the strategic balance exerts a strong influence not only on the maintenance of deterrence and on war-fighting options, but also on the conduct of peacetime foreign policy. The Soviets are well aware that since World War II the West has been unable to establish a credible conventional defense against potential Soviet regional aggressions and expansionism, and therefore has relied on maximizing the political leverage of American nuclear forces to deter Soviet misconduct. Hence the Soviet determination to negate this leverage and decouple American nuclear forces from regional conflicts, particularly in Europe.

Although Moscow has claimed since as early as the mid-1960s that the United States "objectively" lacked nuclear capabilities to coerce the USSR in a crisis, the Soviets apparently believed that Washington sought to compensate by resorting to bluff and brinkmanship and later by incorporating limited nuclear options (LNOs) into its deployment policy. The latter were thought to be a wide range of limited attack options, based on such U.S. force advantages as superior accuracy, that could demonstrate U.S. political resolve, demonstrate to Soviet leaders the danger of escalation, and lead to an early end of a crisis of conflict on terms favorable to the West. During various periods in the nuclear age the Kremlin believed that Soviet strategic defenses could negate the effectiveness of American LNOs.

In theory, for most of the nuclear era the Soviets could have offset American nuclear leverage to some extent with a declaratory policy emphasizing that any American resort to nuclear weapons would lead quickly to an all-out war. Yet this policy inherently lacked credibility. Thus a dearth of operational counters to American LNOs has always made the Soviets uncomfortable.

Yet the Soviets have also believed that, given their superiority in non-nuclear forces and the opportunity to time judiciously their expansionist moves, they would be best served if neither side could engage in highly selective and limited nuclear strikes. In certain strategic environments, Soviet BMD deployments could remove most of the intermediate rungs of the American escalation ladder. In addition, such deployments would seriously undermine the credibility of third-country nuclear forces—that is, British, Chinese, and French forces—and would enhance Soviet political leverage throughout Eurasia.

During the late 1960s, the primitive state of defenses precluded these possibilities. Yet MIRV technology gave Moscow a new way to negate U.S. nuclear leverage through devising a superior war-fighting posture: by credibly threatening a pre-emptive strike. MIRVing opened to the Soviets the eventual possibility of converting their vast ICBM throw-weight into a large number of warheads capable of destroying "hard" (protected) targets and placing at risk American ICBMs, bombers not on alert status, ballistic missile submarines in port, and the entire U.S. command, control, and communications infrastructure. Although the potential pre-emptive capability created by MIRVs did not approach the level of a disarming strike, since U.S. submarines would remain invulnerable, Soviet leaders believed that their extensive civil and air defenses could, in theory, provide enough protection to give Soviet LNOs some credibility.

Deployment of U.S. strategic defenses would have tremendously complicated these nascent Soviet pre-emptive options and eroded any confidence the Soviets might have had in their ability to develop a credible first-strike threat. Even a light U.S. BMD, if deployed as a wide-area, preferential defense, would have vastly complicated Soviet attack plans. Overall, the Soviets began to realize that within the context of a war-fighting strategy there was an inherent tension between defending their own nuclear assets and ensuring their ability to attack an adversary's targets. Efforts to defend their forces were certain to be reciprocated by the other side, thereby decreasing the ability of Soviet forces to destroy assigned targets. During the early 1970s the Soviets opted to emphasize penetrating capability over survivability.

Moscow's view at that time was that an offense-dominated force posture would provide both the best war-fighting options and the most robust deterrence possible. Remaining Soviet concerns about the political leverage of U.S. nuclear forces could be managed, Moscow believed, through diplomacy and arms control measures. This major shift in Soviet strategic thinking and Moscow's subsequent signing of the ABM Treaty were caused by specific circumstances. In no way do they suggest that Moscow has given up on strategic defense. In fact, the ongoing Soviet BMD program and the continued heavy investment in air and civil defense indicate that, despite the treaty, Moscow wants to keep strategic defense options alive and to be prepared to proceed with deployments if strategic circumstances ever warrant them.

Recently, a distinguished group of American authors interpreted the ABM agreement as a "milestone" unmistakably and forever enshrining the condition of mutual societal vulnerability so that neither side's leadership might be tempted to start a war. But although this interpretation may reflect at least some of America's reasons for entering into the ABM Treaty, available writings do not show the Soviets to be in agreement.

After the ABM Treaty, Moscow maintained a conspicuous silence about strategic defense. References to BMD's virtues were rare and were restricted by and large to Soviet air defense journals. By the mid-1970s, assertions that assured retaliation was an inescapable fact of life and constituted the bedrock of deterrence dominated Soviet writings and speeches. Yet this shift, too, stemmed from Soviet assessments of the current strategic situation, not from categorical judgments about the inherent pros and cons of mutual national vulnerability.

The SDI Debate

Equally compelling evidence of the USSR's continued agnosticism on defense is contained in Moscow's attacks on the SDI. As has been the case throughout the nuclear age, Moscow's position is closely tied to its reading of current strategic circumstances. What Soviet analysts invariably stress today in their criticisms of the SDI is that it is the combination of U.S. offensive modernization and space-based defensive deployments within the context of an apparent U.S. war-fighting doctrine that makes the "Star Wars" plan so dangerous.

Thus, perhaps the most authoritative Soviet SDI statement, made 4 days after Reagan's original March 1983 Star Wars speech by the late Soviet leader Yuri Andropov, claimed:

In fact the strategic offensive forces of the United States will continue to be developed and upgraded at full tilt and along a quite definite line at that, namely that of acquiring a first-strike nuclear capability. Under these conditions, the intention to acquire the capability of destroying the strategic systems of the other side with the aid of BMD, that is, of rendering the other side incapable of dealing a retaliatory strike, is a bid to disarm the Soviet Union in the face of the American nuclear threat.

Similarly, a December 3, 1984, article in *Pravda* entitled "Space: Alarm and Hopes" claimed that "the 'comprehensive'

ABM system not only does not do away with ballistic missiles in the U.S. strategic arsenal, but, on the contrary, envisages their buildup and improvement primarily as a means for delivering a nuclear first strike."

A February 24, 1985, *Pravda* editorial pointedly asked, "If the said 'initiative' is put forward in order to make offensive nuclear weapons unnecessary, why [is it] accompanied with an unprecedented buildup of the American strategic nuclear arsenal."

The Soviets also argue that the falsity of U.S. claims that the SDI is a purely defensive effort and does not threaten Soviet security is amply demonstrated by the efforts of Americans to improve the penetrating capabilities of their own offensive forces.

In a Hungarian television interview on March 8, 1985, Soviet foreign affairs official Vladimir Lomeyko asserted:

Only a few days ago the *New York Times* and the *International Herald Tribune* reported that at present the U.S. Air Force is realizing its own work program, the objective of which is the creation of new exceptionally refined missiles with changing trajectory. These missiles are intended to break through an eventual Soviet space shield insofar as the Soviet Union would create one, too. . . . They [the Americans] do not only want a space shield for themselves; they would not only like to retain their nuclear missiles. At the same time, they also hold talks so that they might create missiles suited to breaking through our eventual space shield.

This theme, that it is the combination of U.S. strategic defenses and "offensive first strike forces" that threatens Soviet security, has been reiterated in virtually all Soviet statements on the SDI.

Soviet analysts have also claimed that a space-based BMD system itself would be vulnerable to destruction and hence could not provide an effective defense against a first strike. Yet to the extent that such a BMD system might do well against a ragged retaliatory strike, it might prompt a first strike by the side that deploys it. Thus in a recent interview with a Hungarian newspaper, Georgi Arbatov, director of the Institute of the U.S.A. and Canada, stated:

The star wars conception is part of the first-strike concept. That is, the MX missiles, the missiles of the Trident II submarines, are directed against the missiles of the other side, the Pershing II missiles are used against guidance centers, and the defense system is used to defend against the counterstrikes of the small number of remaining missiles.

Arbatov went on to claim that, given these problems, it should be "clear to the Americans that we will not agree to any reduction of offensive weapons if they do not give up this missile defense system." He further alleged that if

these [arms control] negotiations take 7 to 8 years to reach the first serious agreement, they are useless. During this time, military technology will indeed advance so much that completely different issues will be on the agenda. . . . They [U.S. decision makers] simply want to drag out the negotiations in order to arrive in a position in a few years, when— concerning many issues—it will simply be impossible to achieve an agreement.

It also has been suggested that even if highly effective strategic defense were feasible, the transition to defense dominance would engender major strategic instabilities. Explained Aleksei Arbatov, perhaps the brightest Soviet civilian strategist, in his 1984 monograph *Military-Strategic Parity and U.S. Policy*: "Before the growth in the effectiveness of space-based BMD would enable one to accomplish the most difficult task of defending against a massive nuclear strike, hopes might arise that one can defend against a retaliatory strike."

All of these Soviet criticisms of the SDI are linked to specific circumstances. They focus on particular offense-defense configurations and suggest only that some forms of offense-defense mix may be undesirable. Contrary to many American analyses, not one of these statements qualifies as a wholesale condemnation of strategic defense.

What the Soviets do not say about strategic defenses is almost as significant as what they do say. It is surely no accident that even in the midst of their anti-SDI campaign Soviet analysts have never claimed that defenses inherently undermine deterrence or upset strategic stability. On the contrary, 1 year after Reagan's Star Wars speech, a well-known Soviet military commentator, Lev Semeyko, in a radio broadcast directed at the United States, declared that Moscow's own defensive program was necessary "to show concern about millions of Soviet lives. To save just 1 per cent of the Soviet population would mean to save 3 million people. No one in this country [the Soviet Union] would understand the government if it failed to strive for this."

Allegations that the Soviets consider any transition to a defense-dominated world likely to create dangerous instabilities may be overstated as well. Aleksei Arbatov stated in his monograph that because BMD and space-based systems cannot be deployed until the 1990s, each side will be able "to identify the threat in time, assess it, and undertake the necessary steps." Thus, during the long transitional period that can be expected, both sides will have ample opportunities to avoid major transitional asymmetries.

There is little doubt that the strategic environment condemned by Moscow's anti-SDI statements—featuring high offensive- and defensive-force levels—may be dangerous and, in many respects, perhaps worse than the current strategic situation. Yet there is no reason to believe that this possibility exhausts the range of possible defense-dominated environments. So far the Soviet analysts, at least in the writings available to foreigners, have not come to grips with these possibilities. In particular, it does not appear that the Soviets have given much thought to the possibility of a strategic regime under which deterrence would be based largely on strategic defenses while strategic offenses would remain at low levels or be eliminated altogether. None of the anti-SDI arguments the Soviets have articulated thus far would hold true in such an environment.

Moreover, some long-standing tenets of Soviet strategic thought suggest that different circumstances could increase the attractiveness of different offense-defense force mixes. First, Moscow has never been overly fascinated with the military efficacy of strategic bombardment. Even as the Soviet nuclear arsenal has grown in numbers and sophistication, the Soviets have continued to maintain that nuclear strikes alone cannot bring about victory in war.

Second, the Soviets have never viewed offensive nuclear systems as absolute weapons. As noted by the well-known Soviet military scholar V. M. Bondarenko in his 1976 study *Contemporary Science and the Development of Military Affairs*:

The history of military arms development is full of examples when weapons, which seemed irresistible and frightening, after some time are opposed by sufficiently reliable means of defense. Thus, an absolute limit to the development of military power from the position of the integral development of military affairs and military-technical progress cannot exist.

More recently, former chief of the Soviet General Staff Marshal Nikolai Ogarkov asserted in his 1982 pamphlet *Always Ready to Defend the Motherland* that "the experience of past wars convincingly demonstrates that the appearance of new means of attack has always invariably led to the creation of corresponding means of defense. . . . This applies fully even to the nuclear-missile weapons."

Third, the Soviets appear to agree that BMD could be highly beneficial and cost-effective in a context of certain nuclear-war-fighting scenarios. Commenting on alleged U.S. strategy and the role of BMD, Aleksei Arbatov, in his previously cited monograph, stated:

Even if in the foreseeable future ballistic missile defense of the American territory against a massive nuclear strike remains unlikely, such a system could play a significant role within such contexts as the various exchanges of "limited" nuclear strikes, "protracted" war and the ratio of relative damage and "correlation of forces after the exchanges." Moreover, it is being proven that after a certain time these or those versions of BMD within the context of such plans [war-fighting] would be more cost effective than offensive systems.

It is highly significant that Arbatov did not try to rebut these claims. Moreover, all of the recent Soviet anti-SDI statements have asserted only that any American strategic defense would be unable to protect population and would not prevent the Soviet Union from delivering a devastating nuclear strike against the United States. The Soviets have never denied in principle the military utility of BMD in the context of nuclear-war-fighting scenarios.

In addition, Moscow has many reasons to be unhappy with the current offense-dominated strategic environment and may become convinced that defenses are worth a second look. Although the Soviets have always maintained that nuclear deterrence based on the threat of retaliation leaves much to be desired, by the early 1980s Moscow evidently had concluded that technological developments, worsened U.S.-Soviet relations, and the high crisis potential present in the current international system were making deterrence especially brittle.

Worse, just as the Soviets were about to achieve many of their long-standing nuclear objectives through their massive build-up, ongoing and projected U.S. modernization programs began posing a threat to Moscow's war-fighting options. Time-urgent weapons unveiled in the mid- and late 1970s, such as the MX (missile experimental) and Trident II missile, along with slower but still-potent cruise missiles, endangered Soviet land-based forces and the Soviet command, control, communications, and intelligence systems. The high percentage of Soviet nuclear forces represented by fixed-silo ICBMs made these U.S. counterforce programs a source of major concern to Moscow.

Although the U.S. Joint Chiefs of Staff have reported that the U.S. modernization program, even if completed, would not entirely erase the Soviet counterforce advantage, it is still viewed by the Soviets with extreme alarm. After all, Soviet decision makers undoubtedly engage in their own worst-case analyses and probably credit the United States with greater capabilities than would a U.S. planner presented with identical data. And Soviet military planners have always sought to establish high margins of peacetime advantage to compensate for the unexpected problems that crop up in wartime.

Projected changes in U.S. and West European nuclear force postures are also likely to decrease seriously the effectiveness of Soviet pre-emptive counterforce operations. These changes include the planned addition to the U.S. strategic arsenal of thousands of cruise missiles—in effect, creating a "fourth leg" of the U.S. triad—as well as Pershing II and ground-launched cruise missile deployments in Western Europe; the potential proliferation of mobile assets, such as Midgetman; and the anticipated growth in British, Chinese, and French nuclear forces.

Finally, Moscow has charged that Washington is developing more sophisticated and discriminating nuclear employment concepts, such as counterrecovery targeting—attacks against sectors of the Soviet economy critical to postwar recovery. The combined impact of these developments began to persuade the Soviets that the relatively straightforward, brief counterforce operations envisioned as composing the main nuclear scenario in the early 1970s were becoming less probable; protracted nuclear war was emerging as the most likely contingency.

Strategic Choices

To partially satisfy evolving Soviet capability requirements stemming from these developments, the Soviets have embarked on a vigorous offensive modernization program. Nevertheless, in light of the emerging changes in the strategic nuclear environment, Moscow cannot hope to re-establish its war-fighting options through the simple quantitative expansion of its offensive nuclear forces.

Overall, the Soviets now appear to be in a quandary. Current strategic trends cause them to worry about the erosion of their war-fighting options and the weakening of deterrence. Yet they clearly do not like the SDI approach. All of this suggests that the Soviets simply have not made up their minds. And it is important to realize that U.S. conduct can influence the USSR's strategic choices, such as the one the Soviets face today.

From a strictly military standpoint, immediate and short-term Soviet options roughly resemble those of 1964–1965 and 1969–1970, although the existence of the ABM Treaty has created important new considerations. The USSR's economic troubles and its perceived need to modernize non-nuclear forces—ground forces, tactical air power, and the navy—indicate that short-term Soviet strategic choices can be reduced to two.

Moscow can continue to maintain the current offense-dominated posture, to abide by the ABM Treaty, and to pressure Washington through the arms control process, "peace offensives," and foreign-policy overtures to abandon the SDI. Even under this option the Soviet offensive-force posture probably would still undergo certain changes. The rate of quantitative build-up of central strategic systems is likely to slow down. As suggested by Soviet military leaders, greater emphasis would be placed on the quality of the new weapons systems. The Soviet offensive profile would become more balanced with the addition of a new bomber and new submarine-launched ballistic missiles. And Soviet theater nuclear forces would grow proportionately faster than central strategic forces.

Or the Soviets can place greater stress on strategic defenses. This would entail the abrogation or renegotiation of the ABM

Treaty and potentially the slowdown of the Soviet offensive modernization program. Theoretically, one can envision that the Soviets could combine a major defensive build-up with deployment of offensive forces designed to defeat the U.S. BMD. Yet this policy would be extremely expensive and would prevent Moscow from upgrading conventional forces. Moreover, despite Moscow's conceptual knowledge of systems with SDI-busting potential—featuring fast-burn boosters and maneuverable warheads—its deployment of such new offensive weapons is many years away.

At the same time, Moscow's current defensive capabilities are not impressive enough to justify the risks of minimizing offensive forces. And the Soviets clearly want to maintain the ABM Treaty in its current form, at least for the time being. Moscow currently believes that a negotiated modification of the ABM Treaty, which could permit both sides to deploy extensive defenses, could be almost as bad as a unilateral U.S. abrogation. The Soviets fear that if they signal a willingness to renegotiate the pact, it would remove most of the restraints on the American SDI program, prevent them from manipulating the intra-NATO rift on the strategic defense issue, and might even lead to unconstrained offensive and defensive arms races. For these reasons, the Soviets probably will maintain their current course for the time being.

But post-1995 Soviet strategic choices are far more difficult to predict. The Soviets themselves probably do not know what kind of nuclear posture they will develop, although it is certain to include deployment of the strategic defenses they are working on so determinedly today.

If Moscow's research showed highly effective defense to be impossible or extremely unlikely, it would maintain its offense-oriented strategy, whatever its imperfections. But if effective defenses appeared technologically feasible, Moscow would face yet another difficult strategic choice: embark on a crash antidefense program while shoring up its own defenses, or settle for a defense-dominated posture, under which most, if not all, types of nuclear offensive operations would be impractical. U.S. actions can also exert a major influence on these long-term Soviet strategic choices.

If the Soviets become convinced that Washington can deny them the ability to implement the three major objectives of their strategic policy no matter what offensive forces they deploy, Moscow might agree to restructure the existing strategic environment through a build-down of offensive forces coupled with a defensive build-up. In fact, the Soviets should find a world in which the importance of long-range offensive nuclear forces has been greatly reduced or even eradicated appealing in many ways, since they then might feel freer to flex conventional muscles that the West cannot yet match.

Yet the nature of the transition remains the key issue. Even if Moscow one day endorses a move toward defense, existing offensive- and defensive-force asymmetries would make the transition difficult and dangerous to implement without a mutually agreeable arms control process outlining prior limits on offensive forces.

Specifically, the Soviets fear above all that instead of attempting an orderly and stabilizing transition, the United States might strive for victory in an unrestrained offense-defense arms competition emphasizing space-based systems. They believe that if the United States succeeds, the quality of Soviet deterrence would plummet, the political leverage of Soviet forces would dwindle, and Moscow would have few, if any, credible war-fighting options. In many respects, this situation would be much worse than living with unfavorable force asymmetries in an offense-dominated environment, since even the Soviet ability to inflict devastating retaliatory attacks against the United States might be eroded.

Unfortunately, as long as the United States continues to declare ambitious space-based defenses as one possible goal of the SDI without clearly acknowledging that success would require dramatic U.S. offensive-force reductions, Soviet policy will be driven by the fear of U.S. superiority, not by the promise of a safer, defense-dominated world. Since any defensive transition is still many years away, Washington would be foolhardy to tinker unilaterally with its offensive forces now. Yet there is nothing to lose and much to gain by declaring now that the United States understands Soviet concerns about an offense-defense competition, and that should potent defenses appear feasible, it would be prepared to make major offensive reductions to create an orderly transition.

Getting the Soviets on board the strategic defense effort will not be nearly as easy as SDI optimists sometimes suggest. Yet contrary to the warnings of SDI opponents, it is not inconceivable. The Soviet position is not set in concrete, but for the time being, changing Moscow's mind will require much more determined and skillful American efforts than those made to date.

BIBLIOGRAPHY

An asterisk (*) preceding a reference indicates that the article or part of it has been reprinted in this book.

BOOKS AND PAMPHLETS

Bellany, Ian and Blacker, Coit D., eds. Antiballistic missile defense in the 1980s. F. Cass. '83.

Canan, James. War in space. Harper & Row. '82.

Carter, Ashton and Schwartz, David, eds. Ballistic missile defense. Brookings Institution. '84.

Drell, Sidney D., Farley, Philip J., and Holloway, David. The Reagan strategic defense initiative. Stanford Center for International Security and Arms Control. '84.

Dyson, Freeman. Weapons and hope. Harper & Row. '84.

Ford, Daniel. The button. Simon and Schuster. '85.

Goure, Leon et al. The emerging strategic environment: implications for ballistic missile defense. Institute for Foreign Policy Analysis. '79.

Graham, Daniel O. The non-nuclear defense of cities. University Press of America. '83.

Graham, Daniel O. Shall America be defended? Arlington House. '79.

Hecht, Jeff. Beam weapons. Plenum Press. '84.

Jastrow, Robert. How to make nuclear weapons obsolete. Little, Brown. '85.

Langford, David. War in 2080. Morrow. '79.

McDougall, Walter A. . . . the heavens and the earth: a political history of the space age. Basic Books. '85.

Oberg, James. Red star in orbit. Random. '81.

Peebles, Curtis. The battle for space. Beaufort Books. '83.

Stine, G. Harry. Confrontation in space. Prentice-Hall. '81.

Union of Concerned Scientists. Space-based missile defense. (report) Union of Concerned Scientists. '84.

U. S. Department of Defense. The strategic defense initiative: defense technologies study. U. S. Department of Defense. '84.

PERIODICALS

Aviation Week and Space Technology. 119:11, 16–18. O. 17, '83. Panel urges defense technology advances. W. H. Gregory.

Aviation Week and Space Technology. 119:50–1+. O. 24, '83. U. S. Strategic defense options. Fletcher Commission report.

Aviation Week and Space Technology. p 14+. Ja. 16, '84. Soviets accelerate missile defense efforts. Clarence A. Robinson.

Bulletin of the Atomic Scientists. 39:5–8. My. '83. Lasers for missile defense. D. Kaplan.

Bulletin of the Atomic Scientists. 40:18–23. O. '84. Defense-protected build-down. J. N. Barkenbus and A. M. Weinberg.

*Business Week. p 68+. Jl. 15, '85. The selling of Star Wars to businesses abroad. David Griffin, Ronald Taggiasco, Thane Peterson, and Frederic A. Miller.

Christian Science Monitor. p 1+. Ap. 12, '85. Space defense problems.

Christian Science Monitor. p 9. Je. 28, '85. Western Europe decides to pull together on defense research. Elizabeth Pond.

*Commentary. 79:19–25. D. '84. The war against 'Star Wars.' Robert Jastrow.

*Congressional Digest. 63:69–96. Mr. '85. The star wars controversy.

Current Digest of the Soviet Press. 37:13+. Mr. 20, '85. Gromyko warns U. S. against space arms. Andrei A. Gromyko.

Current Digest of the Soviet Press. 37:7+. My. 29, '85. US wants space strike weapons. S. L. Sokolov.

*Current Digest of the Soviet Press. 37:7+. Jl. 27, '85. Playing with fire. G. Arbatov.

*Department of State Bulletin. 85:65–72. Mr. '85. The president's Strategic Defense Initiative [text of pamphlet].

Department of State Bulletin. 85:55–7. My. '85. US-USSR negotiations on nuclear and space arms. R. Reagan and G. McFarlane.

The Economist. 295:21–22. My. 25, '85. Star wars, terrestrial campaigns.

Foreign Affairs. 62:820–42. Spr. '84. Nuclear policy and the defensive transition. K. B. Payne and C. S. Gray.

Foreign Affairs. 62:843–56. Spr. '84. Ballistic missile defense: the illusion of security. W. F. Burrows.

Foreign Affairs. 63:264–78. Wint. '84/85. The president's choice: Star Wars or arms control. McGeorge Bundy et al.

Foreign Affairs. 63:810–26. Spr. '85. Nuclear strategy—can there be a happy ending? F. C. Ikle.

Foreign Policy. 54:164–70. Spr. '84. Stabilizing Star Wars. A. M. Weinberg and J. N. Barkenbus.

*Foreign Policy. 55:73+. Sum. '85. What is "proof"? Gary L. Guertner.

*Foreign Policy. 55:85+. Sum. '85. What does Moscow think? David B. Rivkin, Jr.

Harvard Business Review. 63:28+. Mr. '85. Nuclear dilemmas. Joseph S. Nye.

High Technology. 5:72+. Ag. '85. Zapping missiles in space. T. A. Heppenheimer.

*Issues in Science and Technology. 1:15+. Fall '84. Technologies for strategic defense. James C. Fletcher.

*Issues in Science and Technology. 1:30+. Fall '84. The case for strategic defense: an option for a world disarmed. George A. Keyworth II.

Issues in Science and Technology. 1:45. Fall '84. The case against: technical and strategic realities. Sidney D. Drell and Wolfgang K. H. Panofsky.

Los Angeles Times. sec VI p 6+. Jl. 10, '83. Teller's obsession became reality in 'Star Wars' plan. Robert Scheer.

Los Angeles Times. sec II p 5. F. 27, '85. 'Star Wars' erodes confidence in nuclear waiting game. Robert E. Hunter.

Maclean's. 98:10–11. Ap. 8, '85. Mixed signals on star wars. R. MacGregor.

Nation. 237:661–4. D. 24, '83. Star wars—from scenario to fact. J. Tirman.

National Review. 36:26+. O. 5, '84. A catechism of strategic defense. B. Bruce-Briggs.

New Republic. 188:7–10. Ap. 18, '83. Nuclear fantasies.

New Republic. 192:20–1+. Mr. 11, '85. Nuclear idealism, nuclear realism. L. Wieseltier.

New Republic. 193:16+. Jl. 8, 1985. A Star Wars solution. Zbigniew Brzezinski.

New York Review of Books. 31:47–52. Ap. 26, '84. Reagan's star wars.

New York Review of Books. 32:38–44. Ap. 11, '85. The war for Star Wars. George W. Ball.

New York Times. p A1+. Mr. 24, '83. Speech by Pres. Reagan on strategic defense; and analysis. Charles Mohr.

New York Times. p 27. F. 19, '85. A moral case for 'Star Wars.' Lewis E. Lehrman.

New York Times. p A1+. Mr. 8, '85. Star Wars and mankind: consequences for the future.

*New York Times. p A1+. Jl. 22, '85. Campuses' role in arms debated as 'Star Wars' funds are sought. David E. Sanger.

New York Times. p A1+. Dec. 15, 16, and 17, 1985.

New York Times Magazine. p 32+. Ag. 11, '85. The secret behind 'Star Wars.' William J. Broad.

*New Yorker. p 37+. Jl. '85. Test. John Newhouse.

Newsweek. 101:16-22. Ap. 4, '83. Rethinking the unthinkable.

Newsweek. 105:18-22. Mr. 18, '85. An ambitious arms agenda. W. Schapiro.

Newsweek. 105:34-8+. Je. 17, '85. The Star Warriors.

Physics Today. 38:24-32. Je. '85. Strategic defense initiative: the politics and science of weapons in space. G. Yonas.

Physics Today. 38:34-40+. Je. '85. The strategic defense initiative: perception vs. reality. W. K. H. Panofsky.

Popular Mechanics. 161:84-7+. Jl. '84. Bringing star wars down to earth. Edward Teller.

*The Progressive. 49:20+. Jl. '85. Star Wars: the final solution. Matthew Rothschild and Keenen Peck.

Science. 221:133-5+. Jl. 8, '83. The search for a nuclear sanctuary. R. J. Smith.

Science. 224:32-4. Ap. 6, '84. Weapons bureaucracy spurns Star Wars goal. R. J. Smith.

Science News. 126:26+. Jl. 14, '84. Beams for defense. Janet Raloff.

Science News. 126:42+. Jl. 21, '84. Building the ultimate weapons. Janet Raloff.

Scientific American. 248:74. Je. '83. Ill-starred wars.

*Scientific American. 251:39-49. O. '84. Space-based ballistic missile defense. H. A. Bethe et al.

Technology Review. 87:30+. Ap. '84. The fallacy of laser defense. Jonathan B. Tucker.

Technology Review. 87:38-9+. Ap. '84. Face-off on nuclear defense. Edward Teller and Hans Bethe.

Technology Review. 88:16+. Jl. '85. The software for Star Wars: an Achilles heel? Herbert Lin.

Time. 121:8-14+. Ap. 4, '83. Reagan for the defense.

Time. 123:81+. My. 7, '84. The case against Star Wars weapons. Strobe Talbott.

Time. 124:16+. N. 26, '84. Roaming the high frontier. Evan Thomas.

Time. 125:12+. Mr. 11, '85. Putting it on the table. William R. Doerner.

Time. 125:14+. Mr. 11, '85. Upsetting a delicate balance. Strobe Talbott.

Time. 125:26–7. Jl. 1, '85. Holier-than-thou on Star Wars. Strobe Talbott.

U. S. News & World Report. 94:28–9+. Ap. 4, '83. Behind Reagan's Star Wars strategy. J. Fromm.

*Vital Speeches of the Day. 49:386–90. Ap. 15, '83. Peace and national security. Ronald Reagan.

Vital Speeches of the Day. 5l:101–3. D. 1, '84. Peace through strength and dialogue. Caspar W. Weinberger.

Vital Speeches of the Day. 51:546–8. Jl. 1, '85. The need for a strategic defense initiative. B. Chappell.

Wall Street Journal. p 1+. S. 28, '84. Technology and chill create dim outlook for arms-control pact. David Ignatius.

Wall Street Journal. p 20. Ja. 7, '85. As Geneva talks open, U. S. is determined to reduce its vulnerability to Soviet strike. David Ignatius.

Washington Monthly. p 32–36. Mr. '85. Why Star Wars is not like the Manhattan project. John Tierney.

Washington Post. p A1+. F. 21, '85. Options studied in arms violations. Walter Pincus.

Washington Post. p E5. Mr. 17, '85. A bear hug to avoid Star Wars? Jeremy J. Stone.

*World Press Review. 30:21–4. Je. '83. The 'Star Wars' delusion. K. Subrahmanyam.

pram